Origami Symphony No. 4

Capturing Vibrant Coral Reef Fish

Books by John Montroll
www.johnmontroll.com
Instagram: @montrollorigami

Origami Symphonies

Origami Symphony No. 1: The Elephant's Trumpet Call
First movement: Allegro: Theme and Variation on the Classic Crane
Second Movement: Andante: Crawling Simple Bugs
Third Movement: Minuet of Platonic Solids with a Trio of Sunken Solids
Fourth Movement: March of the Large African Animals

Origami Symphony No. 2: Trio of Sharks & Playful Prehistoric Mammals
First Movement: Allegro Agitato: Sharks in the Sea
Second Movement: Andante: Dulce, Peaceful Creatures
Third Movement: Minuet of Dimpled Polyhedra with a Trio of Archimedean Solids
Fourth Movement: March of the Prehistoric Mammals

Origami Symphony No. 3: Duet of Majestic Dragons & Dinosaurs
First Movement: Allegro: Quacking Chorus of Dinosaurs
Second Movement: Andante: Colorful Australian Birds
Third Movement: Minuet of Diamonds with a Trio of Dimpled Diamonds
Fourth Movement: Presto: Flight of the Dragons

Origami Symphony No. 4: Capturing Vibrant Coral Reef Fish
First Movement: Allegro: Songs of the Tropical Birds
Second Movement: Andante: Colorful Coral Reef Fish Swimming in Harmony
Third Movement: Minuet of Deltahedra with a Trio of Duo-Colored Octahedra
Fourth Movement: Allegro: Deep Melodies of the Sea Invertebrates

General Origami

Origami Fold-by-Fold
DC Super Heroes Origami
Origami Worldwide
Teach Yourself Origami: Second Revised Edition
Christmas Origami: Second Edition
Storytime Origami
Origami Inside-Out: Third Edition

Animal Origami

Dogs in Origami
Perfect Pets Origami
Dragons and Other Fantastic Creatures in Origami
Bugs in Origami
Horses in Origami
Origami Birds
Origami Gone Wild
Dinosaur Origami
Origami Dinosaurs for Beginners
Prehistoric Origami: Dinosaurs and other Creatures: Third Edition
Mythological Creatures and the Chinese Zodiac Origami
Origami Under the Sea
Sea Creatures in Origami
Origami Sea Life: Third Edition
Bringing Origami to Life: Second Edition
Bugs and Birds in Origami
Origami Sculptures: Fourth Edition
African Animals in Origami: Third Edition
North American Animals in Origami: Third Edition

Geometric Origami

Origami Stars
Galaxy of Origami Stars: Second Edition
Origami and Math: Simple to Complex
Origami & Geometry
3D Origami Platonic Solids & More: Second Edition
3D Origami Diamonds
3D Origami Antidiamonds
3D Origami Pyramids
A Plethora of Polyhedra in Origami: Third Edition
Classic Polyhedra Origami
A Constellation of Origami Polyhedra
Origami Polyhedra Design

Dollar Bill Origami

Dollar Origami Treasures: Second Edition
Dollar Bill Animals in Origami: Second Revised Edition
Dollar Bill Origami
Easy Dollar Bill Origami

Simple Origami

Fun and Simple Origami: 101 Easy-to-Fold Projects: Second Edition
Super Simple Origami
Easy Dollar Bill Origami
Easy Origami Animals
Easy Origami Polar Animals
Easy Origami Ocean Animals
Easy Origami Woodland Animals
Easy Origami Jungle Animals
Meditative Origami

Origami Symphony No. 4

Capturing Vibrant Coral Reef Fish

Antroll Publishing Company

John Montroll

To Charley

Origami Symphony No. 4: *Capturing Vibrant Coral Reef Fish*

ISBN-10: 1-877656-52-6
ISBN-13: 978-1-877656-52-1

Antroll Publishing Company

Introduction

Welcome to the world premier of the Fourth Origami Symphony! By combining origami with music, storytelling and the visual arts, an elaborate composition in four movements is brought to life. These movements depict various themes, styles and levels of complexity, showing the richness of origami.

The symphony opens with Tropical Birds singing cheerful songs in high registers, high up in the trees. Colorful birds from the first movement include the long-tailed Quetzal, Sunbird, and Parrot. The second movement presents a dozen colorful Coral Reef Fish swimming in harmony, half of which have stripes. Fish include varied Angelfish, Butterflyfish, a Clownfish and more. The third movement is a minuet of Deltahedra with a trio of duo-colored Octahedra. These polyhedra all have triangular sides and take us on a cosmic journey through time and space. Complex Sea Invertebrates fill the fourth movement, taking us to the depths of the ocean and back out. Sea Invertebrates include an Octopus, Squid, Jellyfish, Nautilus and more.

Each of the 37 models of this symphony are folded from a single uncut square, and all can be folded from standard origami paper. The models are specifically designed to be as simple as possible for the given detail. The simplicity in folding complex shapes produces models which exhibit a life-force of their own. Half of the Tropical Birds have duo-colored patterns. Half of the Coral Reef Fish have stripes. Using symphonic structure, models from the first two movements alternate between solid color and duo-colored. The Octahedra from the trio also have color-change patterns. These origami color-change patterns create a dazzling effect.

The diagrams are drawn in the internationally approved Randlett-Yoshizawa style. You can use any kind of square paper for these models, but the best results will be achieved with standard origami paper, which is colored on one side and white on the other (in the diagrams in this book, the shading represents the colored side). Large sheets, such as nine inches squared, are easier to use than small ones.

Origami supplies can be found in arts and craft shops, or at Dover Publications online: www.doverpublications.com. You can also visit OrigamiUSA at www.origamiusa.org for origami supplies and other related information including an extensive list of local, national, and international origami groups.

Please follow me on Instagram @montrollorigami to see posts of my origami.

I thank Christian Gonzalez and Jay Sella for the photography. I thank my editor, Charley Montroll. I also thank the many folders who continued to encourage me to develop the presentation of origami through an origami symphony.

I hope you enjoy this colorful symphony.

John Montroll
www.johnmontroll.com

Contents

★ Simple
★★ Intermediate
★★★ Complex
★★★★ Very Complex

First Movement
Allegro: Songs of the Tropical Birds

11

Quetzal
★★

14

Narina Trogon
★★

17

Hummingbird
★★

21

Sunbird
★★

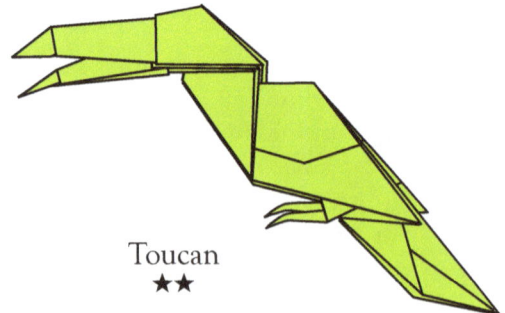

24

Toucan
★★

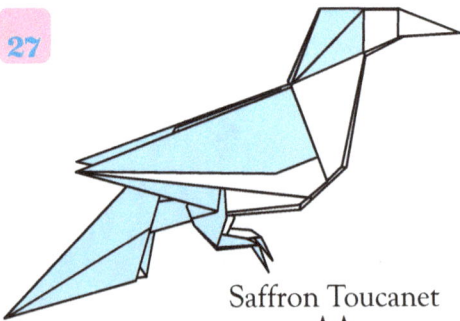

27

Saffron Toucanet
★★

30

Gannet
★★★

34

Parrot
★★

Second Movement
Andante: Coral Reef Fish Swimming in Harmony

 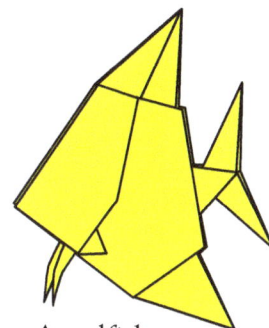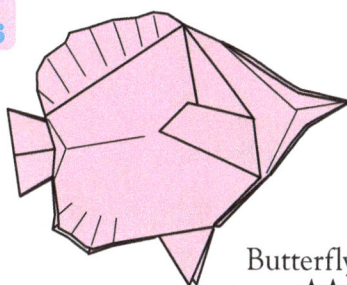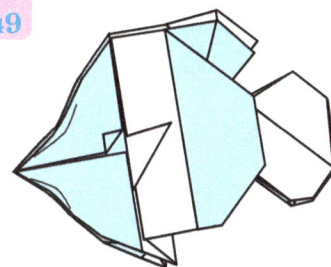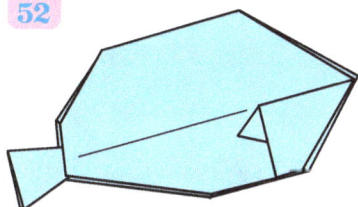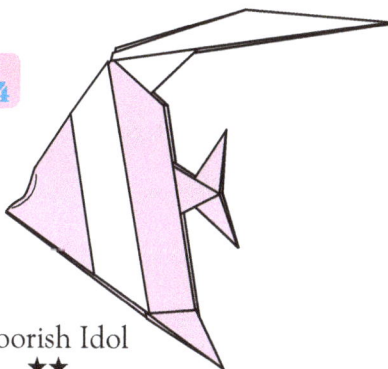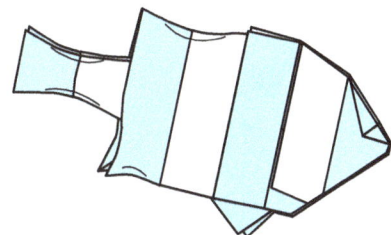

Third Movement
Minuet of Deltahedra with a
Trio of Duo-Colored Octahedra

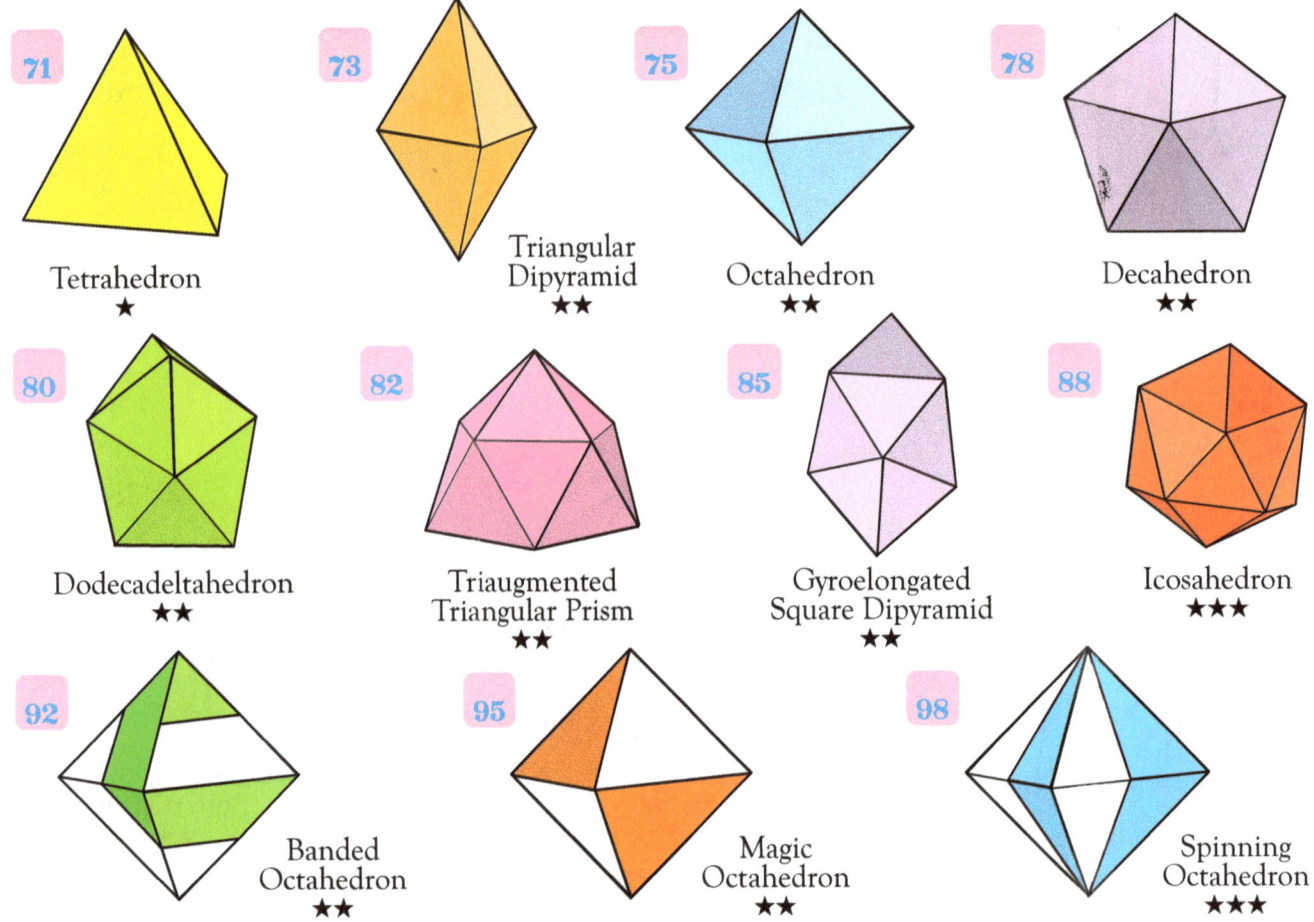

71

Tetrahedron
★

73

Triangular
Dipyramid
★★

75

Octahedron
★★

78

Decahedron
★★

80

Dodecadeltahedron
★★

82

Triaugmented
Triangular Prism
★★

85

Gyroelongated
Square Dipyramid
★★

88

Icosahedron
★★★

92

Banded
Octahedron
★★

95

Magic
Octahedron
★★

98

Spinning
Octahedron
★★★

Fourth Movement
Allegro: Deep Melodies from the Sea Invertebrates

102

Starfish
★★

104

Jellyfish
★★★

107

Octopus
★★★

111

Squid
★★★

117

Nautilus
★★★

122

Crab
★★★★

Symbols

Lines

– – – – – – – –

Valley fold,
fold in front.

–·–·–·–·–·–

Mountain fold,
fold behind.

———————

Crease line.

·····················

X-ray or guide line.

Arrows

Fold in this direction.

Fold behind.

Unfold.

Fold and unfold.

Turn over.

Sink or three dimensional folding.

Place your finger between these layers.

Symphonic Design

I hope you enjoy folding from these symphonies as much as I enjoy writing them. It allows me to present my work in a format that draws on the magnificence of all the arts, from music to sculpture, storytelling to the visual arts. The four-movement structure of varied focused themes is ideal for my design method.

While I cannot possibly explain origami design, I can allude to a specific method I often use. I call this method "Iterative Improvement".

The iterative improvement method means: I am designing several models of a related theme at the same time. Rather than try to create one subject, I plan to create several all together. I will use the second movement of Coral Reef Fish to explain.

1. I look up photos, drawings, and information on the nature of the subject. I am looking for differences and similarities. For the Coral Reef Fish, I see beautiful and varied species and imagine how elegant a scene could be. Of the similarities of these fish, most are flat with a round body shape, several have white stripes, and the tails come in two forms as forked or short and tapered.

2. I decide on a level of detail and complexity, in the context of a specific movement, given that I have about 30 pages. For these fish, I want a range of simple to challenging ones, with and without stripes, all at an intermediate level.

3. I begin designing! I make up fish after fish! This is where the fun begins. I call these "doodles". There is nothing great about them, but it is a start and I am now on the map.

4. Each doodle has some new design element of importance to the general theme. These elements give insight to making more fish and improving previous ones.

5. I now have a new set of fish. A clever tail structure from one fish can become part of the design of another one. The way the stripes work on one fish can be applied to another.

6. I repeat this process until I reach my design criteria (including simplicity of structure, fun to fold...).

7. There really is no end but at some point I begin diagramming. Throughout the entirety of the book work, I still continue making improvements, and end up replacing several fish. It is all part of the Iterative Improvement method.

Origami Symphony No. 4

As the first movement of the symphony opens, we find ourselves on tree branches in tropical forests, listening to the Songs of the Tropical Birds. A Quetzal, with its long flowing tail, sings a high note, carrying the first cheerful melody. Birds with long tails or long bills enter, each with a colorful display. Following symphonic structure, the birds alternate between solid and duo-colored patterns. Photos show a Toucan and other birds perched on polyhedra, hinting of an adventure yet to come. A duo-colored Parrot entertains us with the last melody in the treble clef, and flies away, closing the first movement.

For the peaceful second movement, we go down into the waters watching Colorful Coral Reef Fish Swim in Harmony. We are surrounded by their beauty. In symphonic form, every other fish has stripes of color and white. A variety of Angelfish and Butterflyfish chant harmonies through low notes. Twelve Coral Reef Fish tell a story and weave harmonies, as we enjoy folding these treasures of the sea. A Blue Tang Surgeonfish, Moorish Idol, and Clownfish swim past us. A Damselfish sporting seven color-change bands presents a mind-boggling challenge as we leave the enchanted Coral Reef.

For the minuet of the third movement, we take a cosmic tour of worlds composed only of equilateral triangles. These shapes, Deltahedra, have sides that are all triangles, ranging from four to twenty sides. First we encounter the Tetrahedron with four sides, carrying a melody of four notes. We zoom to the next orbit to explore the Triangular Diamond, with six sides carrying a melody of six notes. As we travel, each new world has more sides, offering more complex melodies. Along the way, we encounter the odd worlds of the 12-sided Dodecadeltahedron and the 14-sided Augmented Triangular Prism, reminding us of the never-ending mysteries of nature. Finally, we reach the roundest world of all, the Icosahedron with its twenty sides. Our adventure continues with the Trio as we encounter three Octahedral worlds with Cosmos-shattering color patterns. The trio concludes with a Spinning Octahedron which hurls us back to Earth, but too dizzy to know where we land as the movement ends.

We discover that we have landed at the bottom of the ocean surrounded by Starfish. The fourth movement with Deep Melodies from the Sea Invertebrates has taken us back into the waters, but far deeper this time. Jellyfish swim around us, an Octopus shows us its den, and a Squid takes us to depths unknown where it glows in the dark, singing the lowest notes ever. Wondering where we will go next, a Nautilus takes us out of the great depths with songs it knew from millions of years ago. Detailed Crabs delight us with their chatter as they bring us to the shores where the sun is shining, ending the symphony.

As with any symphony, the more you hear it, the more things you notice, and the many tones and phrases in this symphony are so complex that they deserve to be played over and over. I hope, after getting out of the water and coming on shore, that you are ready to climb the trees of the Tropical Forests and start over. A visit to the Coral Reef never ends.

First Movement

Allegro: Songs of the Tropical Birds

Tropical Birds live in warm climates. Many have large bills which are perfect for dining on fruits, nuts, and tasty insects. Many have long tails. These birds are colorful yet blend into the trees. In symphonic form, every other bird has a duo-color pattern. Let's climb into the trees and start on a high note as we listen to the Songs of the Tropical Birds.

Quetzal

The Quetzal resides in the mountainous tropical forests of Southern Mexico and Central America. Guatemala has a "Quetzal" currency, as it is their national bird. With a red belly and iridescent green wings, the bird is about a foot long with a two foot long tail. Found on lower layers of the tropical forest trees, it feeds on fruits, berries, insects, and frogs.

1

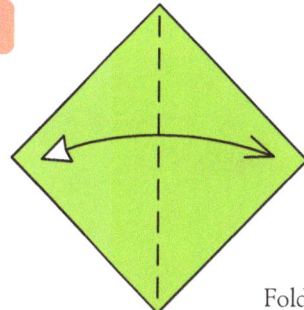

Fold and unfold.

2

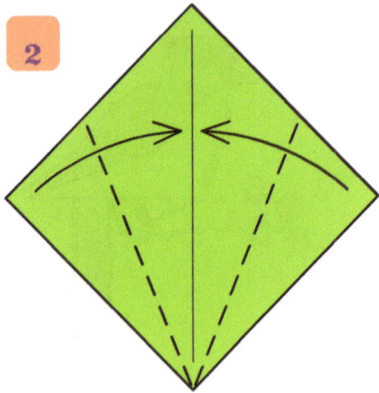

Fold to the center.

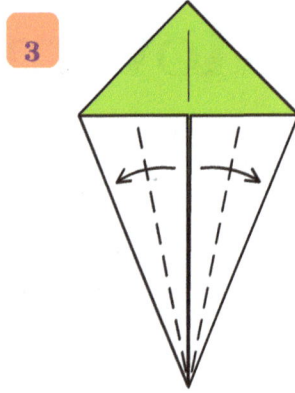

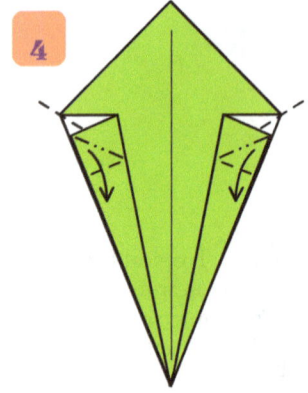

3

4

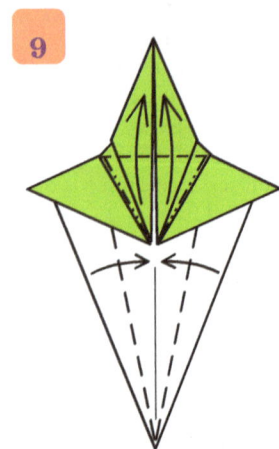

Make squash folds.

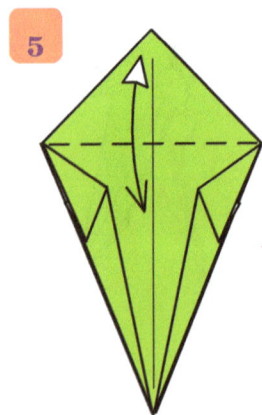

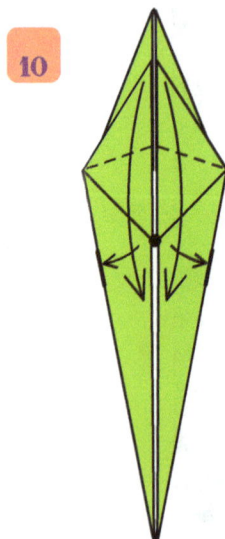

5

Fold and unfold.

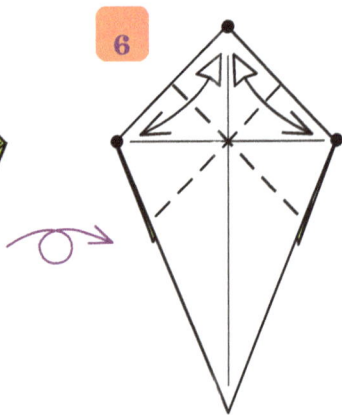

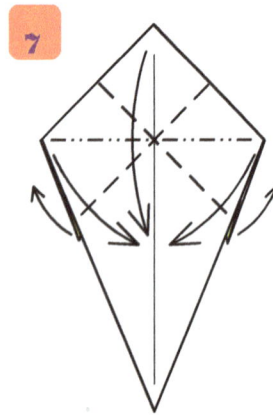

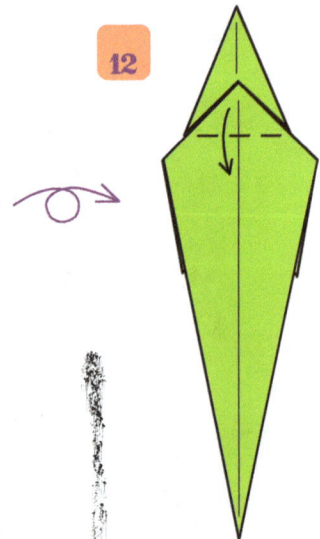

6

Fold and unfold.

7

Fold along the creases.
The flaps on the sides
will swing out.

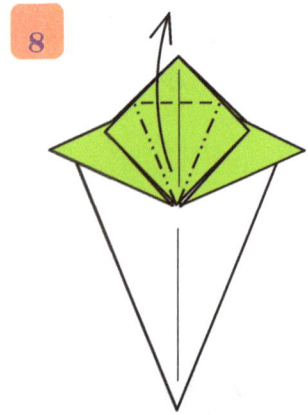

8

Petal-fold.

9

Make squash folds.

10

Slide the corners at the
dot to the bold lines
while folding down.

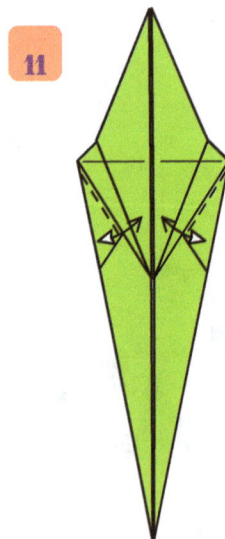

11

Fold and unfold.

12

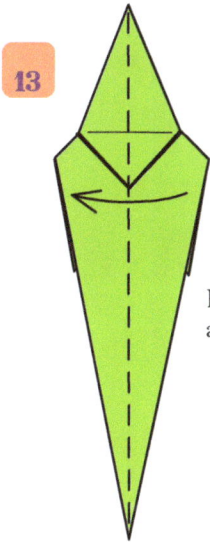

13

Fold in half and rotate.

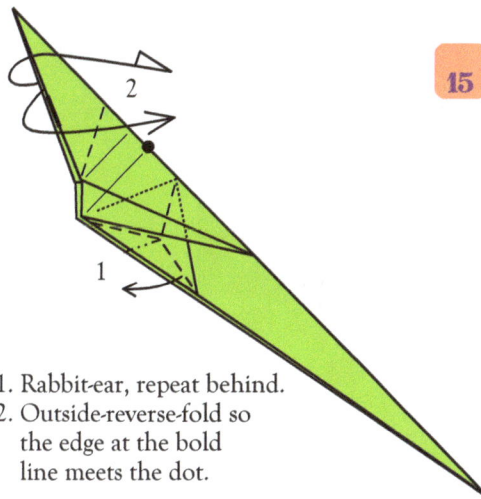

14

1. Rabbit-ear, repeat behind.
2. Outside-reverse-fold so the edge at the bold line meets the dot.

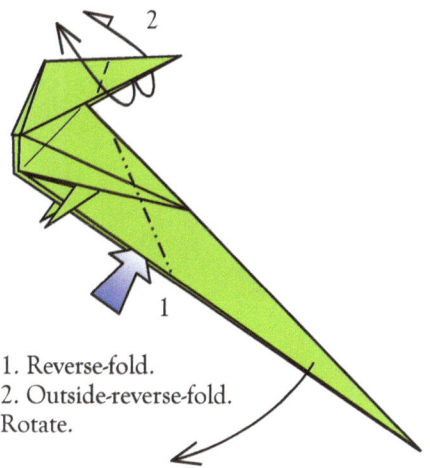

15

1. Reverse-fold.
2. Outside-reverse-fold. Rotate.

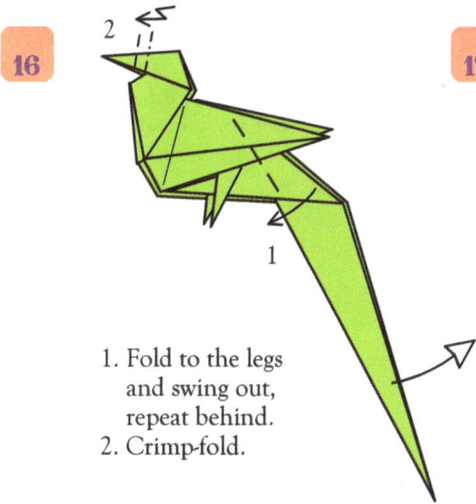

16

1. Fold to the legs and swing out, repeat behind.
2. Crimp-fold.

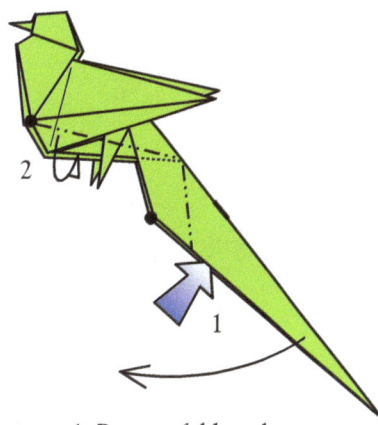

17

1. Reverse-fold so the edge meets the dot.
2. Fold inside, repeat behind.

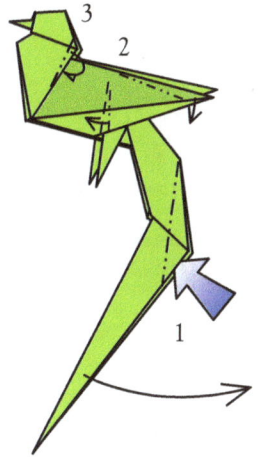

18

1. Reverse-fold.
2. Begin with a pleat-fold under the dark paper. Then slide the wing on the right. Repeat behind.
3. Fold inside, repeat behind.

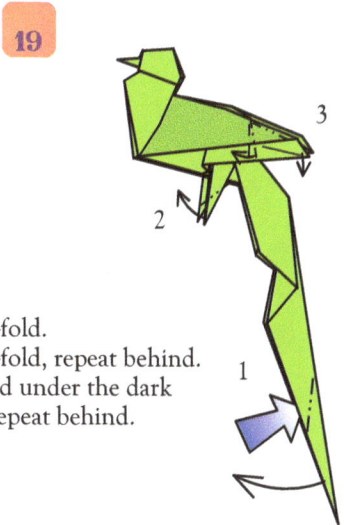

19

1. Reverse-fold.
2. Reverse-fold, repeat behind.
3. Pleat-fold under the dark paper, repeat behind.

20

Quetzal

Narina Trogon

The Narina Trogon is a brilliantly colored bird with a red belly and green wings. It is found in forests and woodlands throughout Africa. Around one foot in length, it feeds on insects and other small creatures. It perches on lower banches for long periods of time.

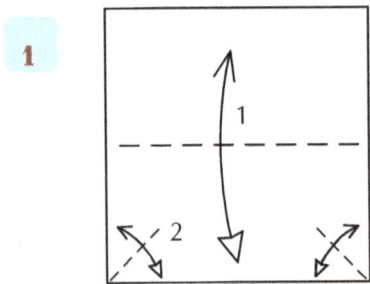

Fold and unfold.

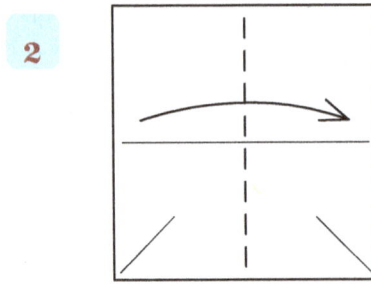

Fold in half.

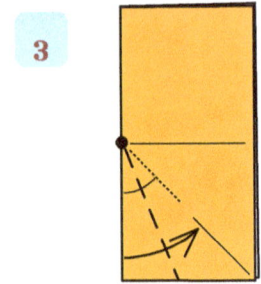

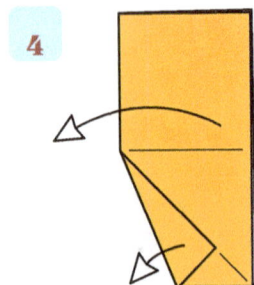

Unfold.

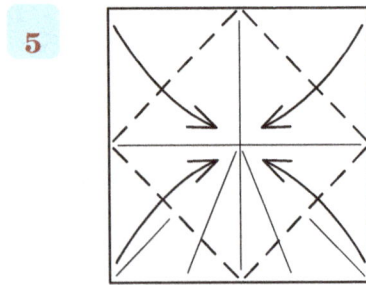

Fold to the center.

7

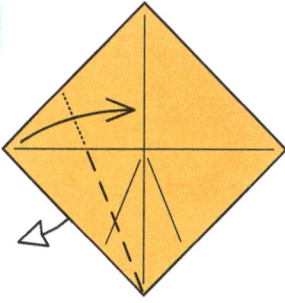

Fold to the center and swing out from behind. Do not crease at the top.

8

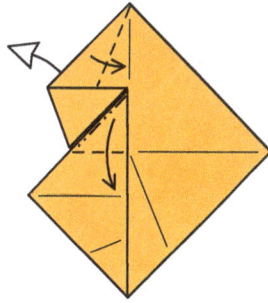

Squash-fold and swing out from behind.

9

Unfold.

10

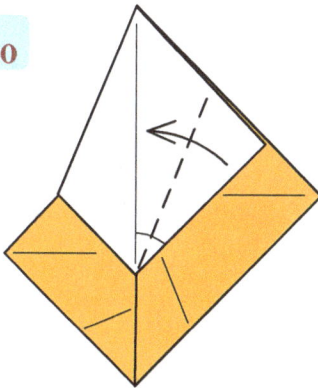

11

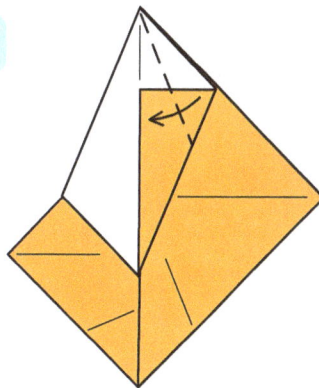

12

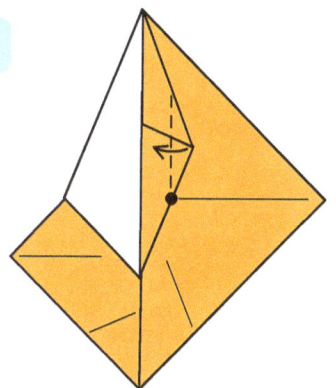

13

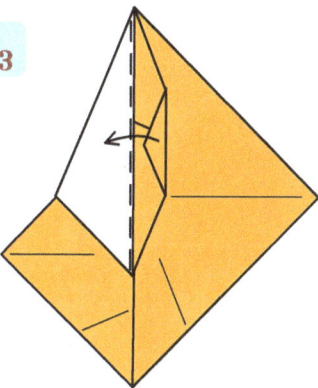

14

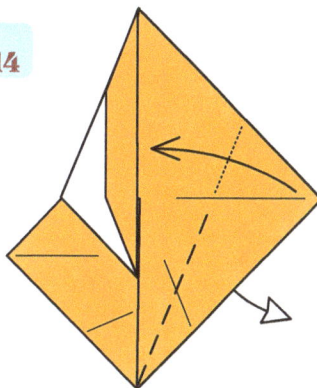

Repeat steps 7–13 on the right.

15

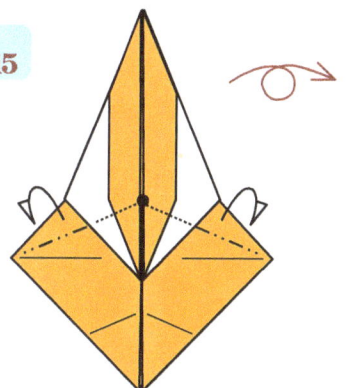

16

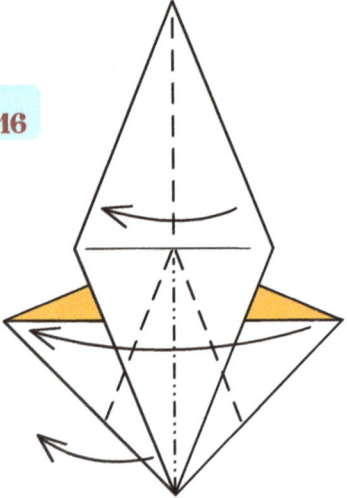

Fold along the
creases and rotate.

17

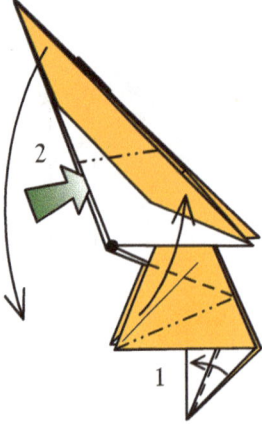

1. Squash-fold, repeat behind.
2. Reverse-fold so the edge, at
   the bold line, meets the dot.

18

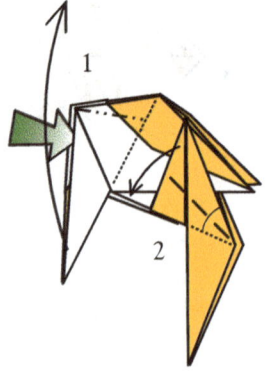

1. Reverse-fold.
2. Repeat behind.

19

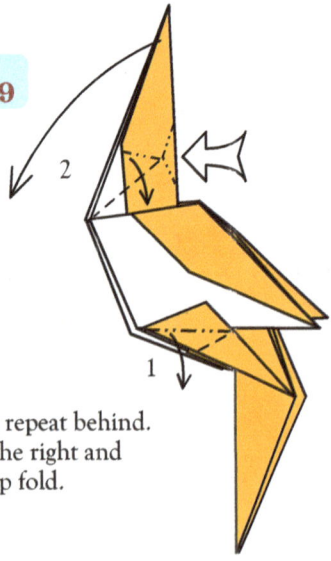

1. Squash-fold, repeat behind.
2. Push in on the right and
   make a crimp fold.

20

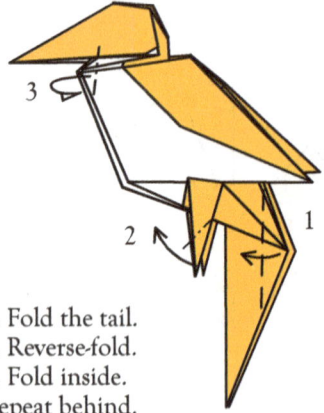

1. Fold the tail.
2. Reverse-fold.
3. Fold inside.
   Repeat behind.

21

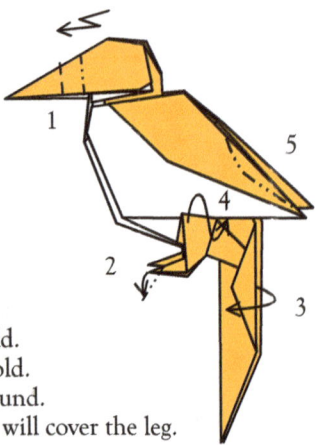

1. Crimp-fold.
2. Reverse-fold.
3. Wrap around.
4. The wing will cover the leg.
5. Shape the wings.
   Repeat behind.

22

Narina
Trogon

Hummingbird

Sporting brilliant glittering colors, Hummingbirds have high energy and are always hungry. Eating half their weight daily, they feed on nectar, small insects, and spiders. This small bird is found throughout North and South America. They make nests as small as walnuts, for their eggs, which are as small as peas.

1

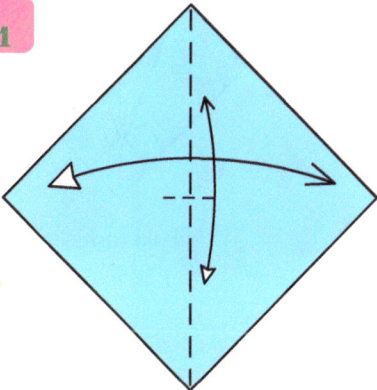

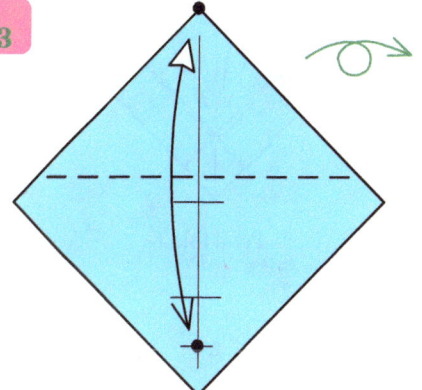

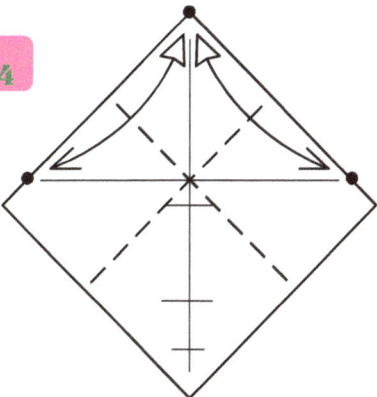

Fold and unfold.

2

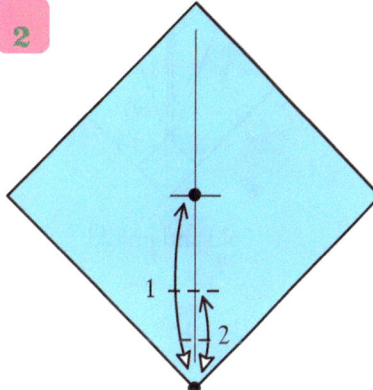

Fold and unfold twice.

3

Fold and unfold.

4

Fold and unfold.

5

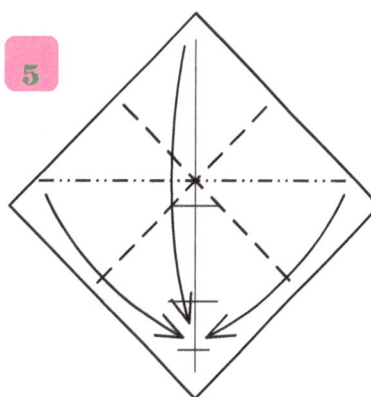

Fold along the creases.

6

Fold to the center.

7

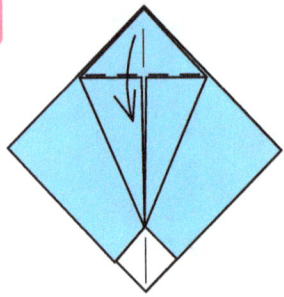

8

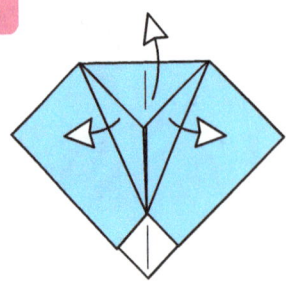

Unfold.

9

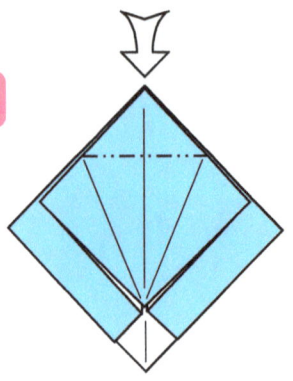

Sink.

10

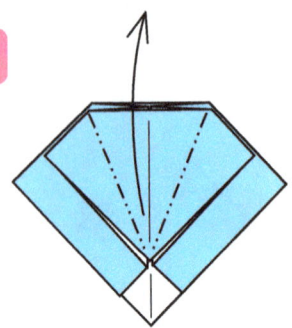

Petal-fold.

11

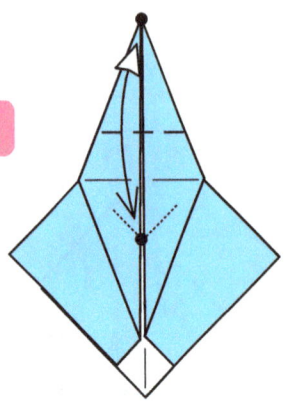

Fold and unfold.

12

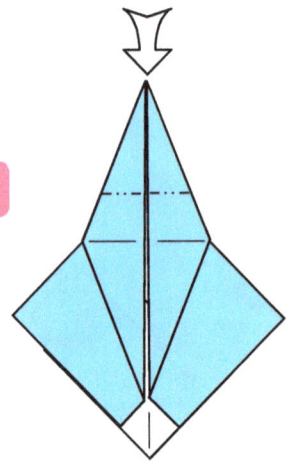

Fold inside.

13

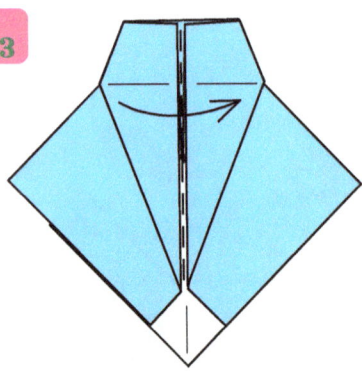

14

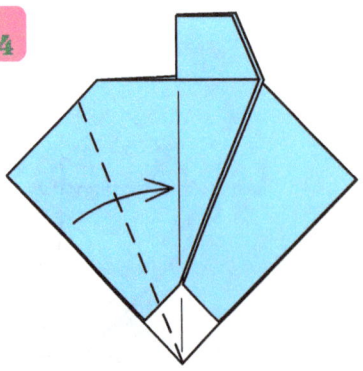

Fold to the center.

15

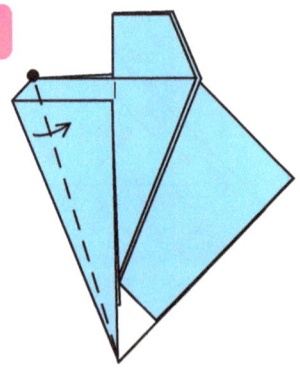

16

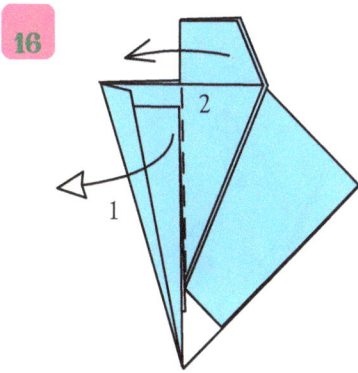

1. Unfold.
2. Valley-fold.

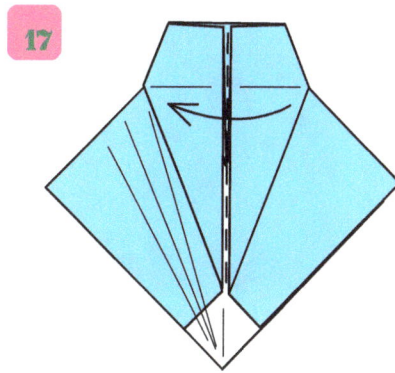

17

Repeat steps 13–16
on the right.

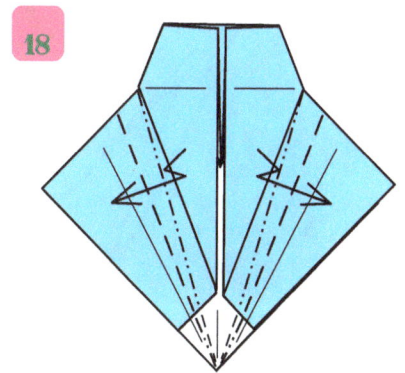

18

Make crimp folds
along the creases.

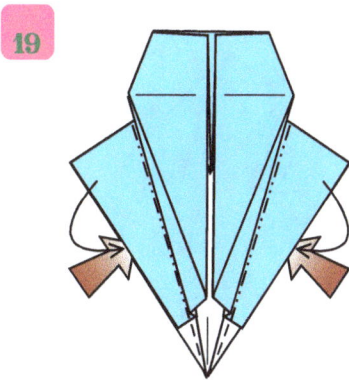

19

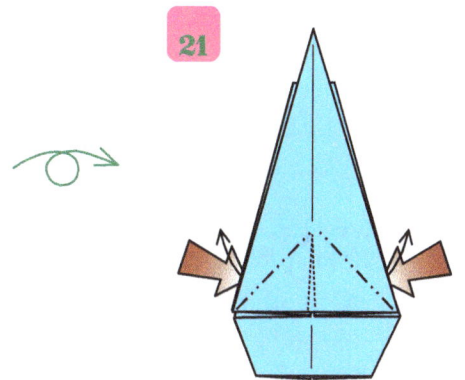

Make reverse folds.

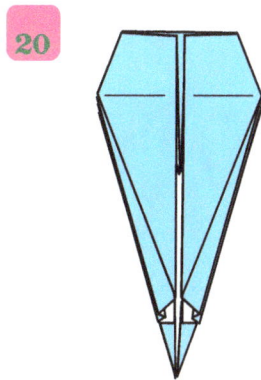

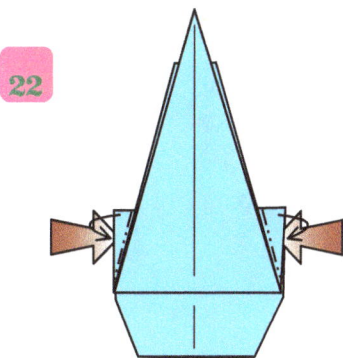

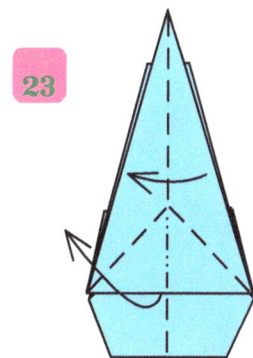

20

Rotate 180°.

21

Make reverse folds.

22

Make reverse folds.

23

Lift up while folding
in half. Rotate.

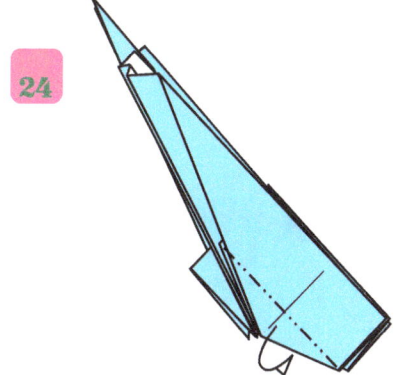

24

Fold inside,
repeat behind.

25

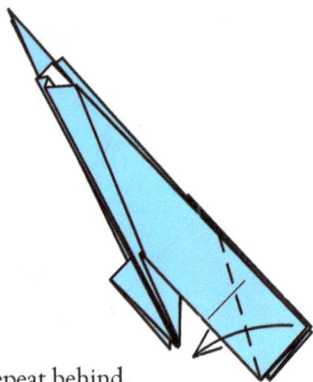

Repeat behind.

26

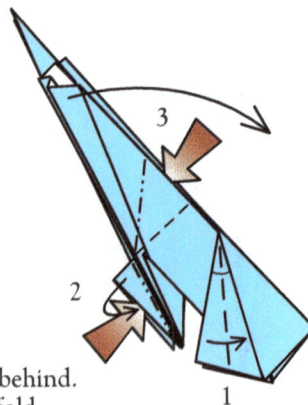

1. Repeat behind.
2. Revese-fold.
3. Squash-fold,
   repeat behind.

27

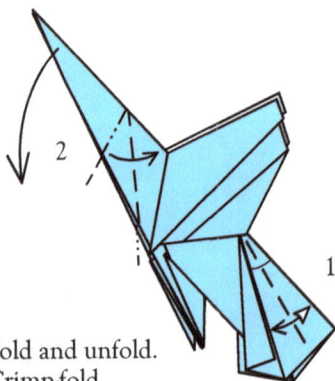

1. Fold and unfold.
2. Crimp-fold.

28

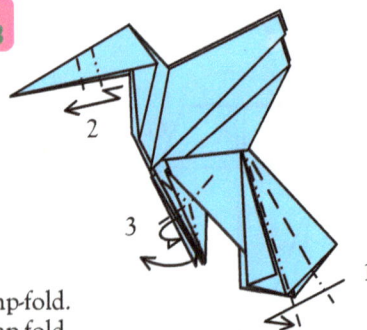

1. Crimp-fold.
2. Crimp-fold.
3. Rabbit-ear all the
   layers, repeat behind.

29

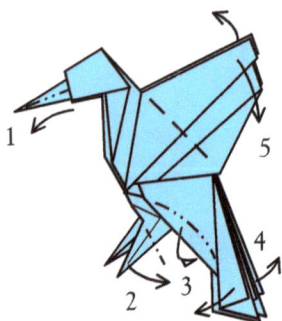

1. Thin and curl the beak.
2. Shape the leg, repeat behind.
3. Shape the body.
4. Spread the tail.
5. Spread the wings.

30

Hummingbird

Sunbird

The Sunbird is a small bird found in Africa, Asia, and Australia. It is considered to be the counterpart to Hummingbirds of the New World, but not quite as small. Brilliantly colored with iridescent feathers, they live in small groups. Using their long curved bills, they feed on nectar and insects.

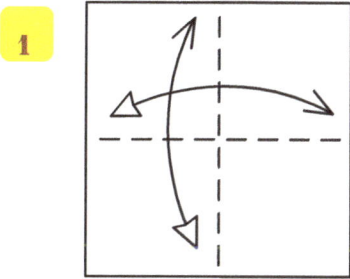

1

Fold and unfold.

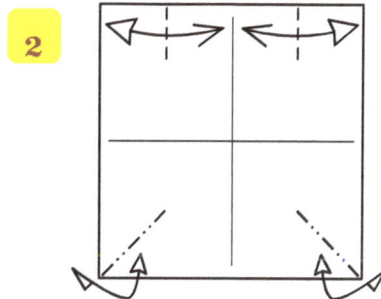

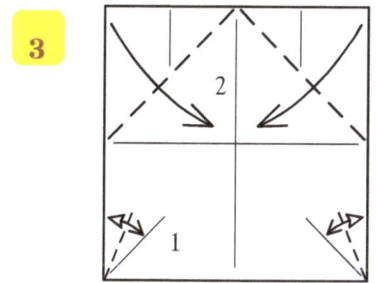

2

Fold and unfold.

3

1. Fold and unfold.
2. Fold to the center.

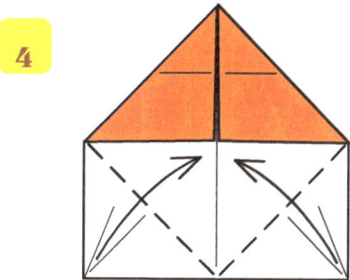

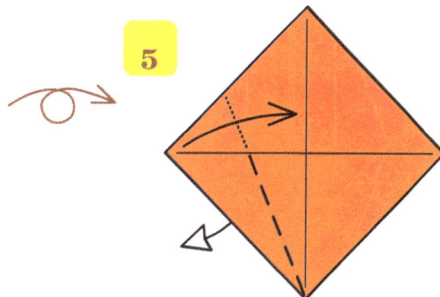

4

Fold to the center.

5

Fold to the center and swing out from behind. Do not crease at the top.

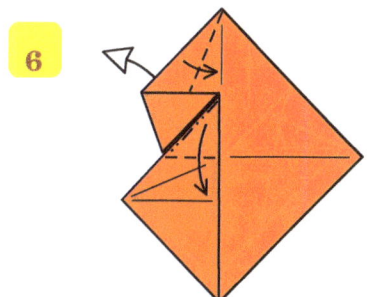

6

Squash-fold and swing out from behind.

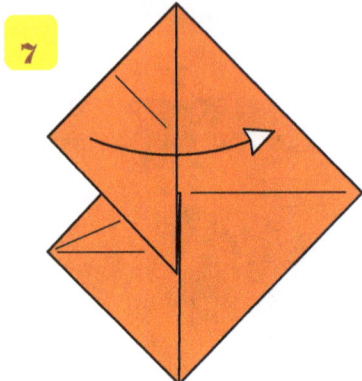

7

Unfold.

8

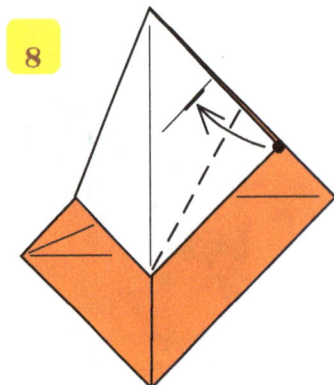

Bring the dot
to the line.

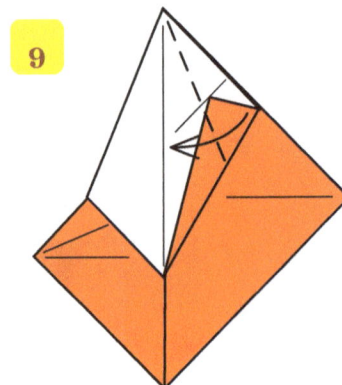

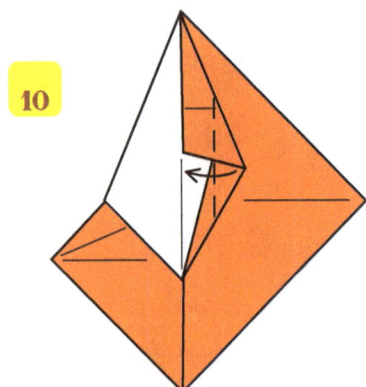

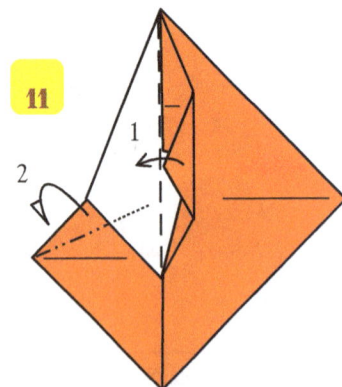

9

10

11

Fold along
the creases.

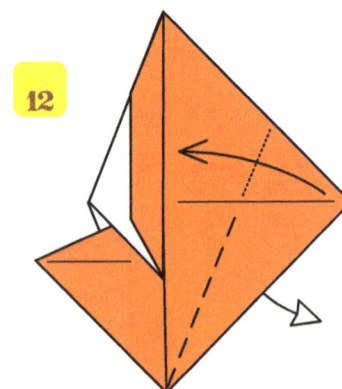

12

Repeat steps 5–11
on the right.

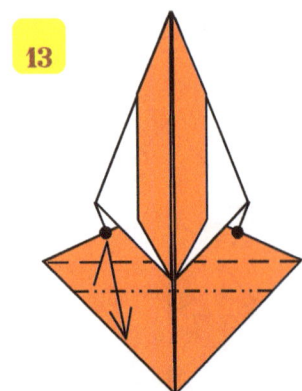

13

Pleat-fold to
the dots.

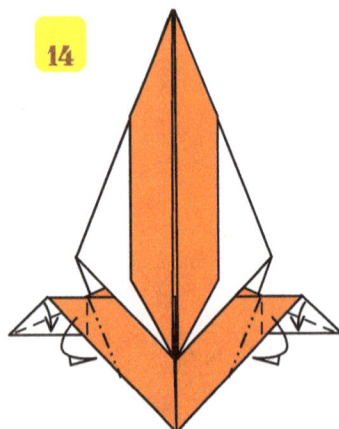

14

Thin the legs.

15

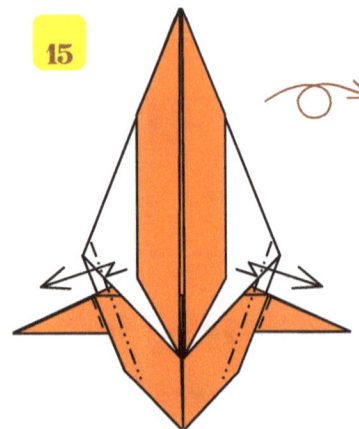

Make pleat folds.

16

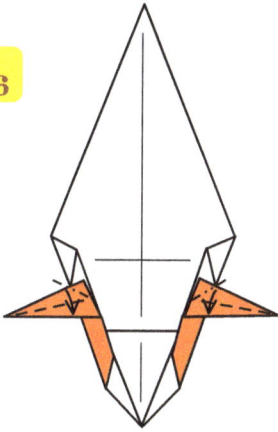

Make squash folds.

17

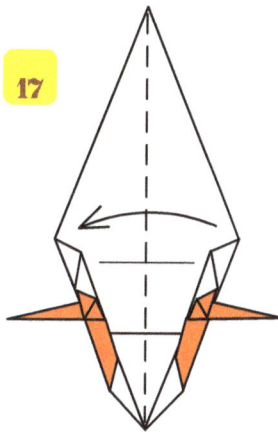

Fold in half
and rotate.

18

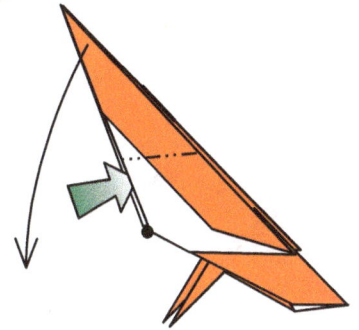

Bring the edge to the
dot for this reverse fold.

19

Reverse-fold.

20

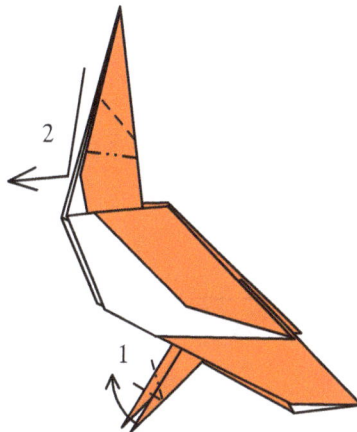

1. Crimp-fold, repeat behind.
2. Make reverse folds.

21

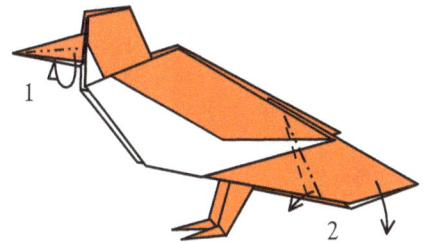

1. Fold inside,
   repeat behind.
2. Crimp-fold.

22

1. Fold inside, repeat behind.
2. Squash-fold, repeat behind.
3. Curve the beak.

23

Sunbird

Toucan

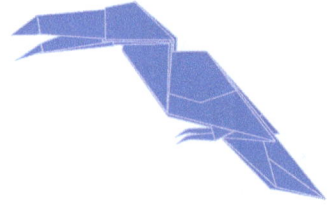

The Toucan is about the size of a crow and carries a magnificent beak. The large colorful beak is very light. The large beak allows them to perch in one spot as they feed on fruits. They plunder nests of smaller birds by scaring them with their beaks. Found in the rainforests of South America, they are social and very noisy. They nest in tree holes which they prefer not to make themselves.

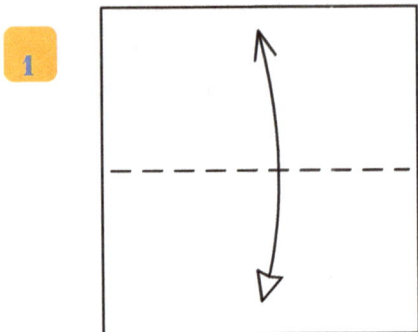

1

Fold and unfold.

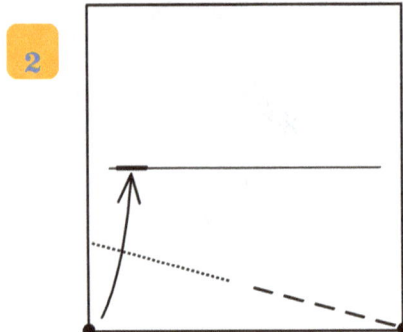

2

Bring the corner to the line and crease on the right.

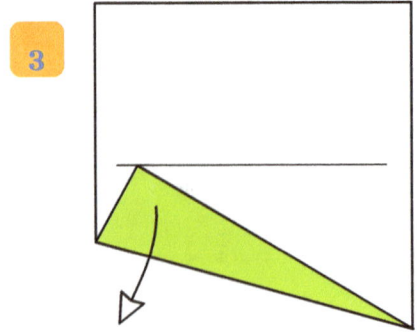

3

Unfold.

4

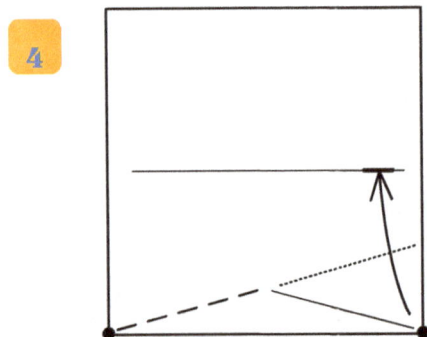

Repeat steps 2–3 on the right.

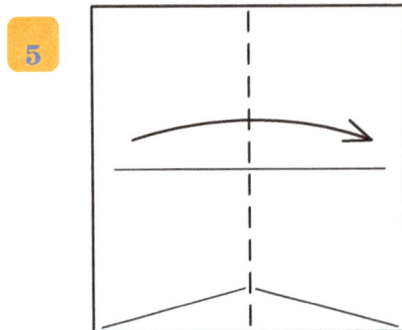

5

Fold in half.

6

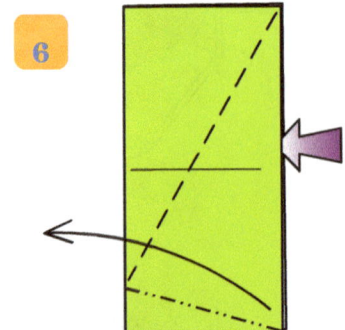

Mountain-fold along the crease for this squash fold. Rotate.

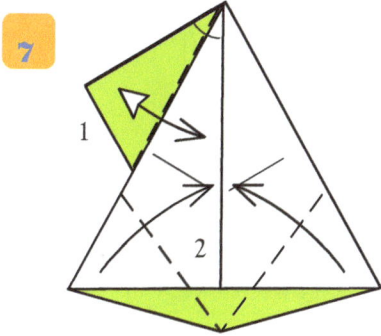

7

1. Fold and unfold.
2. Fold to the center.

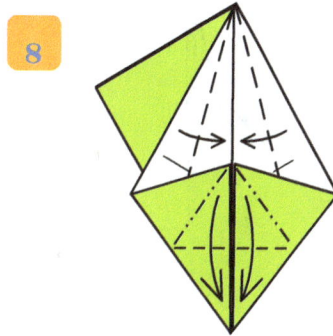

8

Make squash folds.

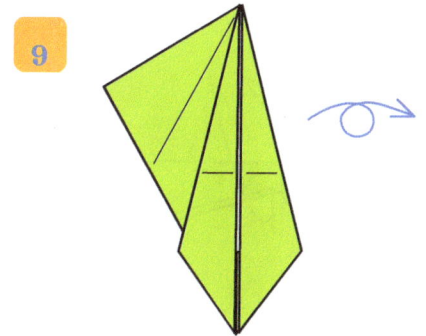

9

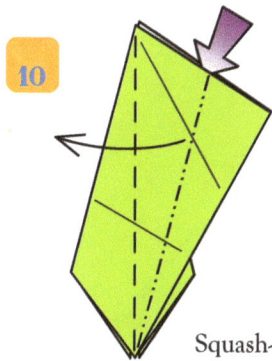

10

Squash-fold.

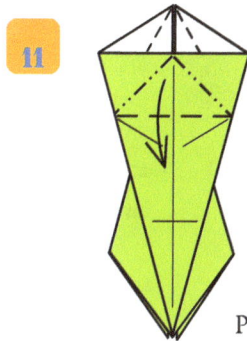

11

Petal-fold.

12

Fold to
the center.

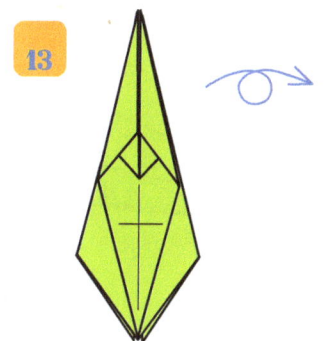

13

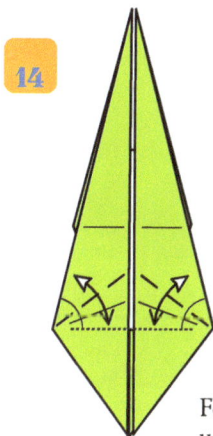

14

Fold and
unfold.

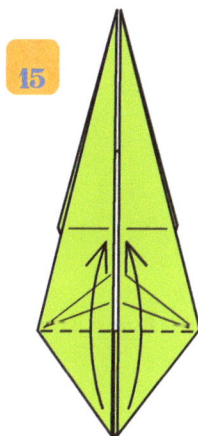

15

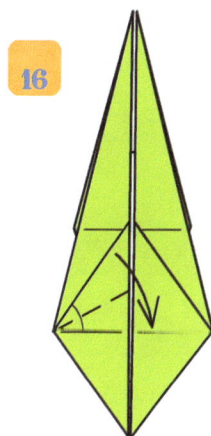

16

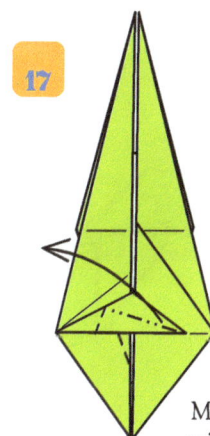

17

Make a squash fold
with a spread-squash
fold at the base.

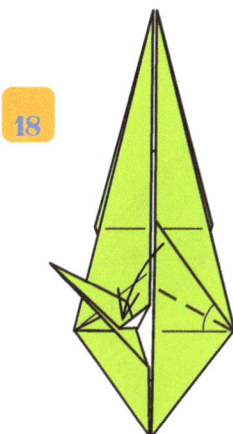

18

Repeat steps 16–17
on the right.

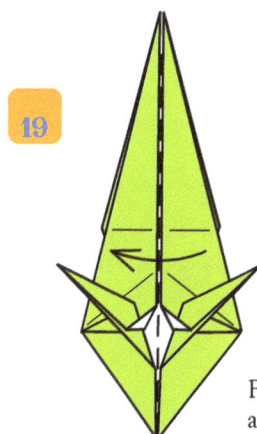

19

Fold in half
and rotate.

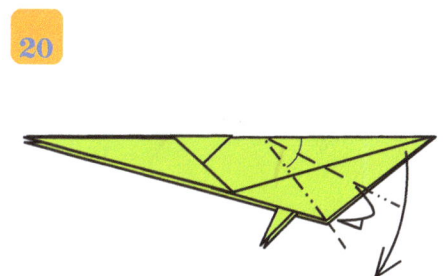

20

Mountain-fold along the
crease for this crimp fold.

21

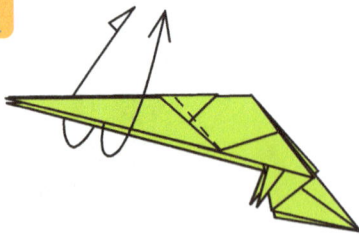

Outside-reverse-fold.

22

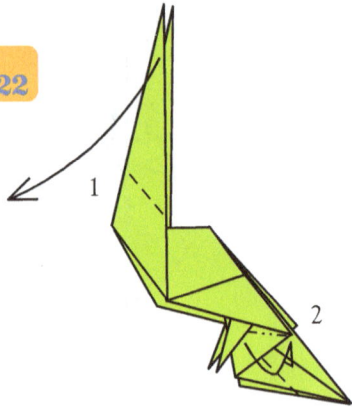

1. Valley-fold the top flap.
2. This is similar to a reverse
   fold, repeat behind.

23

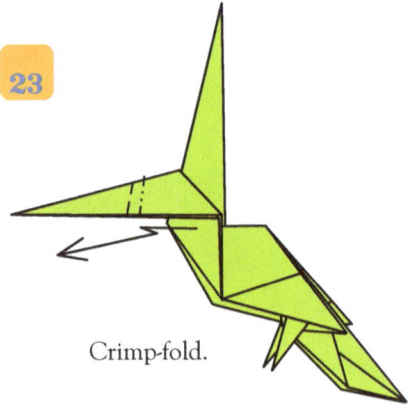

Crimp-fold.

24

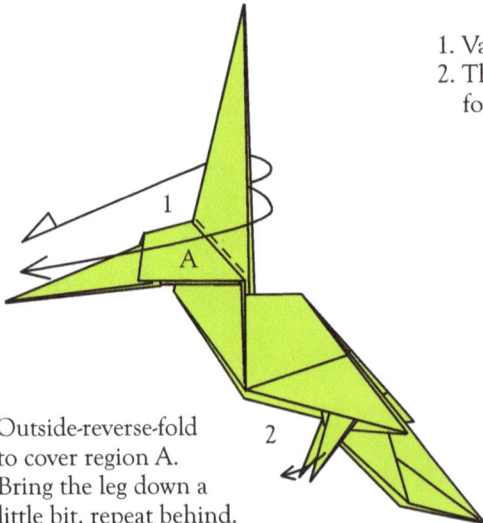

1. Outside-reverse-fold
   to cover region A.
2. Bring the leg down a
   little bit, repeat behind.

25

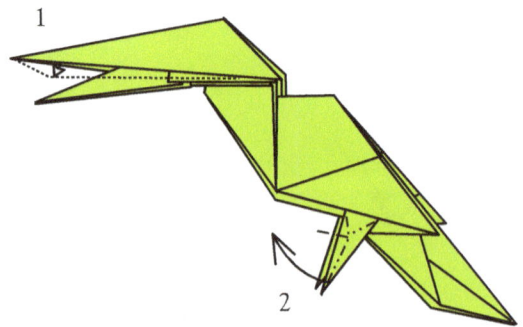

1. Spread the beak.
2. Double-rabbit-ear.
   Repeat behind.

26

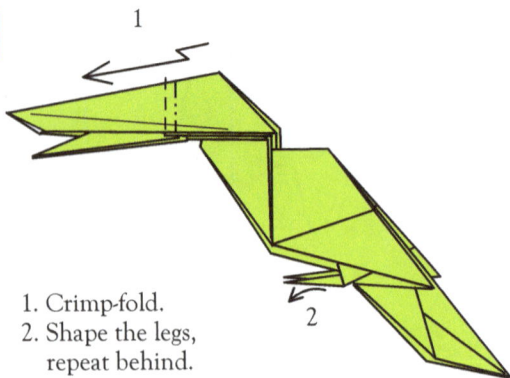

1. Crimp-fold.
2. Shape the legs,
   repeat behind.

28

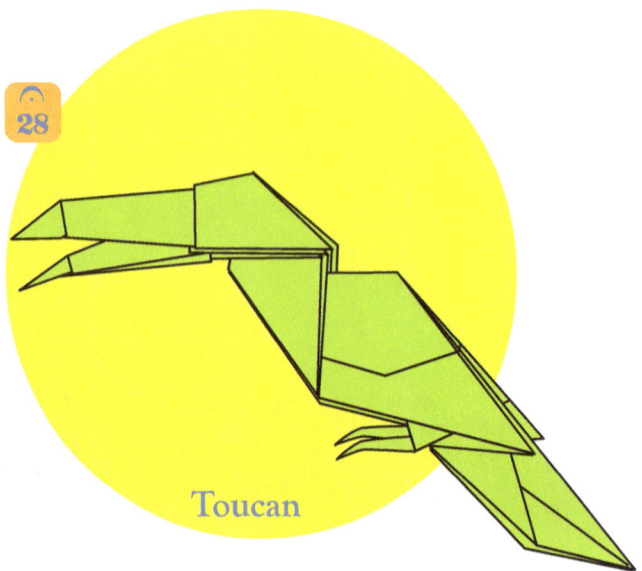

Toucan

27

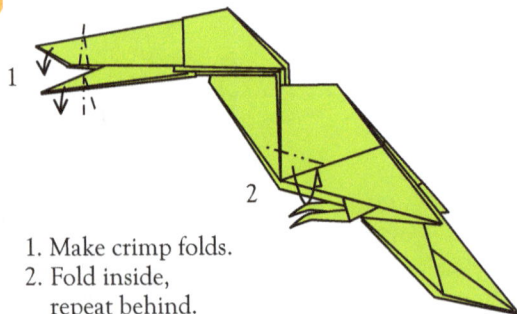

1. Make crimp folds.
2. Fold inside,
   repeat behind.

Saffron Toucanet

The Saffron Toucanet is a Toucan with golden feathers and a larger tail. They live in small groups in the forests of Argentina, Brazil, and Paraguay. It feeds mainly on fruits, high in the treetops.

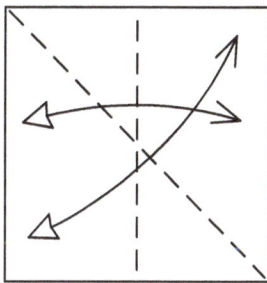

1

Fold and unfold.

2

Fold to the center.

3

4

Bring the corner to the line.

5

6

7

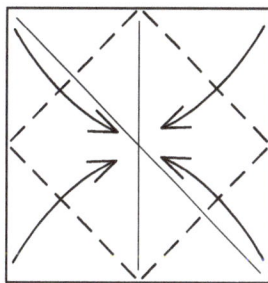
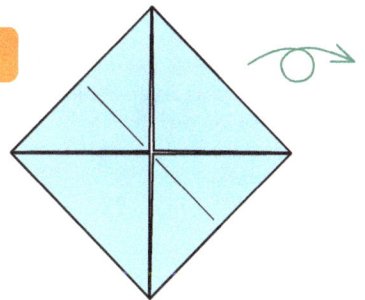
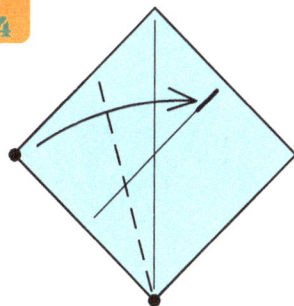
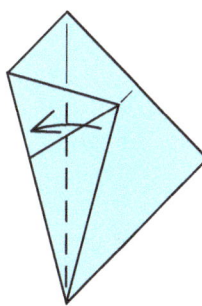
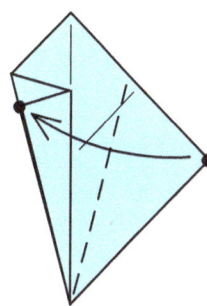
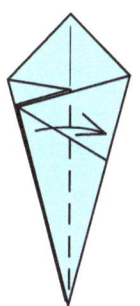

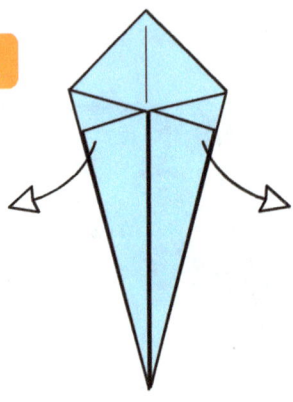

8

Unfold.

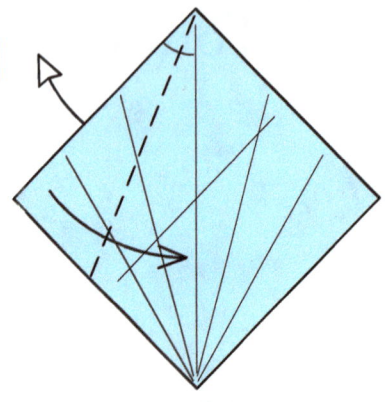

9

Fold to the center and swing out from behind.

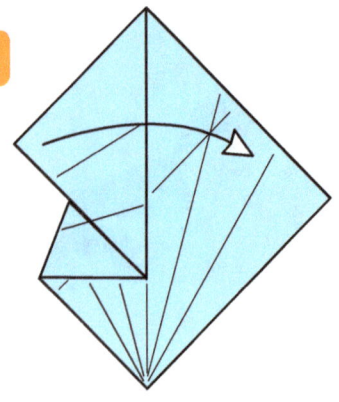

10

Unfold.

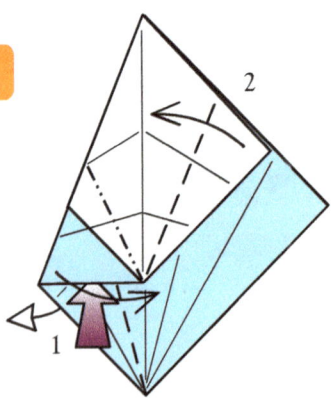

11

1. Valley-fold along the crease for this reverse fold and swing out from behind.
2. Fold to the center.

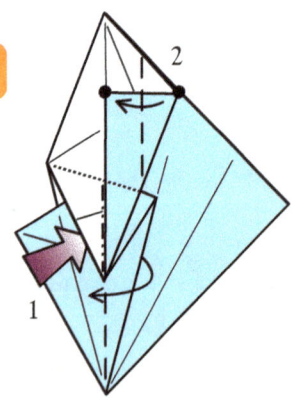

12

1. Reverse-fold.
2. Valley-fold.

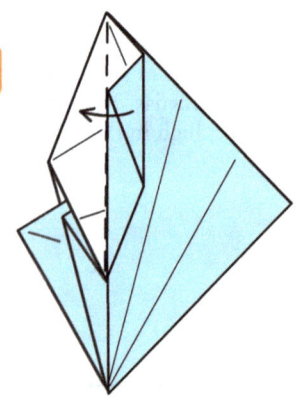

13

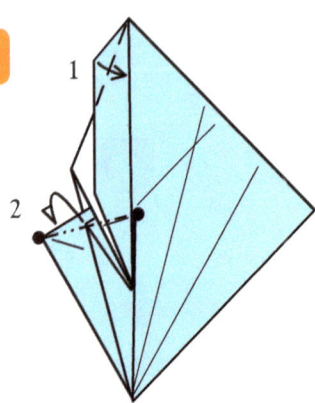

14

1. Valley-fold.
2. Fold behind.

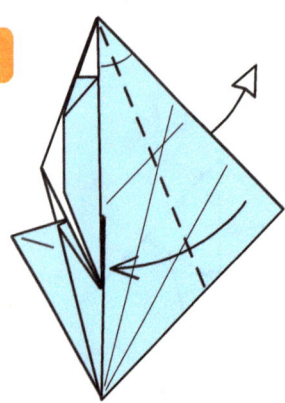

15

Repeat steps 9–14 on the right.

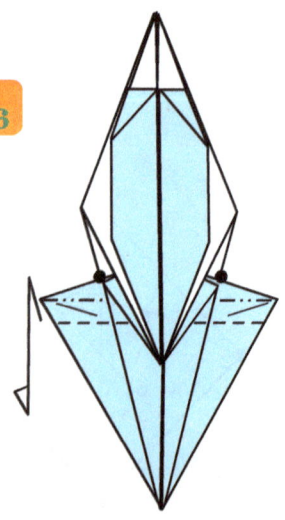

16

Pleat-fold so the edge meets the dots.

17

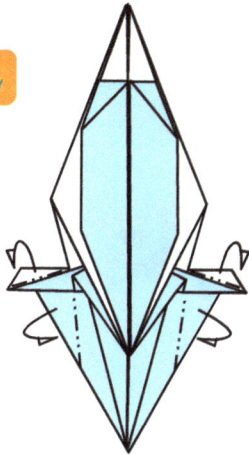

Make squash folds.

18

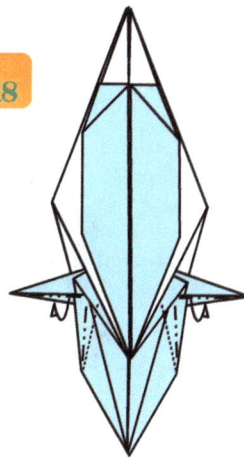

Make thin squash folds. Much of the folding is behind the tail.

19

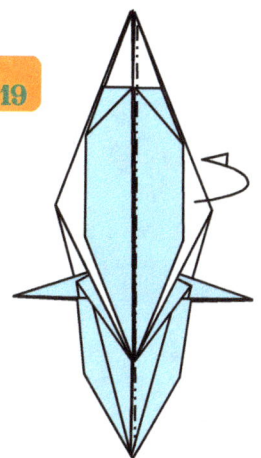

Fold in half and rotate.

20

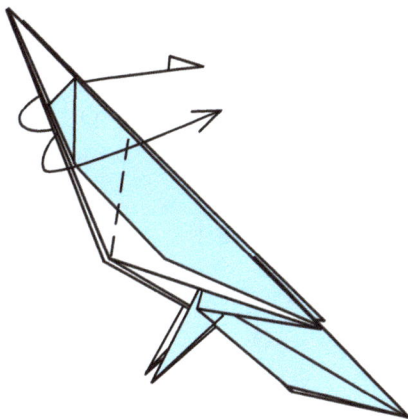

Outside-reverse-fold.

21

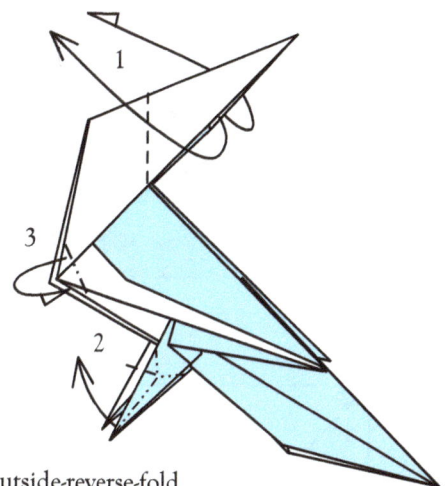

1. Outside-reverse-fold.
2. Double-rabbit-ear, repeat behind.
3. Fold inside, repeat behind.

22

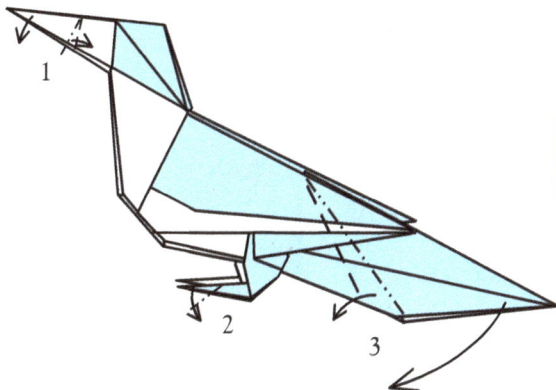

1. Crimp-fold.
2. Reverse-fold, repeat behind.
3. Crimp-fold.

23

Saffron Toucanet

Gannet

The Gannet is a seabird found on the coasts of the northern Altantic, Africa, Australia, and New Zealand. They dive into the seas to catch fish and squid. They live in large dense colonies, often found on cliffs.

1

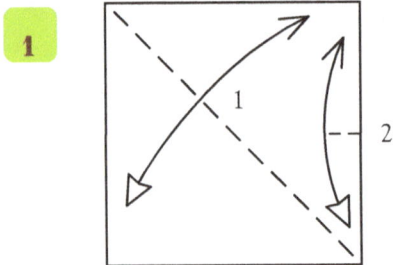

1. Fold and unfold.
2. Fold and unfold on the edge.

2

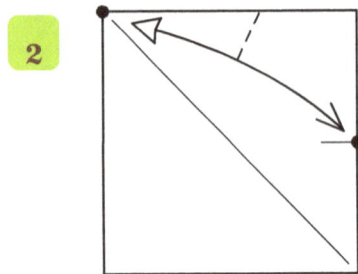

Fold and unfold on the top.

3

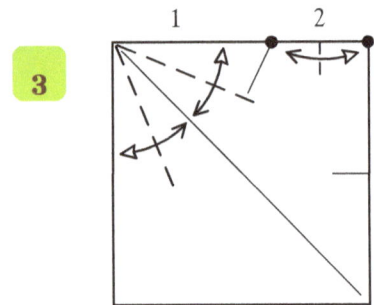

1. Fold to the center and unfold.
2. Fold and unfold on the top.

4

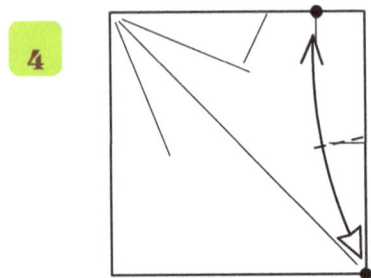

Fold and unfold.

5

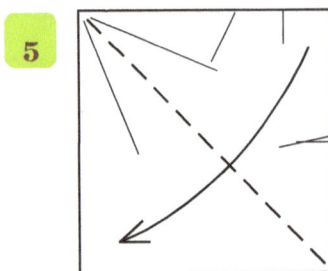

Fold along the crease.

6

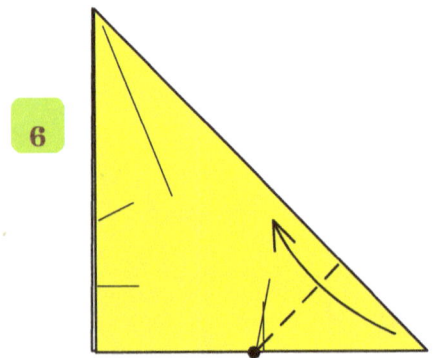

7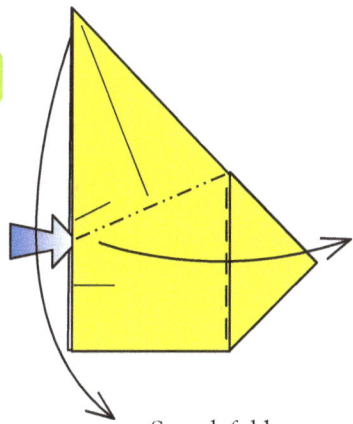

Squash-fold.

8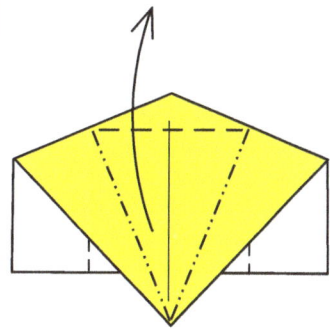

Petal-fold.

9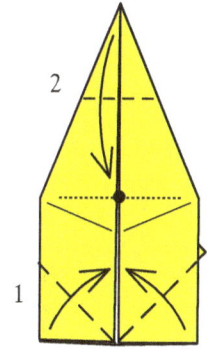

1. Fold to the center.
2. Fold down.

10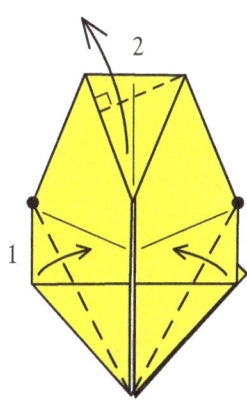

1. Fold at the bottom.
2. Fold at the top.

11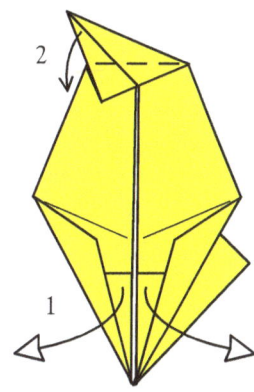

1. Unfold.
2. Fold down.

12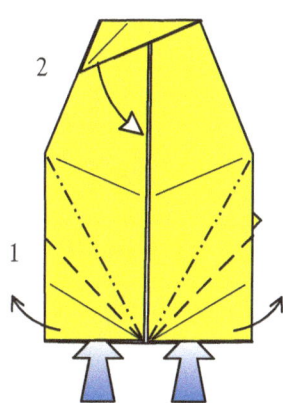

1. Make crimp folds along the creases.
2. Unfold.

13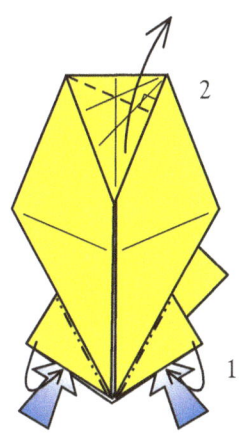

1. Make reverse folds.
2. Repeat steps 10–12 on the right.

14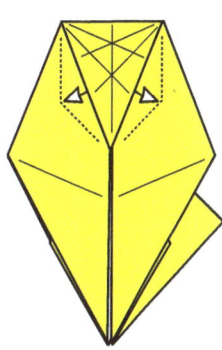

Pull out.

15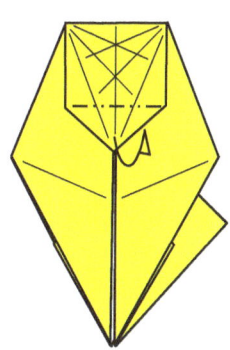

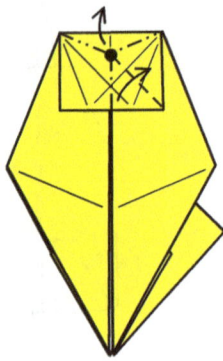

16

Lift up at the dot.
Mountain-fold
along the creases.

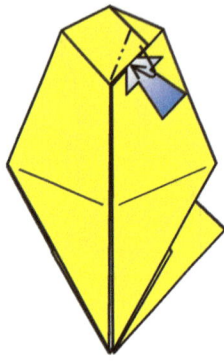

17

Reverse-fold.

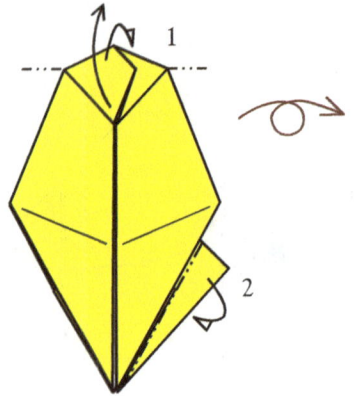

18

1. Swing the top behind
   while folding up.
2. Fold behind.

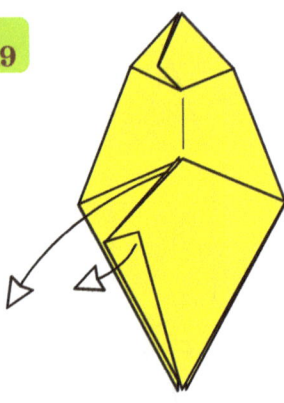

19

Unfold.

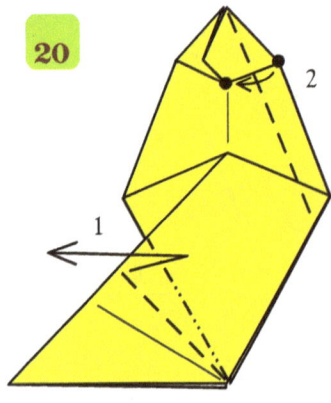

20

1. Crimp-fold along
   the creases.
2. Valley-fold.

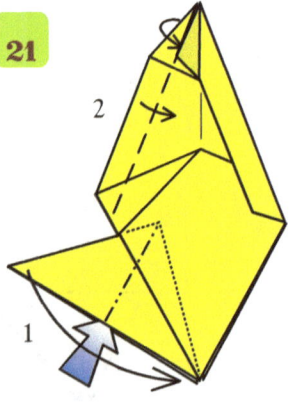

21

1. Reverse-fold.
2. Tuck under the
   darker layers.

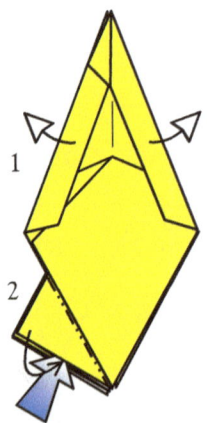

22

1. Unfold.
2. Make two
   reverse folds.

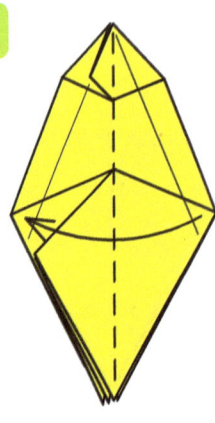

23

Fold in half
and rotate.

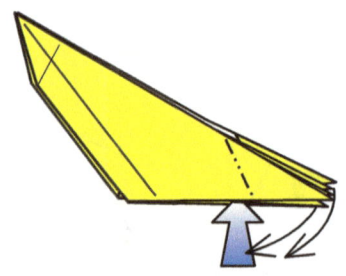

24

There are five flaps on the right.
Reverse-fold the second and fourth
flaps to form the legs. Make small
squash folds at the tops.

25

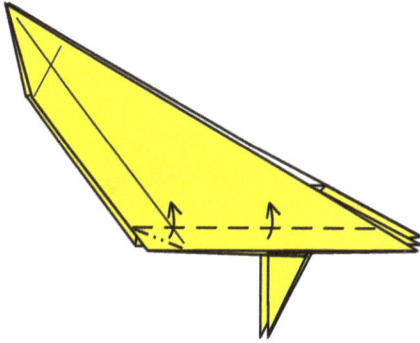

Make two spread-squash
folds. Repeat behind.

26

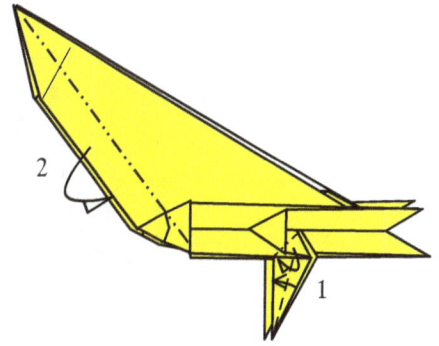

1. Thin the leg with a small reverse
   fold at the top. Repeat on the back
   of the leg. Repeat behind.
2. Fold inside, repeat behind.

27

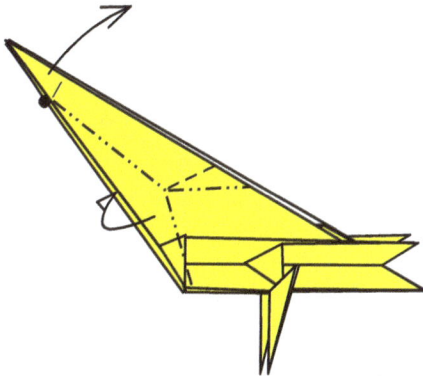

Double-rabbit-ear.

28

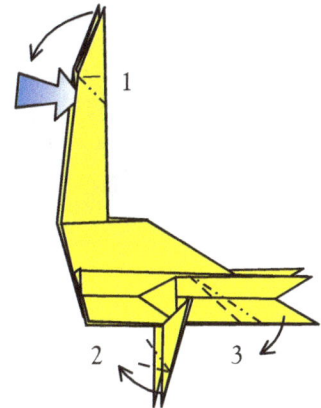

1. Reverse-fold.
2. Crimp-fold, repeat behind.
3. Crimp-fold.

29

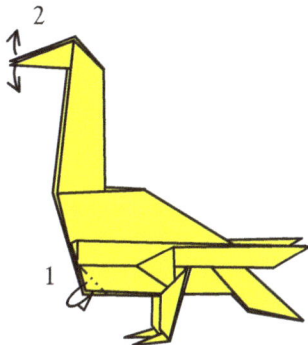

1. Fold inside, repeat behind.
2. Spread the beak.

30

Gannet

Parrot

Parrots are colorful birds with strong, hooked beaks, which are perfect for cracking nuts. These intelligent birds are found in tropical and subtropical regions of South America, Africa, Australia, and New Zealand. These social birds feed on seeds, fruit, and insects. They are the only birds that can pick up food with their feet and feed themselves, as we would with our hands.

1

Fold and unfold.

2

Fold to the center.

3

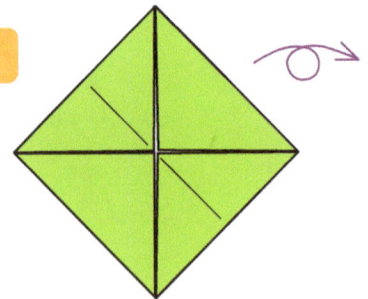

4

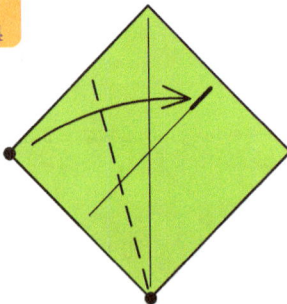

Bring the corner
to the line.

5

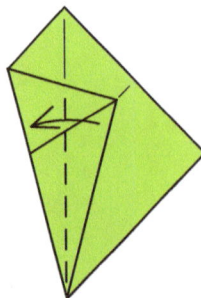

6

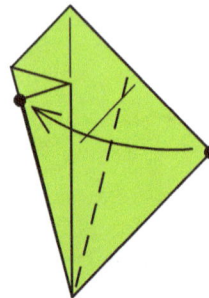

7

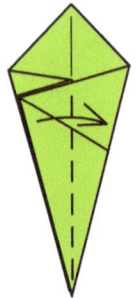

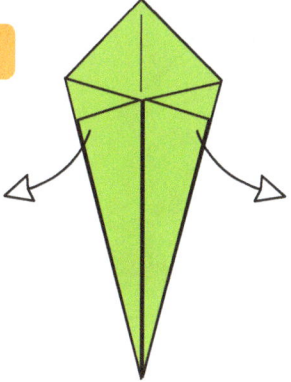

8

Unfold.

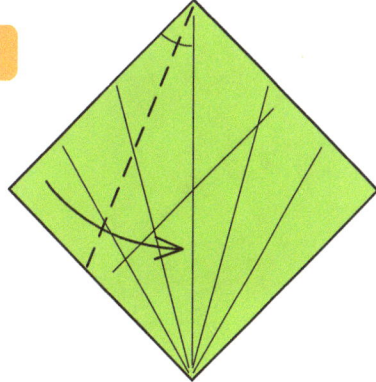

9

Fold to the center.

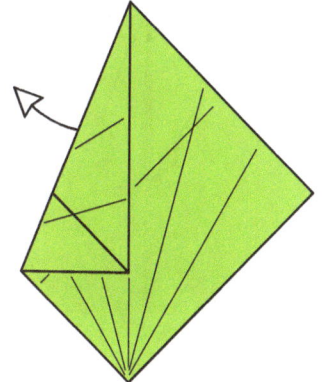

10

Unfold.

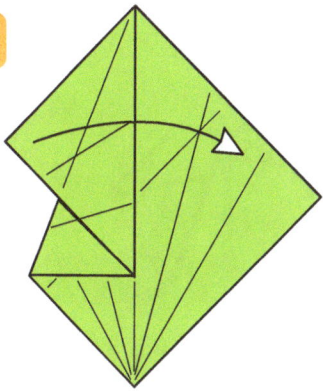

11

Unfold.

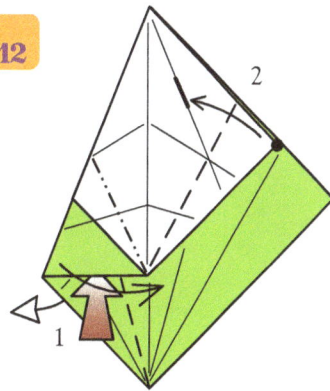

12

1. Valley-fold along the crease
   for this reverse fold and
   swing out from behind.
2. Bring the dot to the line.

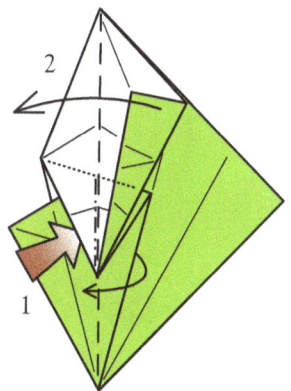

13

1. Reverse-fold.
2. Valley-fold.

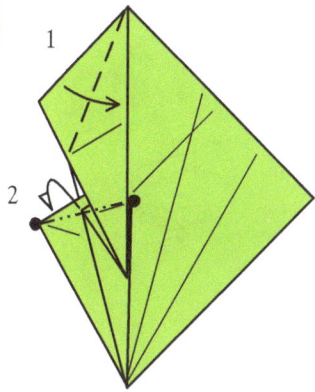

14

1. Fold along the crease.
2. Fold behind.

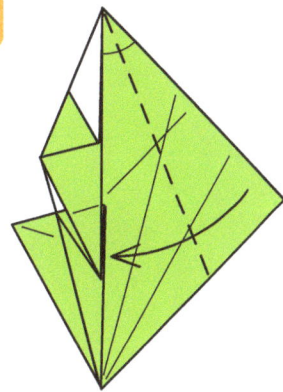

15

Repeat steps 9–14
on the right.

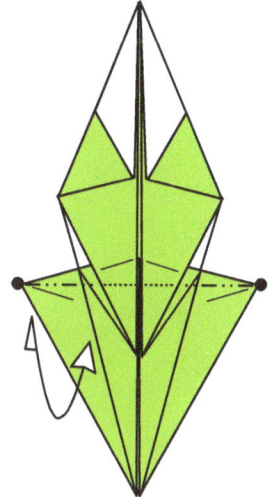

16

Fold and unfold.

Parrot **35**

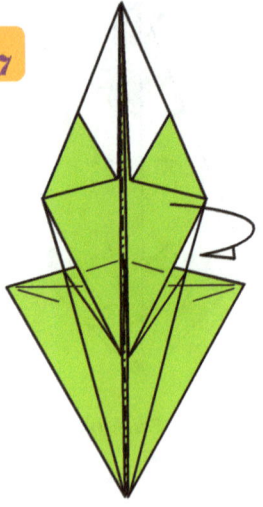

17

Fold in half and rotate.

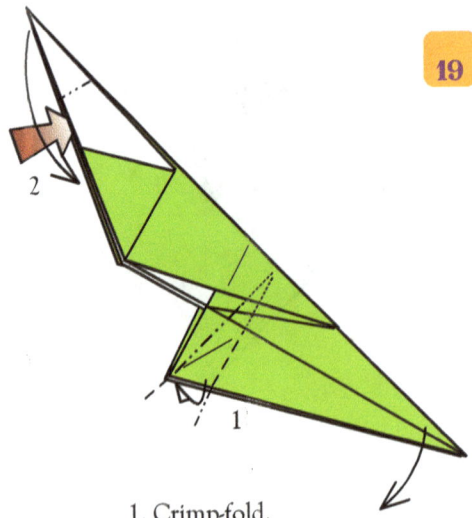

18

1. Crimp-fold.
2. Reverse-fold.

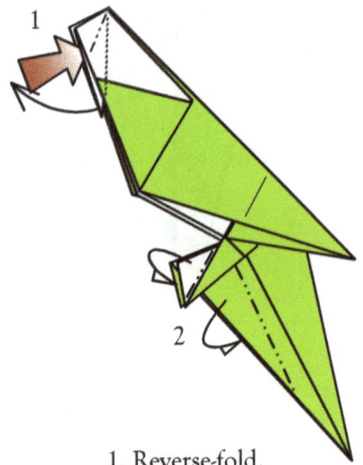

19

1. Reverse-fold.
2. Squash-fold,
   repeat behind.

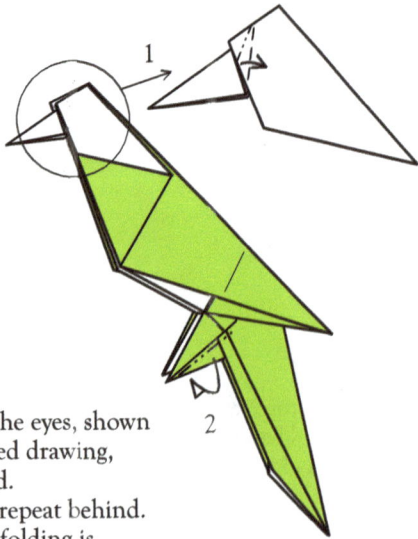

20

1. Squash-fold the eyes, shown
   in the enlarged drawing,
   repeat behind.
2. Squash-fold, repeat behind.
   Much of the folding is
   hidden in the tail.

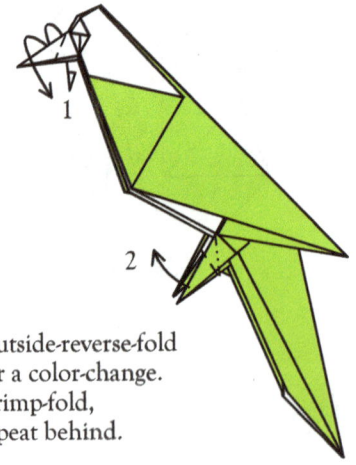

21

1. Outside-reverse-fold
   for a color-change.
2. Crimp-fold,
   repeat behind.

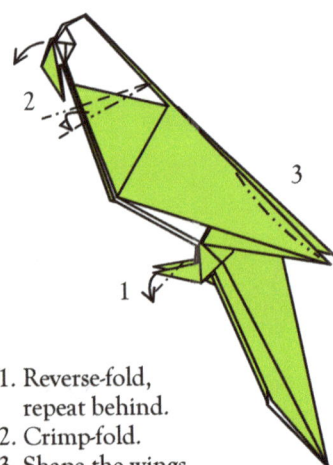

22

1. Reverse-fold,
   repeat behind.
2. Crimp-fold.
3. Shape the wings,
   repeat behind.

23

Parrot

Second Movement

Andante: Colorful Coral Reef Fish Swimming in Harmony

Coral Reefs are animals that grow in shallow water. They create large colonies that provide for incredibly beautiful habitats of a wide range of colorful fish and other sea creatures. Many coral reef fish are flat so they can hide between the coral reefs. Many have stripes for camouflage. In symphonic form, every other fish in this movement is striped. It is time to catch these vibrant fish.

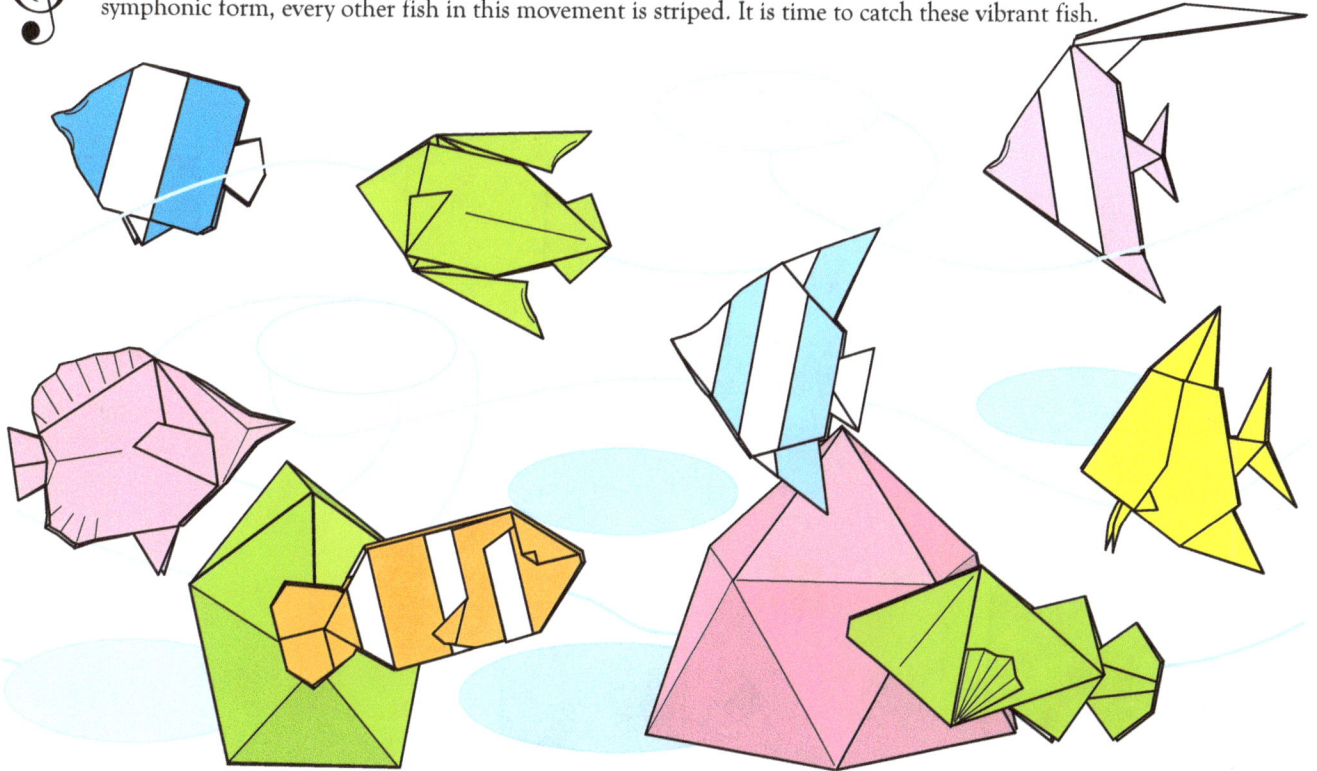

Easy Angelfish

Angelfish are popular in aquariums. They swim gracefully and are happy to go to the top of the tank when being fed. This simple fish begins the journey into the stunning beauty of coral reef fish.

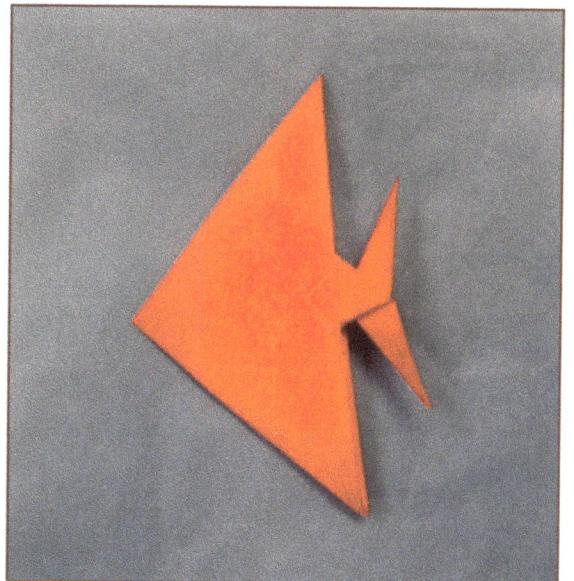

1

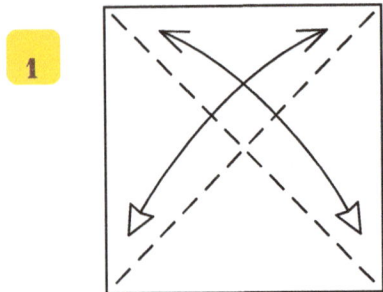

Fold and unfold.

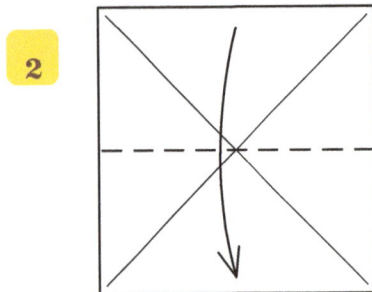

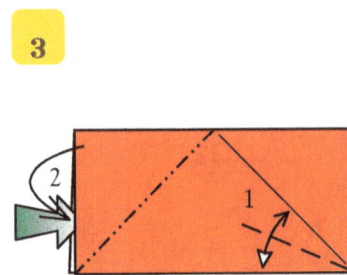

2

3

1. Fold and unfold
   both layers.
2. Reverse-fold.

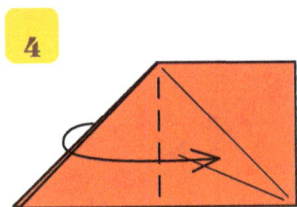

4

Fold both layers.

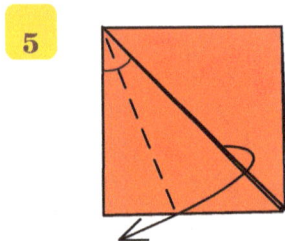

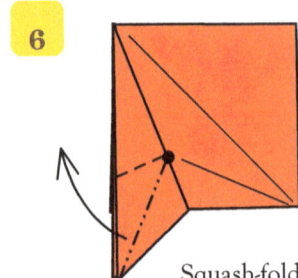

5

Fold both layers.

6

Squash-fold
both layers.

7

The dotted line shows that
the crease (on the right) lines
up with the tail on the left.
Reverse-fold both layers.

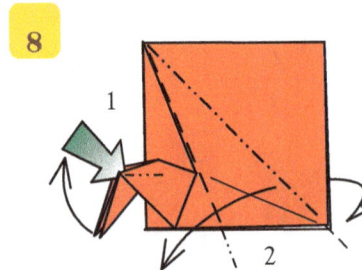

8

1. Reverse-fold the inner flap.
2. Crimp-fold.

9

Mountain-fold two
hidden layers together
to lock the model.

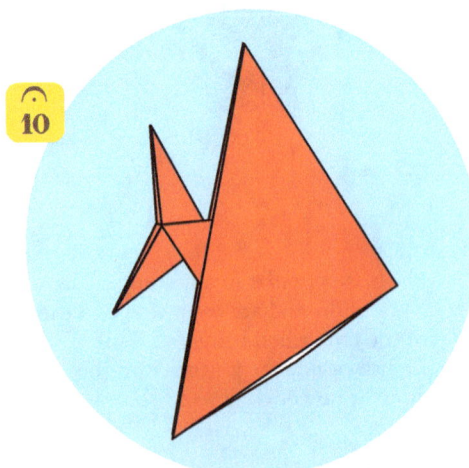

10

Easy Angelfish

Easy Butterflyfish

Butterflyfish are popular in home aquariums. Colorful and banded patterns make these beautiful fish fun to watch as they swim gracefully. This Easy Butterflyfish captures their shape with stripes in 16 steps.

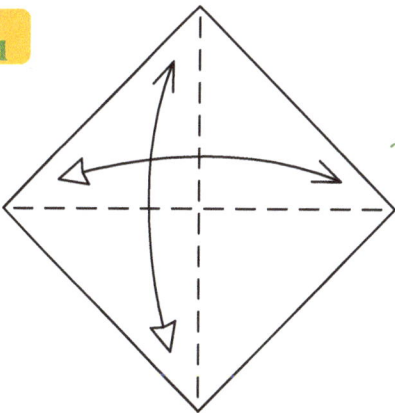

1

Fold and unfold.

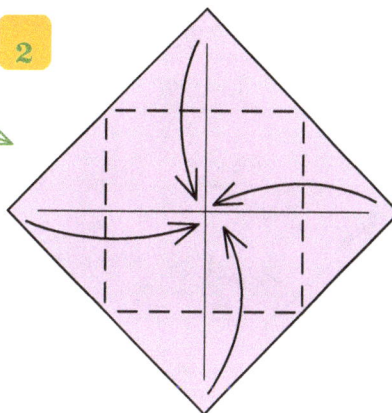

2

Fold the corners to the center.

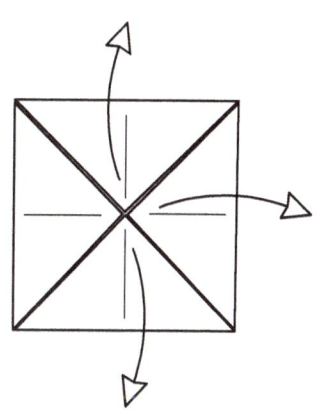

3

Unfold on three sides.

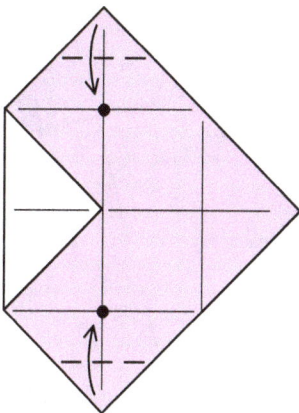

4

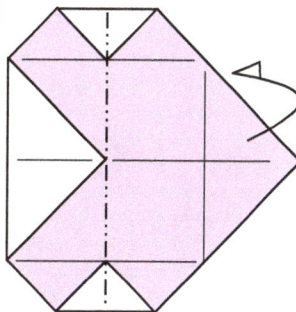

5

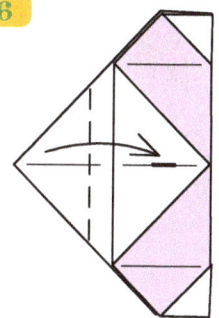

6

Fold a bit to the right of the center of the triangle with the bold line.

7

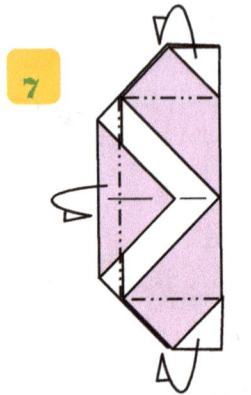

Fold behind
along the creases.

8

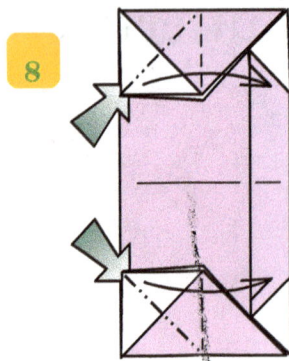

Make squash folds.

9

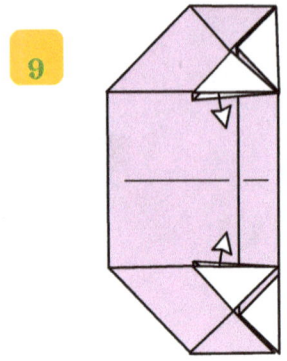

Pull out the
white corners.

10

This is similar to
squash folds.

11

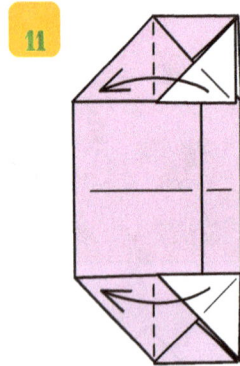

Rotate 90°.

12

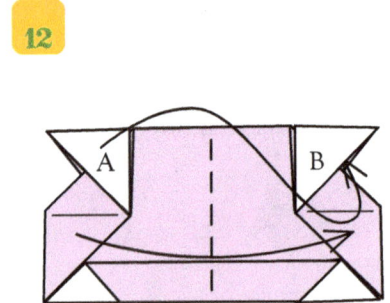

Tuck A into B while
folding in half. Rotate 45°.

13

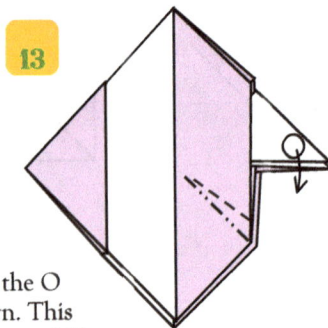

Hold the tail at the O
and slide it down. This
is similar to a crimp fold.

14

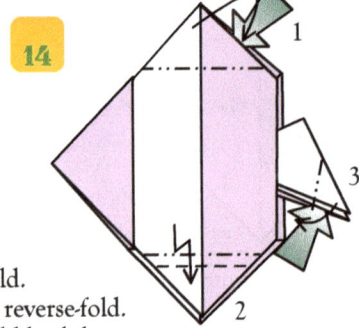

1. Reverse-fold.
2. Pleat-fold, reverse-fold.
3. Reverse-fold both layers.

15

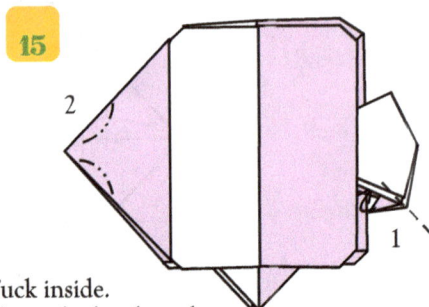

1. Tuck inside.
2. Shape the head, push
   in on the top, repeat
   behind on the bottom.

16

Easy Butterflyfish

Angelfish

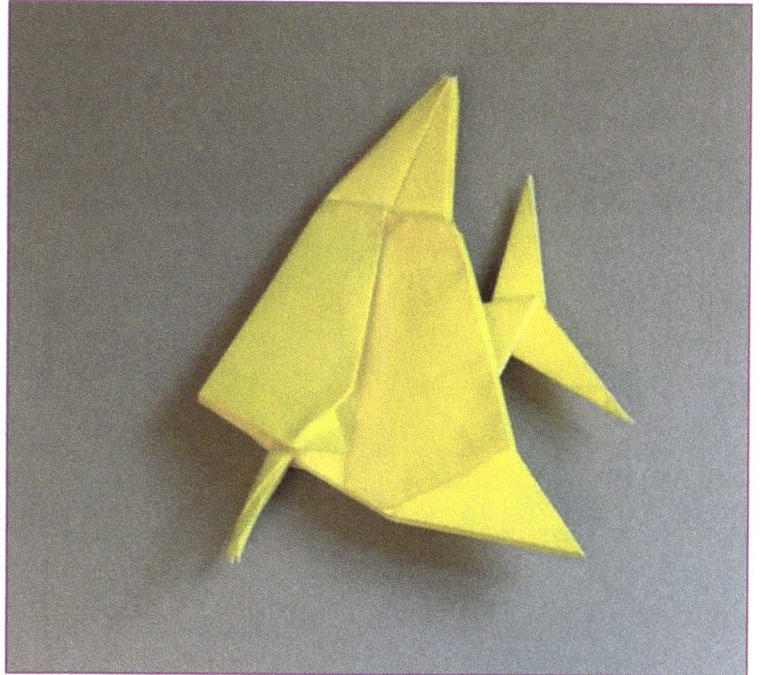

Angelfish are Cichlids with fins that give them a triangular shape. They swim in the Amazon River Basin and other waters of South America. Around 6 to 10 inches long, they feed on small crustaceans and worms.

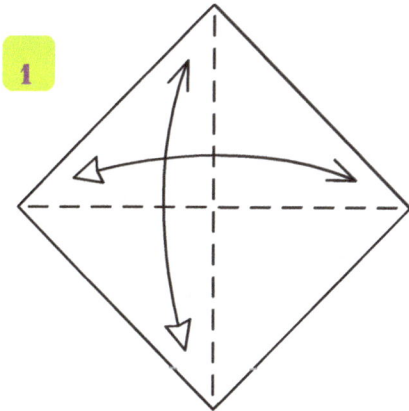

Fold and unfold.

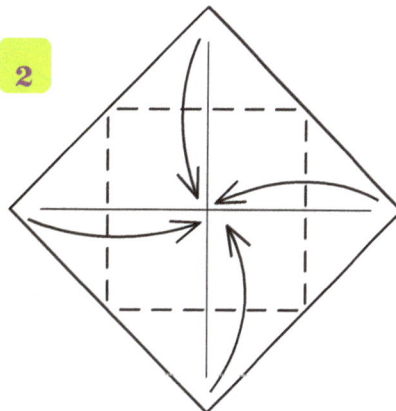

Fold the corners to the center.

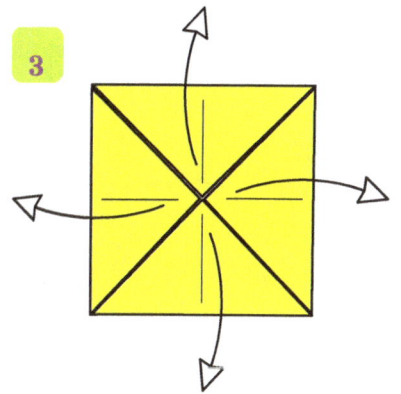

Unfold.

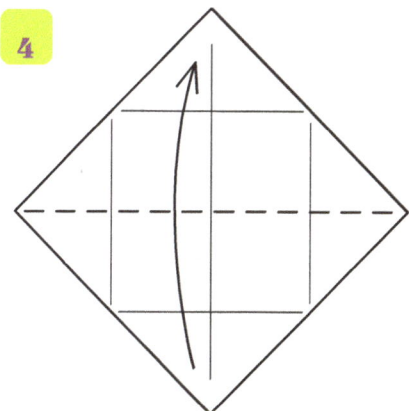

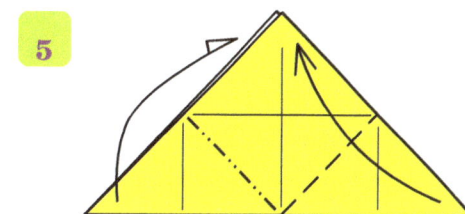

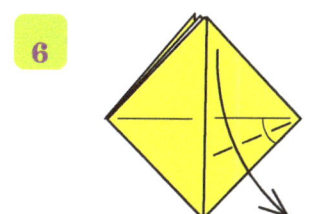

7

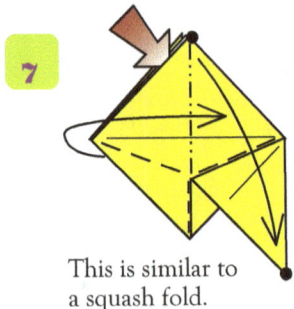

This is similar to a squash fold.

8

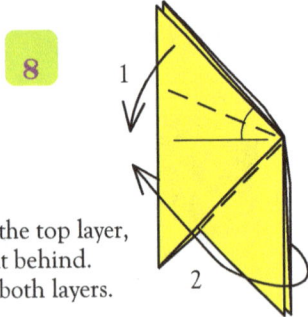

1. Fold the top layer, repeat behind.
2. Fold both layers.

9

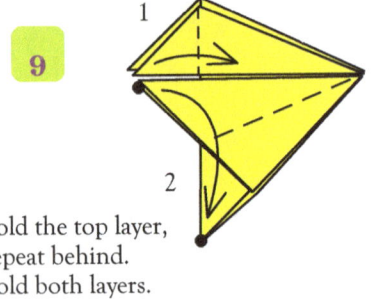

1. Fold the top layer, repeat behind.
2. Fold both layers.

10

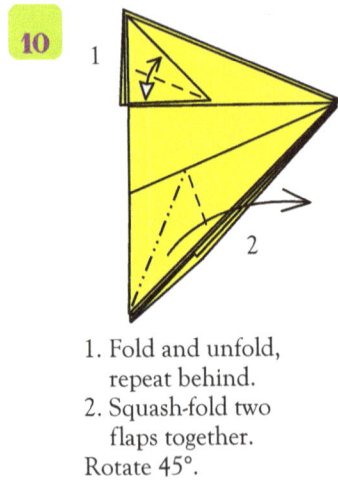

1. Fold and unfold, repeat behind.
2. Squash-fold two flaps together. Rotate 45°.

11

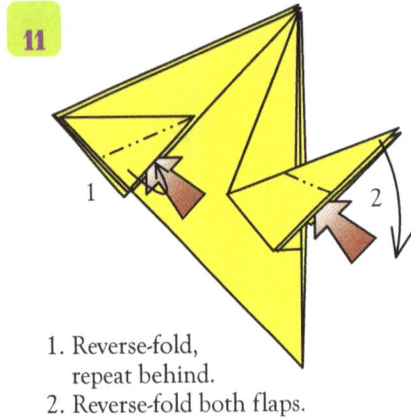

1. Reverse-fold, repeat behind.
2. Reverse-fold both flaps.

12

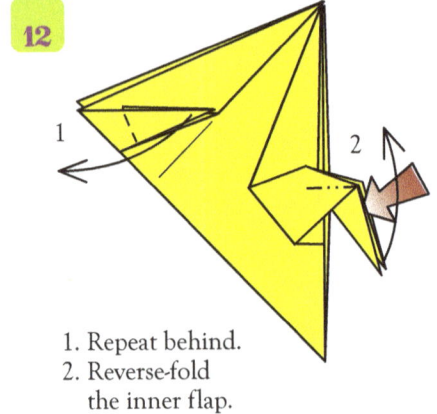

1. Repeat behind.
2. Reverse-fold the inner flap.

13

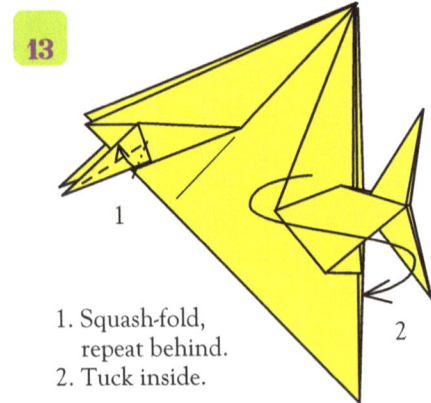

1. Squash-fold, repeat behind.
2. Tuck inside.

14

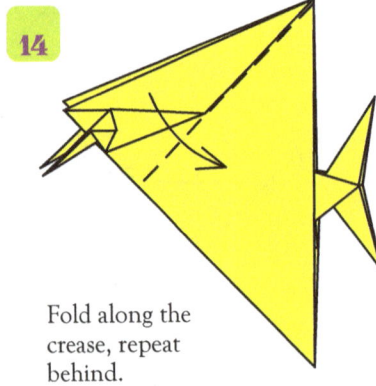

Fold along the crease, repeat behind.

15

Pleat-fold, repeat behind.

16

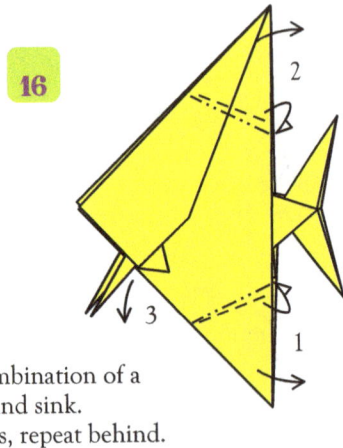

1. Crimp-fold.
2. This is a combination of a crimp fold and sink.
3. Curl the fins, repeat behind.

17

Angelfish

Colorful Angelfish

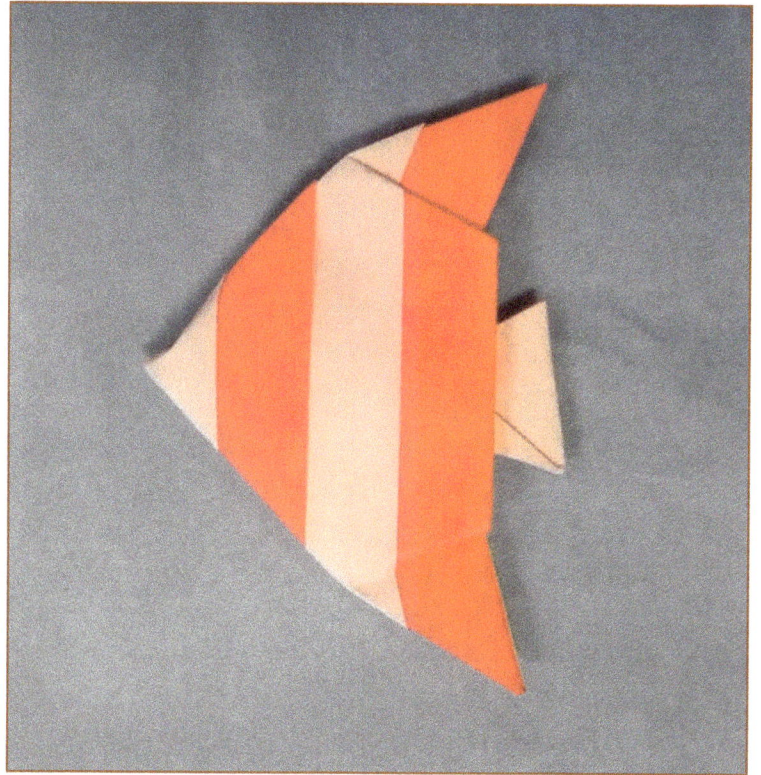

Angelfish have stripes which are used as camouflage with the stems of the plants in the water. Folding stripes on origami models is a fun challenge that produces a stunning effect.

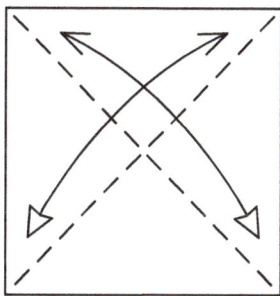

1

Fold and unfold.

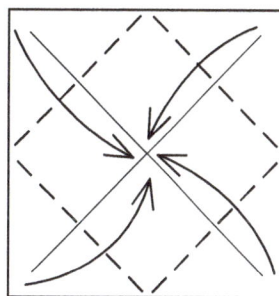

2

Fold the corners to the center.

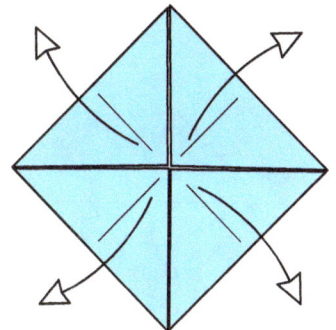

3

Unfold.

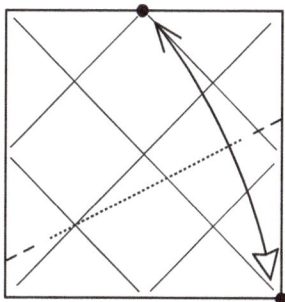

4

Fold and unfold, creasing on the left and right.

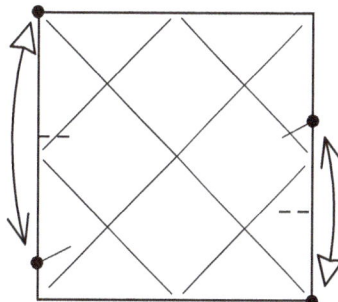

5

Fold and unfold on the left and right.

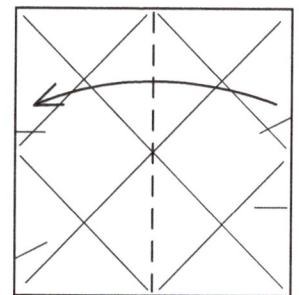

6

Fold in half.

7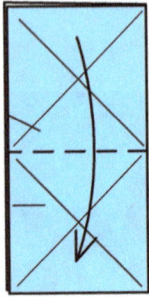

Fold in half.

8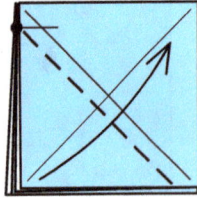

Fold the top layer.

9

Fold the top layer.

10

Fold the top layer, a tiny bit above the landmark at the dot.

11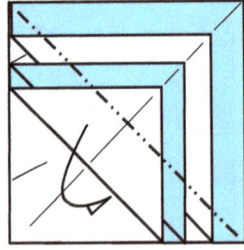

Fold all the layers together.

12

Rotate 45° so the dot goes to the top.

13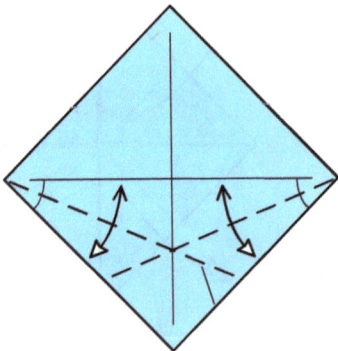

Fold and unfold.

14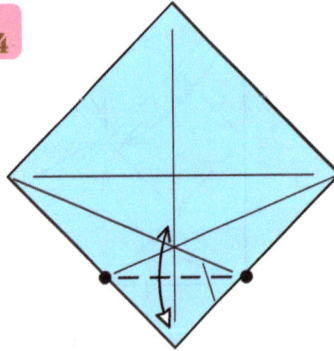

Fold and unfold.

15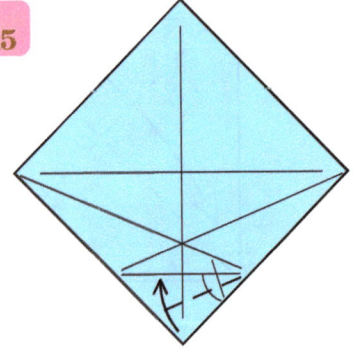

16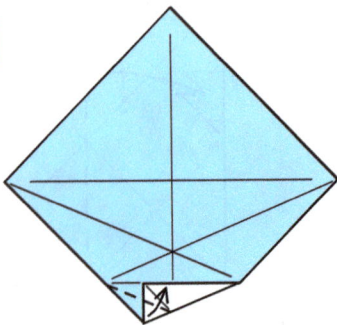

17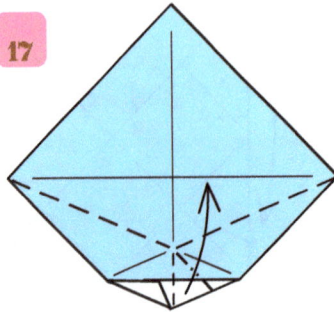

Rabbit-ear.

18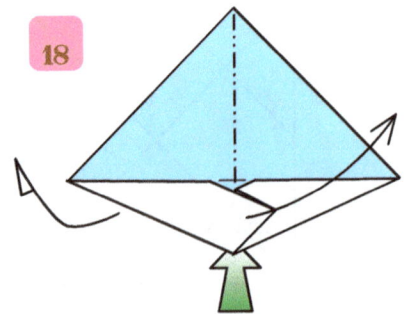

Spread the model.

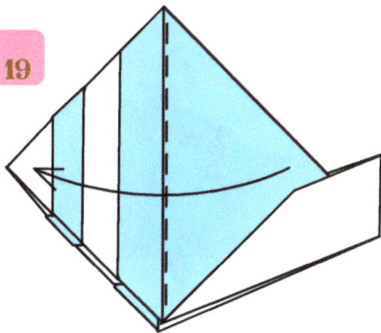

19

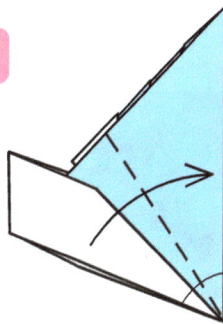

20

21

Squash-fold.

22

Unfold back
to step 21.

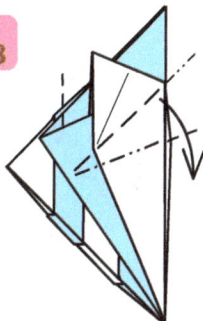

23

This is similar to a
crimp fold. Refold
along the creases.

24

Repeat behind.

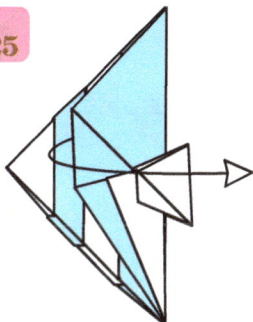

25

Unfold.

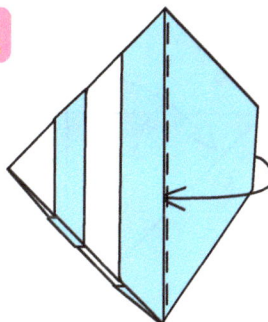

26

Tuck inside.

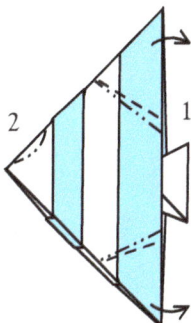

27

1. Make crimp folds.
2. Shape the head.

28

**Colorful
Angelfish**

Colorful Angelfish **45**

Butterflyfish

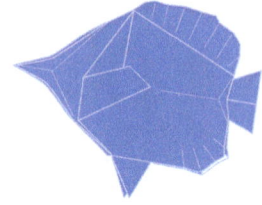

Butterflyfish are beautifully colored tropical marine fish found in reefs around the world. With long, thin snouts, they feed on coral for small invertebrates, worms, and other small creatures. They range in size from 4 to 12 inches.

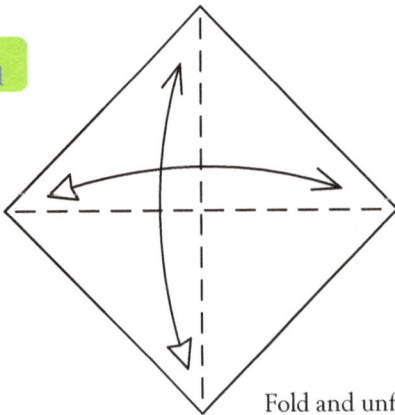

Fold and unfold.

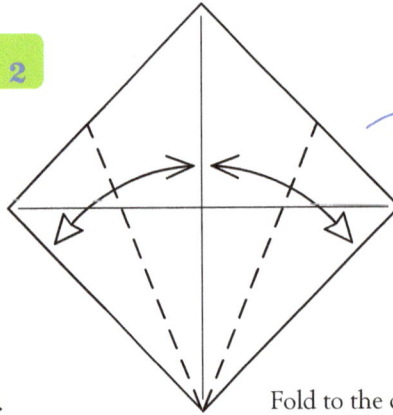

Fold to the center and unfold.

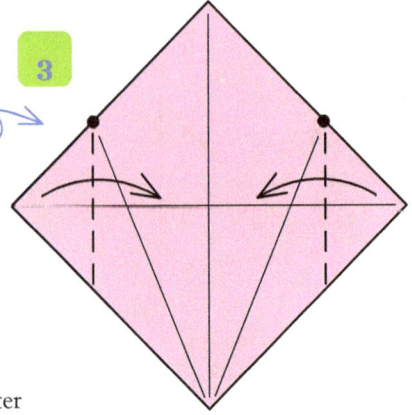

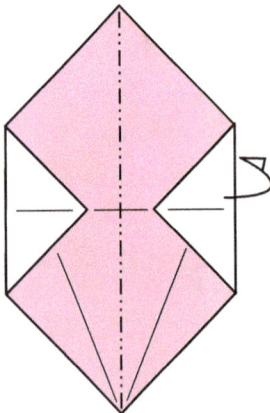

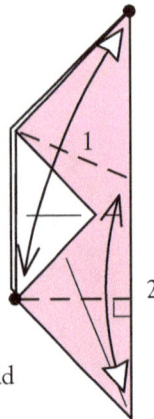

Fold and unfold at 1 and 2.

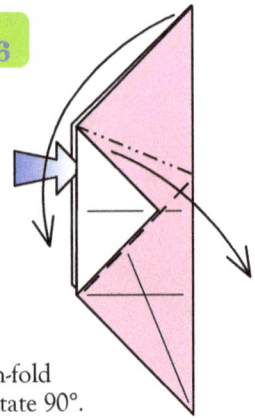

Squash-fold and rotate 90°.

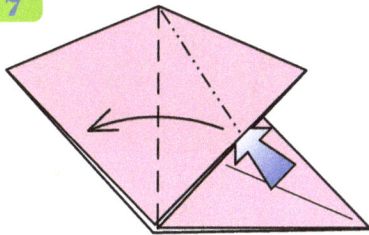

Squash-fold.

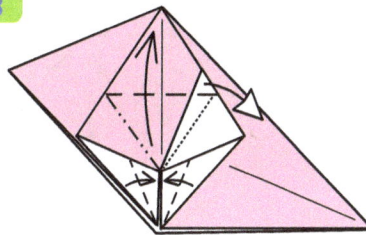

Petal-fold and unwrap the white paper on the right.

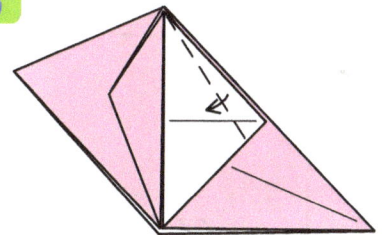

Fold along the hidden edge.

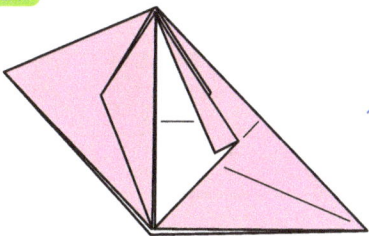

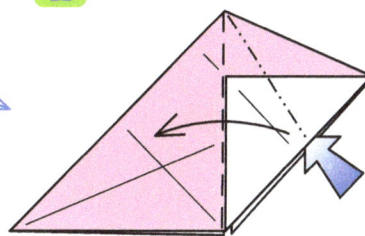

Repeat steps 7–9 on the left.

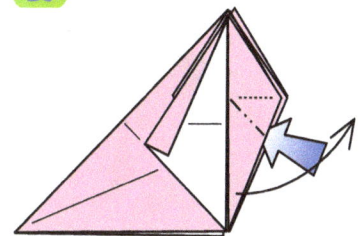

Reverse-fold.

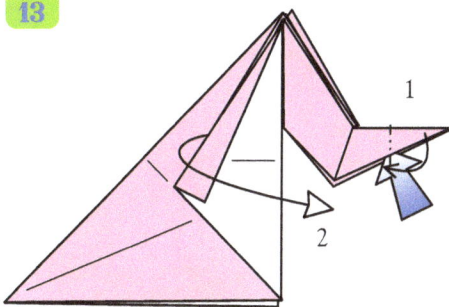

1. Reverse-fold.
2. Unfold, repeat behind.
Rotate 90°.

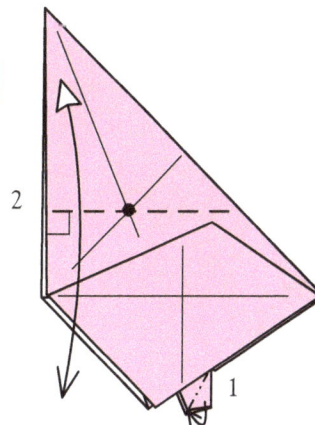

1. Reverse-fold.
2. Fold and unfold.

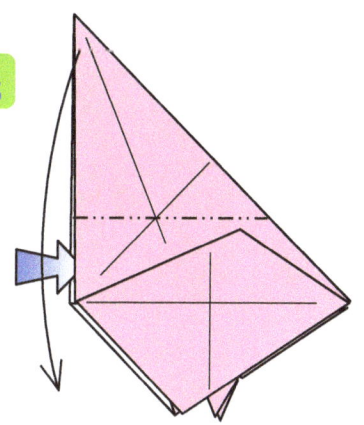

Reverse-fold.

16

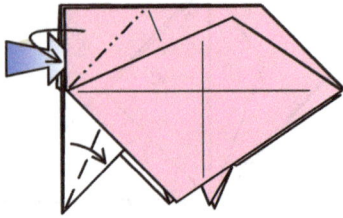

Reverse-fold,
repeat behind.

17

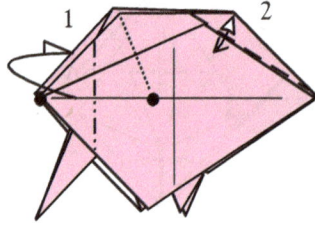

1. Fold inside so the dots
   meet, repeat behind.
2. Fold and unfold.

18

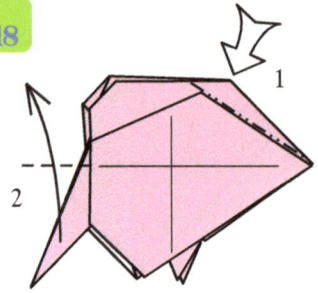

1. Sink.
2. Valley-fold along the
   horizontal crease.

19

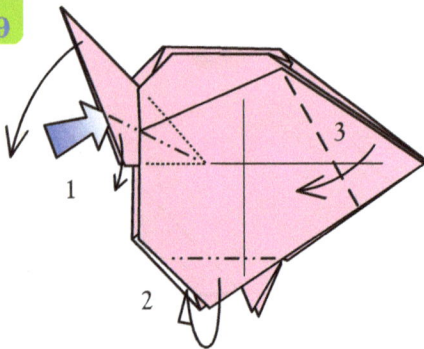

1. Squash-fold.
2. Fold inside, repeat behind.
3. Repet behind.

20

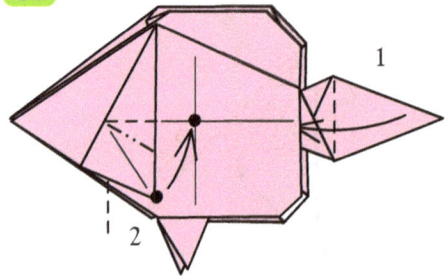

1. Tuck inside.
2. Squash-fold,
   repeat behind.

21

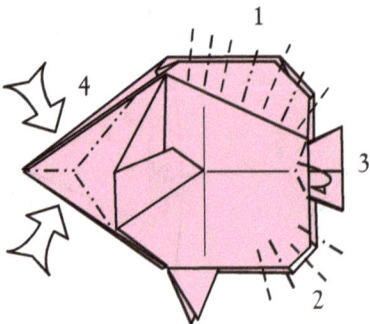

1. Pleat-fold all the layers.
2. Pleat-fold, repeat behind.
3. Make the base of the tail 3D,
   repeat behind.
4. Thin the head by making it 3D.

22

Butterflyfish

Black Pyramid Butterflyfish

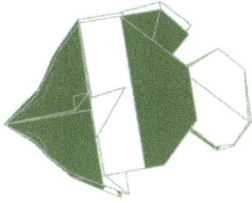

The Black Pyramid Butterflyfish feeds on algae, plankton, and corals. This 9 inch fish swims in reefs of the Indian Ocean.

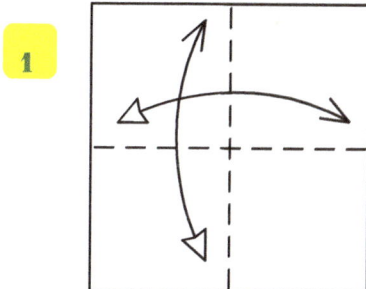

1

Fold and unfold.

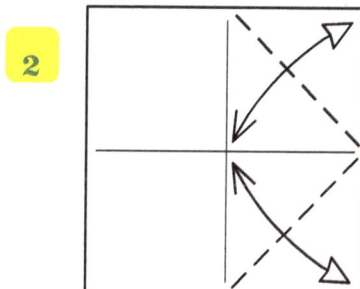

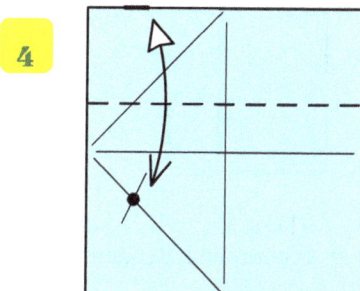

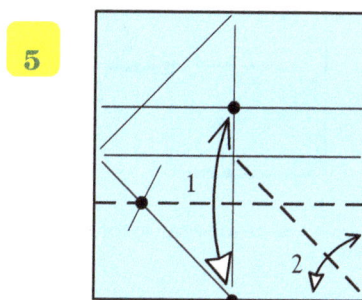

2

Fold to the center and unfold.

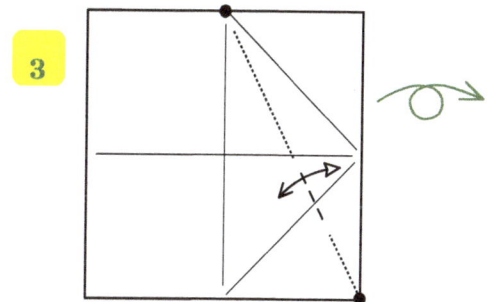

3

Fold and unfold.

4

Fold and unfold.

5

Fold and unfold at 1 and 2.

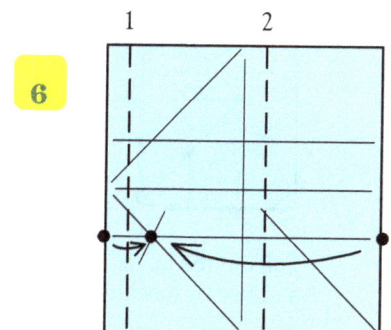

6

7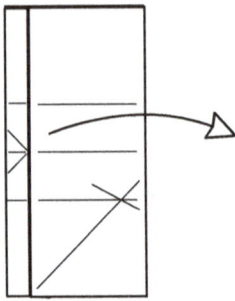

Unfold.

8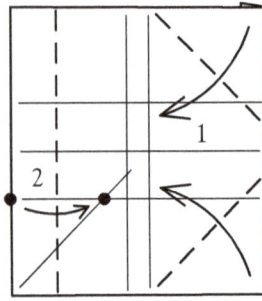

1. Fold along the creases.
2. The dots will meet.

9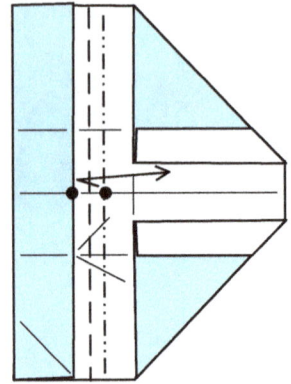

Mountain-fold along the crease for this pleat fold.

10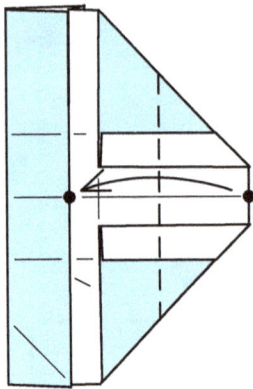

11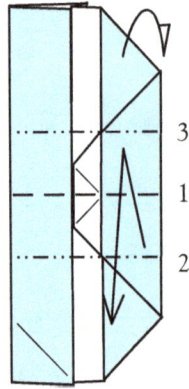

Fold along the creases.

12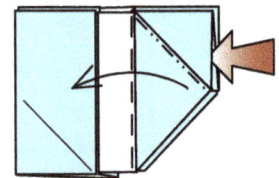

Squash-fold and repeat behind.

13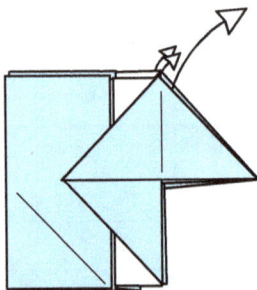

Pull out the hidden flap and two small white flaps.

14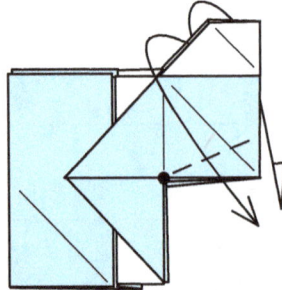

Outside-reverse-fold.

15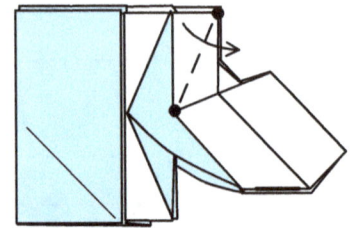

This is 3D. Note the bold line is horizontal. Repeat behind.

16

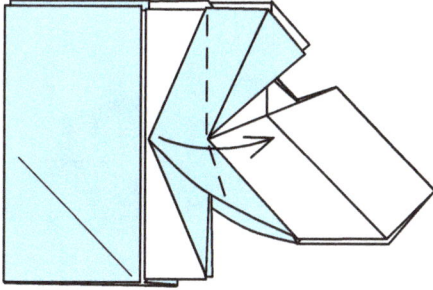

Flatten and repeat behind.

17

1
2

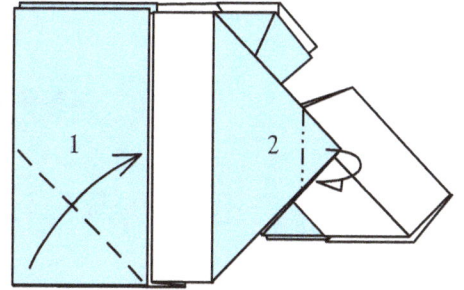

1. Valley-fold.
2. Mountain-fold.
Repeat behind.

18

1
2

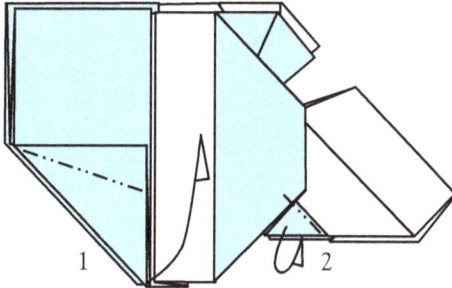

1. Mountain-fold the
   hidden white flap.
2. Fold inside.
Repeat behind.

19

3
2
1

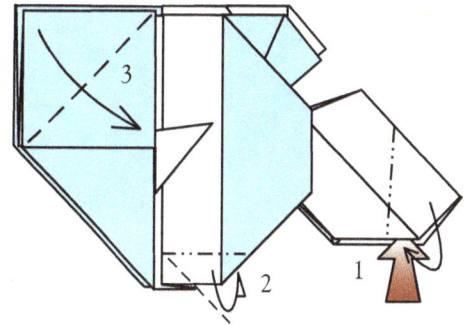

1. Reverse-fold.
2. Fold inside, repeat behind.
3. Valley-fold, repeat behind.

20

1
2

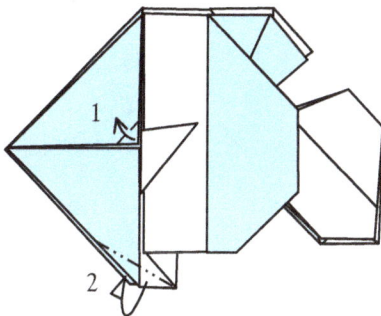

1. Fold the eye.
2. Fold inside.
Repeat behind.

21

2
1

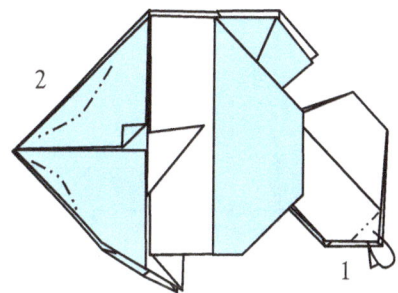

1. Fold inside.
2. Shape the head.
Repeat behind.

22

**Black Pyramid
Butterflyfish**

Blue Tang Surgeonfish

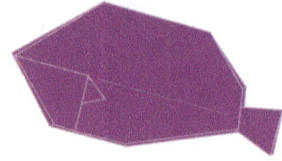

The Blue Tang Surgeonfish has a deep royal blue body with a yellow tail. It is found in abundance in the reefs of Indonesia, Japan, and the Great Barrier Reef of Australia. This 12 inch fish lives in pairs or small groups and feeds on plankton and algae.

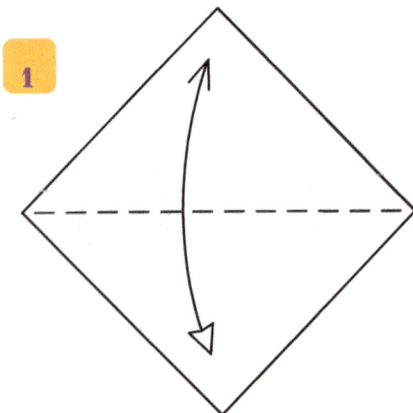

1

Fold and unfold.

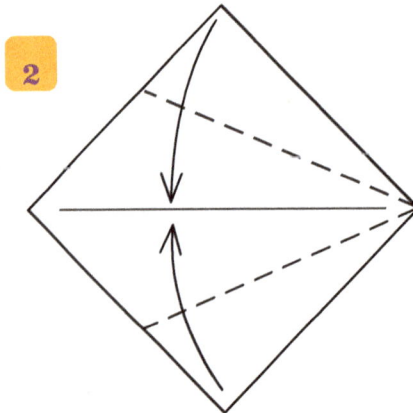

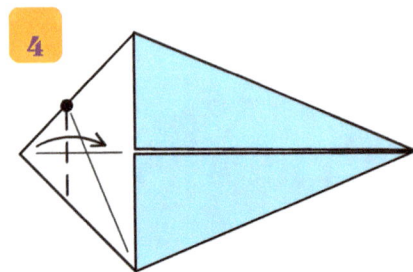

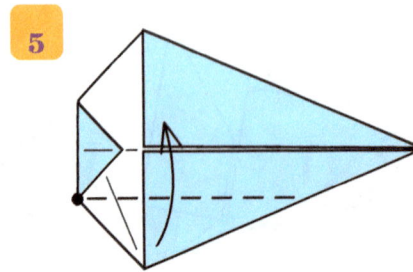

2

Fold to the center.

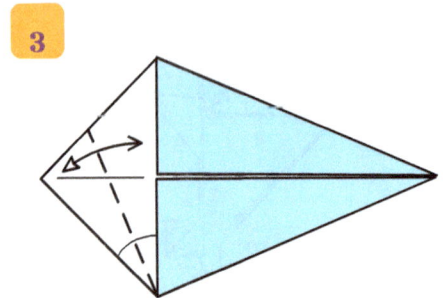

3

Fold and unfold.

4

5

Crease lightly.

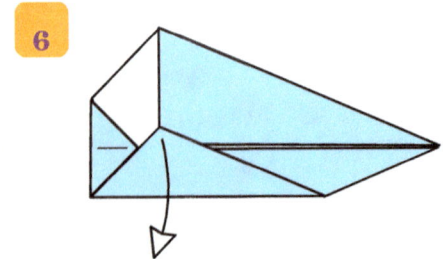

6

Unfold.

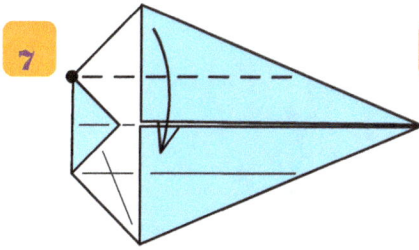

7

Repeat steps 5–6 on the top.

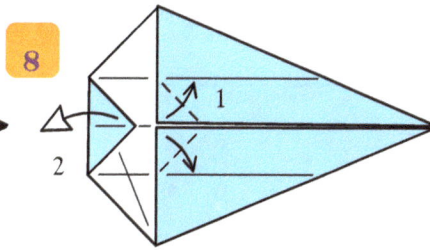

8

1. Fold to the creases.
2. Unfold.

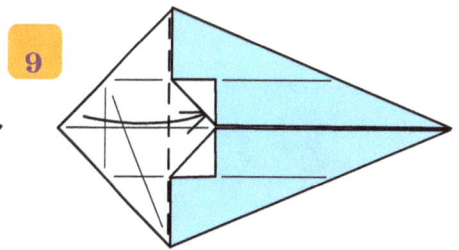

9

Tuck inside.

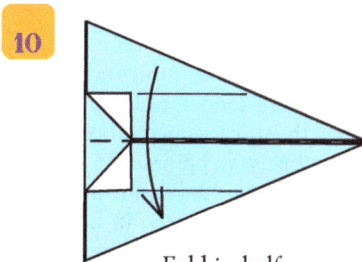

10

Fold in half.

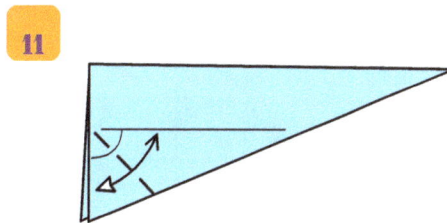

11

Fold and unfold the top flap. Repeat behind.

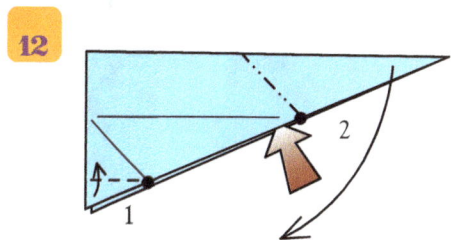

12

1. Repeat behind.
2. Reverse-fold.

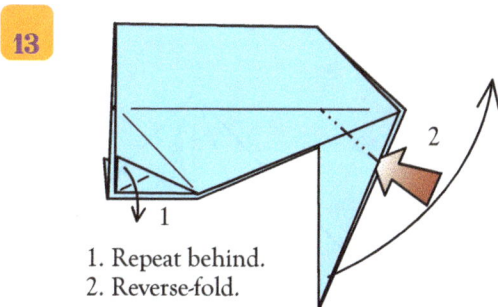

13

1. Repeat behind.
2. Reverse-fold.

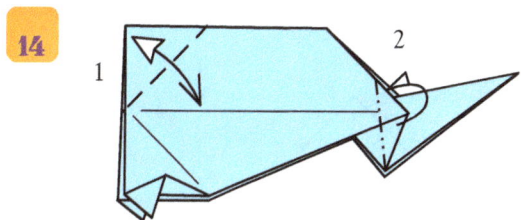

14

1. Fold and unfold.
2. Repeat behind.

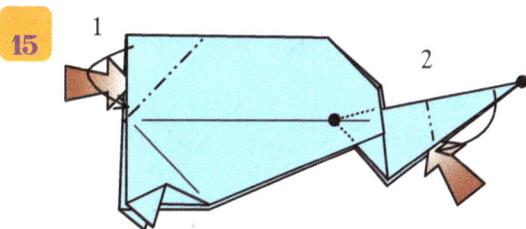

15

1. Reverse-fold into the white layers to lock.
2. Reverse-fold so the dots meet.

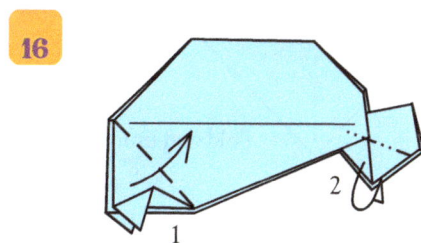

16

Repeat behind at 1 and 2.

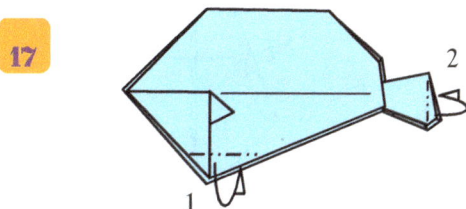

17

Repeat behind at 1 and 2.

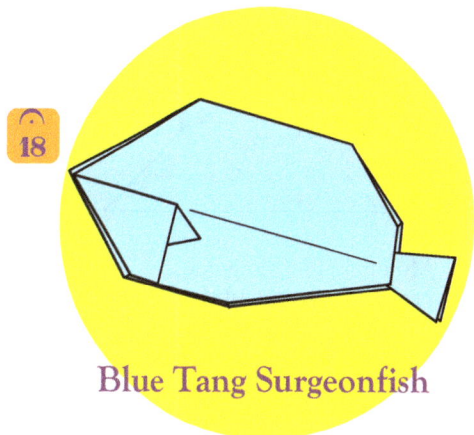

18

Blue Tang Surgeonfish

Moorish Idol

The Moorish Idol is a beautiful and peaceful fish with a long dorsal fin. The Moors of North Africa named it because they believe it brings happiness. At 7 to 9 inches, the Moorish Idol swims in shallow waters of tropical reefs in East Africa, the Indian Ocean, and other parts of the Indo-Pacific. It feeds on corals, sponges, and small invertebrates.

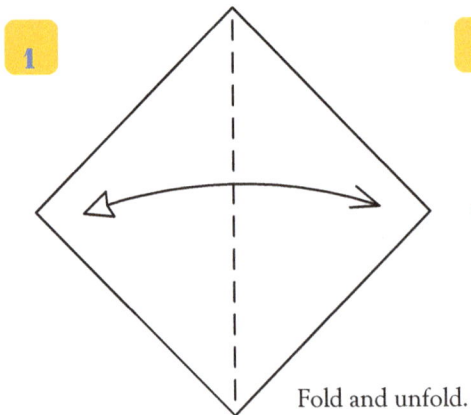

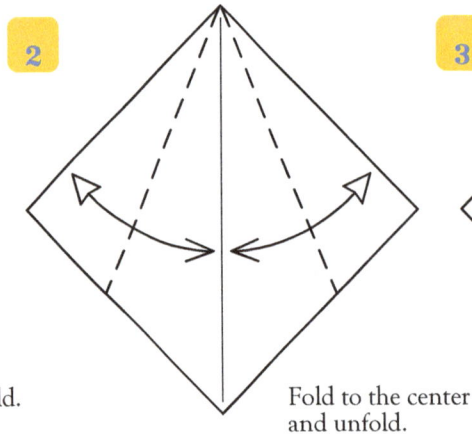

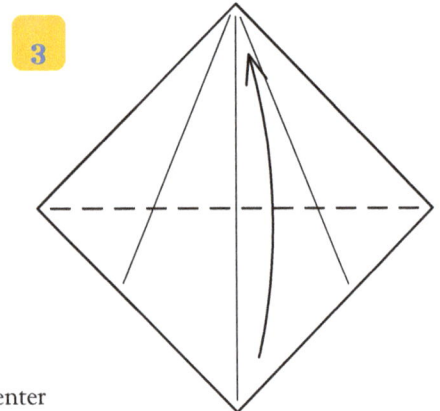

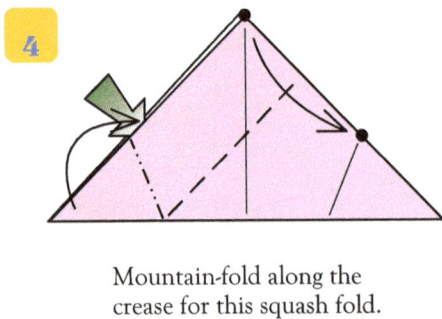

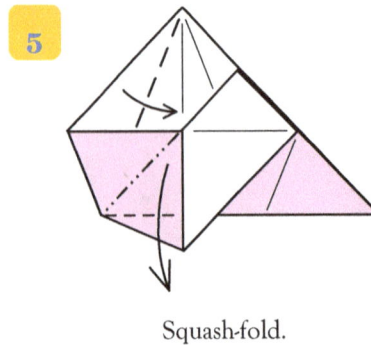

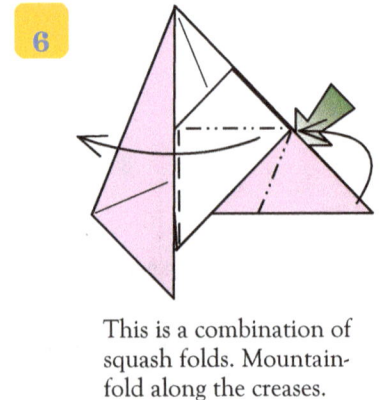

1

Fold and unfold.

2

Fold to the center and unfold.

3

4

Mountain-fold along the crease for this squash fold.

5

Squash-fold.

6

This is a combination of squash folds. Mountain-fold along the creases.

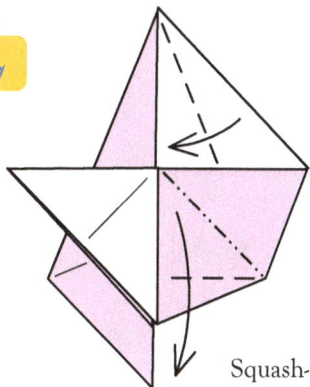

Squash-fold.

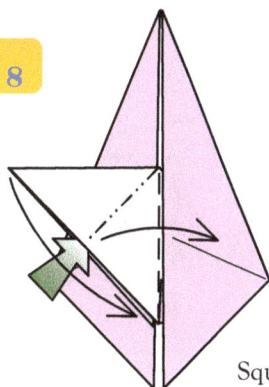

Squash-fold.

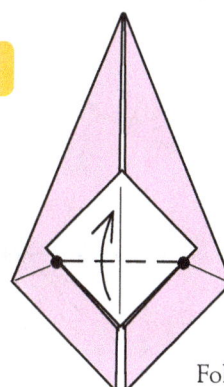

Fold the top layer up.

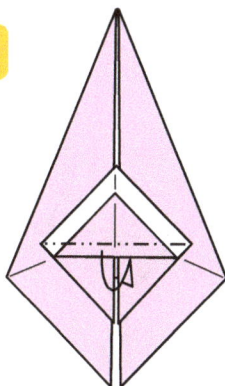

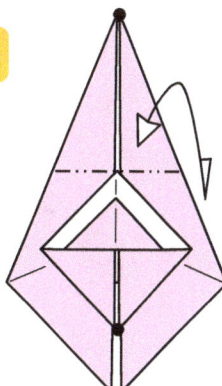

Fold and unfold so the dots meet.

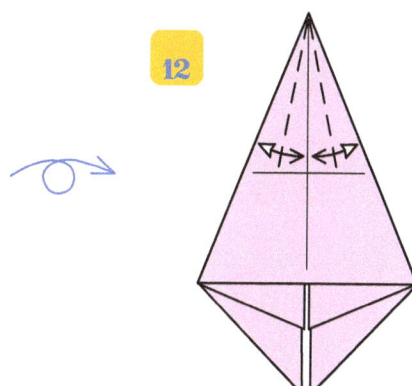

Fold and unfold.

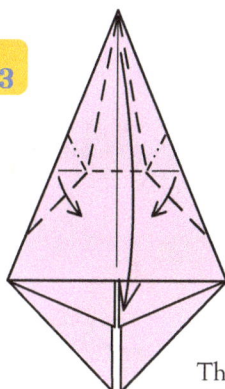

Thin the flap while folding down.

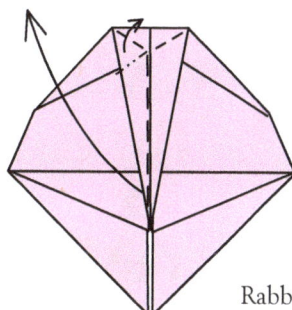

Rabbit-ear.

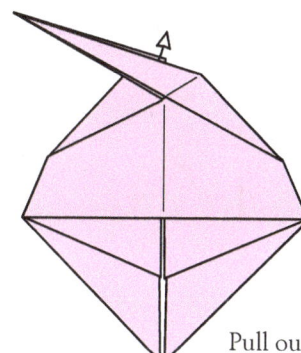

Pull out one layer.

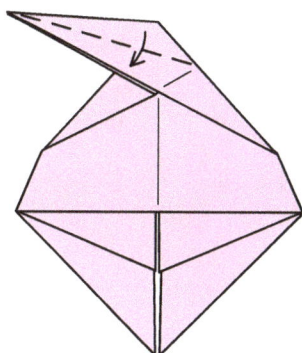

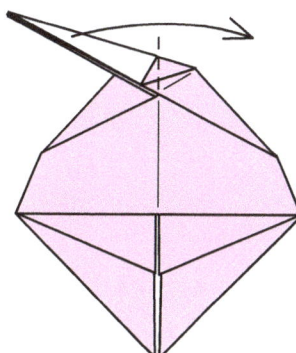

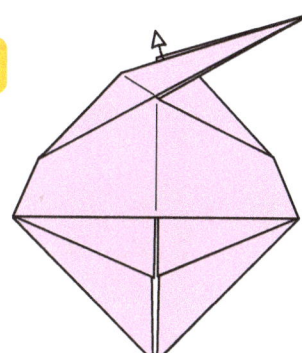

Repeat steps 16–17.

Moorish Idol **55**

19

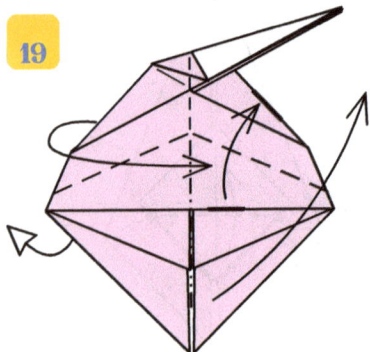

Fold in half and bring the bottom flaps up so the bold lines meet. Swing up from behind. Rotate.

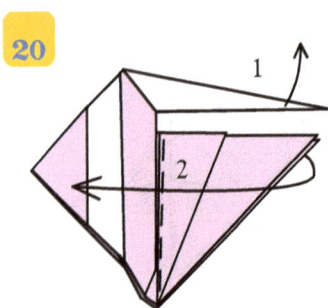

20

1. Slide up.
2. Fold all the layers.

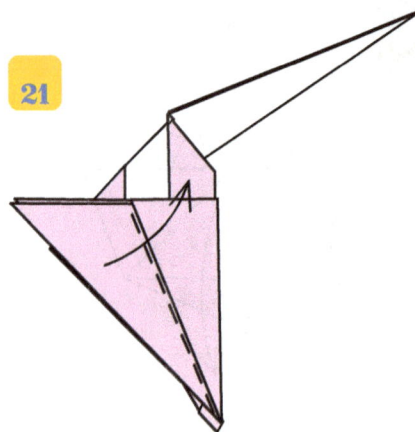

21

Fold both layers.

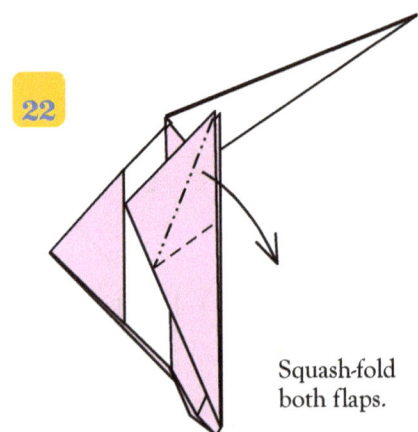

22

Squash-fold both flaps.

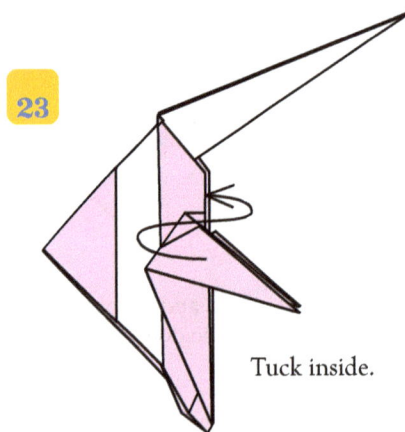

23

Tuck inside.

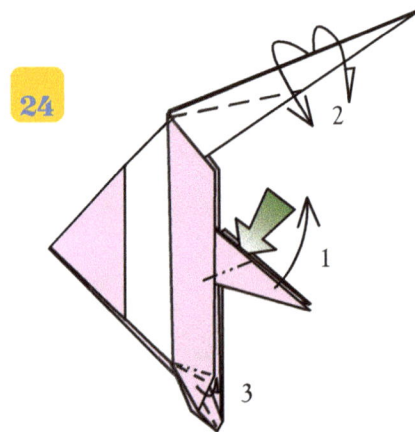

24

1. Reverse-fold both flaps.
2. Outside-reverse-fold.
3. Repeat behind.

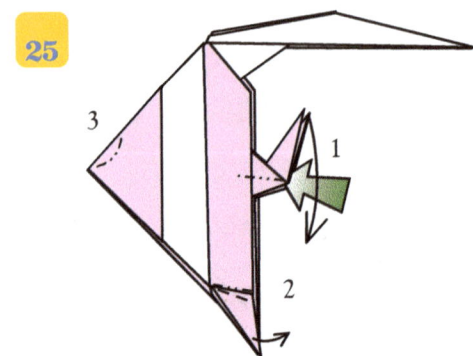

25

1. Reverse-fold the inner flap.
2. Crimp-fold.
3. Shape the head.

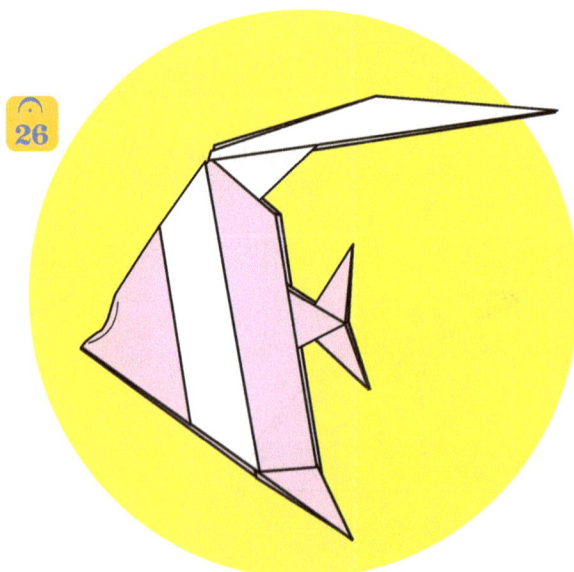

26

Moorish Idol

Triggerfish

The Triggerfish is found in shallow waters of the Indo-Pacific and other tropical seas worldwide. The 40 species of this brightly colored, oval shaped fish varies in size from 8 to 20 inches. It has a powerful jaw and strong teeth which are perfect for crushing shells. It feeds on crustaceans, mullusks, and sea urchins. It is territorial and can grunt like a pig.

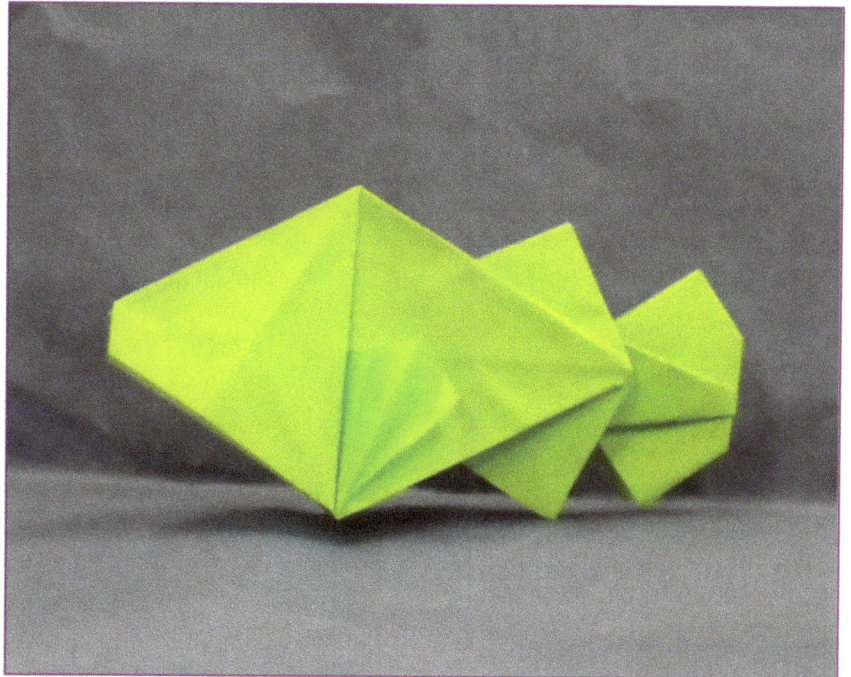

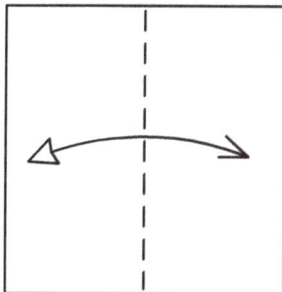

Fold and unfold.

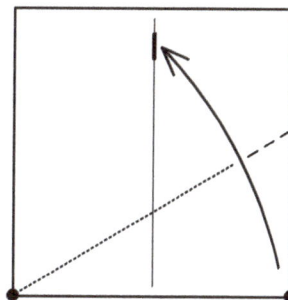

Bring the corner to the line. Fold on the right.

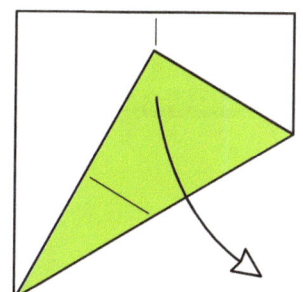

Unfold.

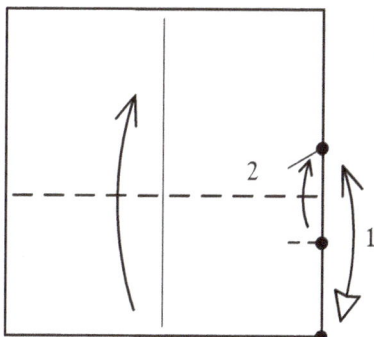

1. Fold and unfold on the right.
2. Fold up.

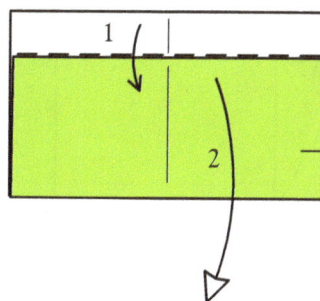

1. Fold along the edge.
2. Unfold.

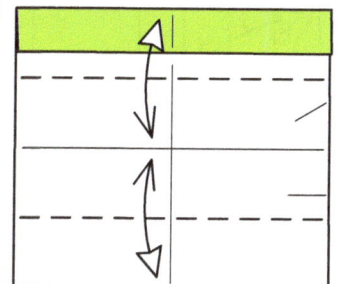

Fold to the center and unfold.

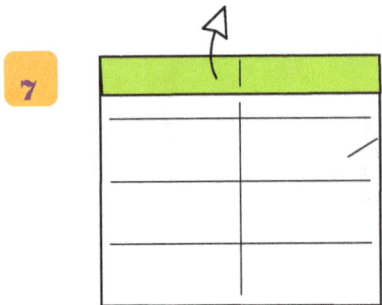

7 Unfold.

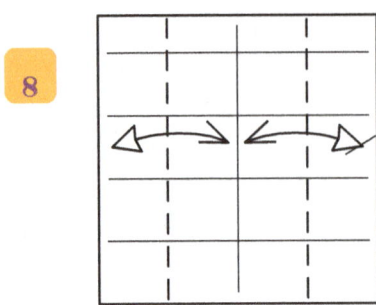

8 Fold to the center and unfold.

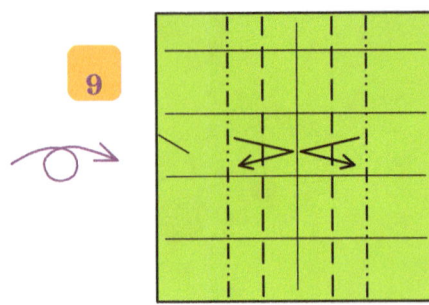

9 Mountain-fold along the creases for these pleat folds.

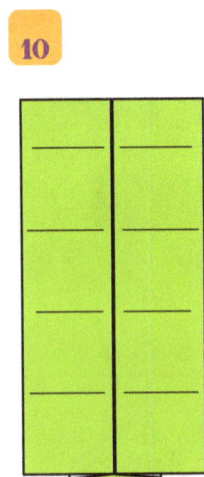

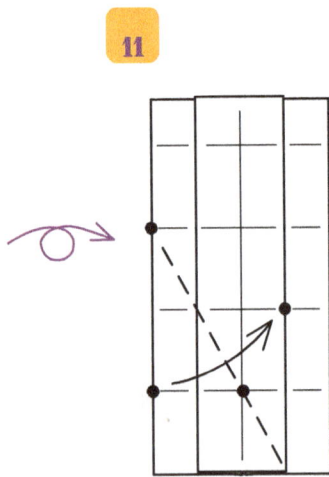

10

11 Fold all the layers.

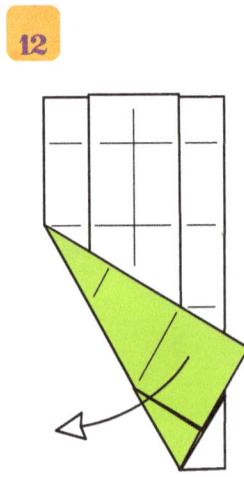

12 Unfold.

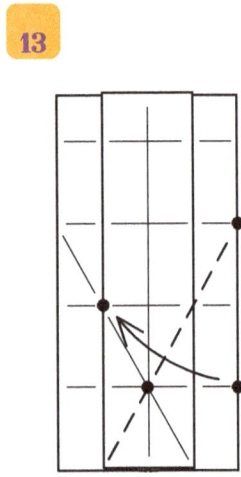

13 Repeat steps 11–12 on the right.

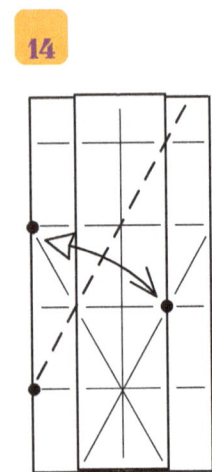

14 Fold and unfold.

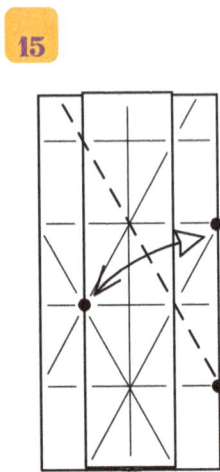

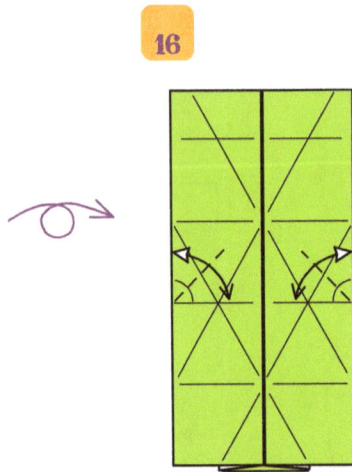

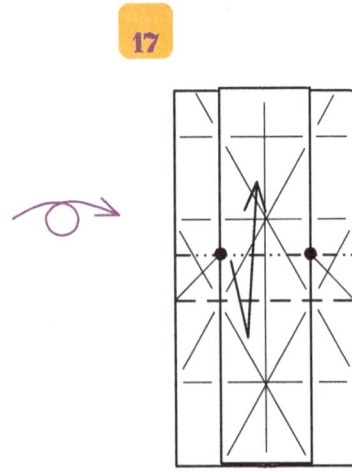

15 Fold and unfold.

16 Fold and unfold.

17 Valley-fold along the crease for this pleat fold.

18

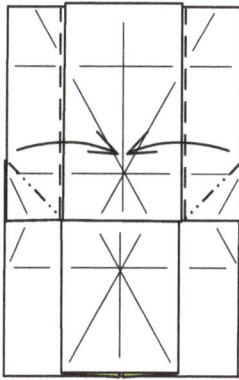

Make squash folds.

19

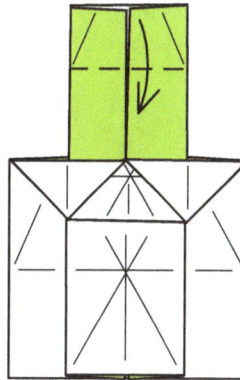

Fold along the creases.

20

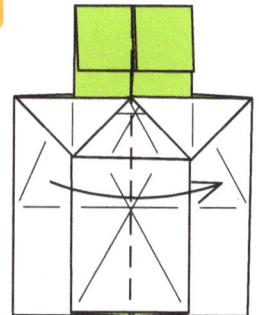

Fold in half
and rotate 90°.

21

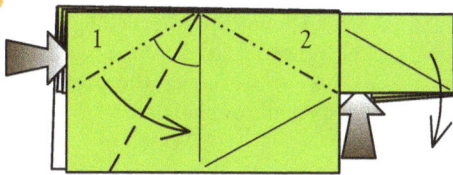

1. Squash-fold, repeat behind.
2. Reverse-fold.
Mountain-fold along the creases.

22

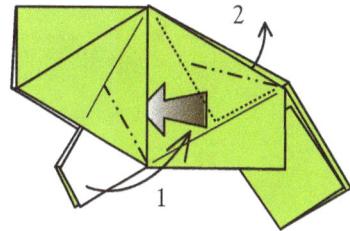

1. Reverse-fold, repeat behind.
2. Reverse-fold.

23

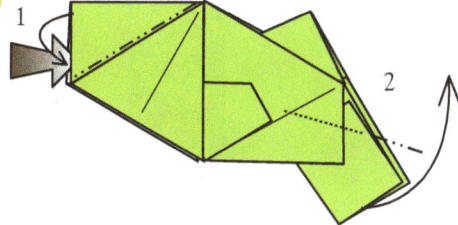

1. Reverse-fold.
2. Reverse-fold the inner layers.

24

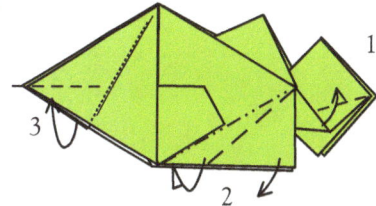

1. Squash-fold, repeat behind.
2. Pleat-fold, repeat behind.
3. Fold the inner flap.

25

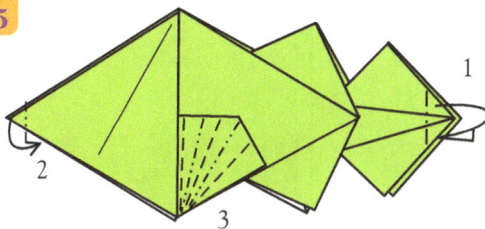

1. Fold inside, repeat behind.
2. Reverse-fold.
3. Pleat the fin, repeat behind.

26

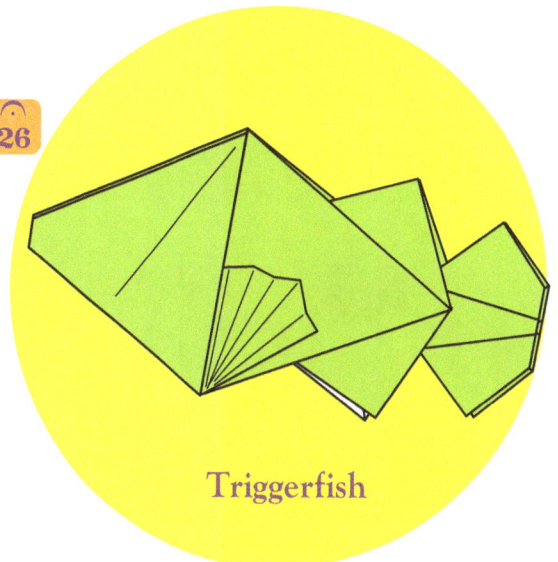

Triggerfish

Clownfish

The Clownfish lives in shallow waters of the Indian and Pacific Oceans, the Red Sea, and Great Barrier Reef of Australia. It is also called an Anemonefish, as it has a symbiotic relation with sea anemones. It hides among the poisonous tentacles of sea anemones, which protect the Clownfish. Meanwhile, the Clownfish lures other fish into the tentacles. At three to six inches, the Clownfish feeds on small zooplankton.

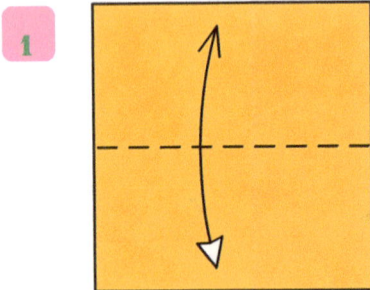

Fold and unfold.

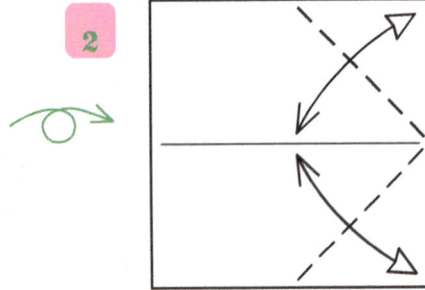

Fold to the center and unfold.

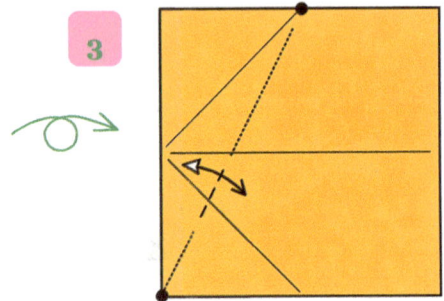

Fold and unfold.

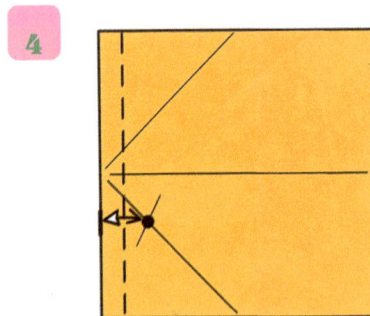

Fold and unfold.

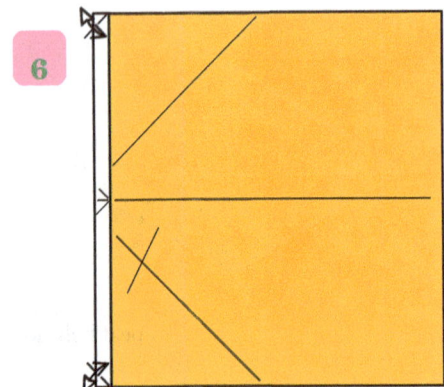

Fold and unfold.

7

8

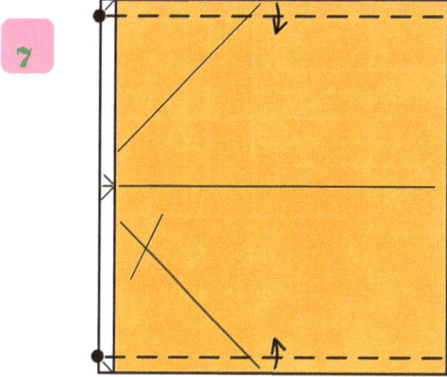

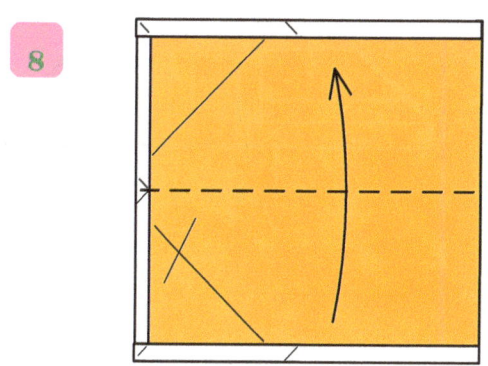

Fold along the crease.

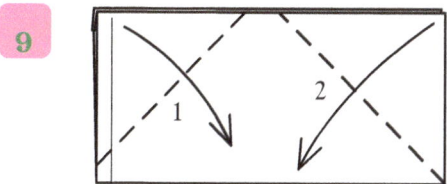

9

1. Fold along the crease.
2. Fold down.
Repeat behind.

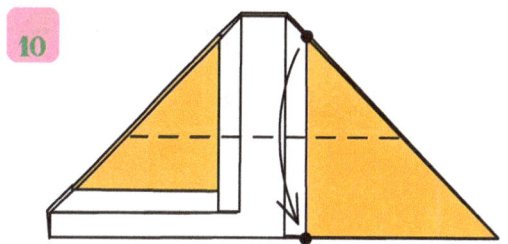

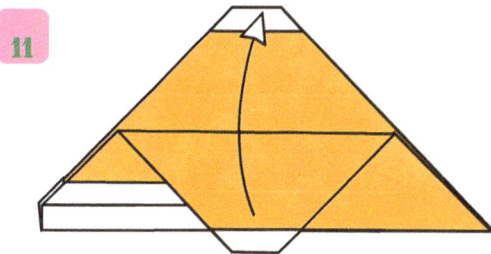

10

11

Unfold.

12

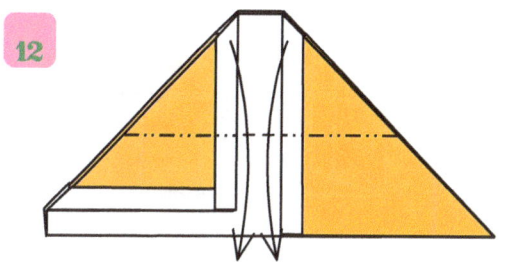

Make reverse folds.

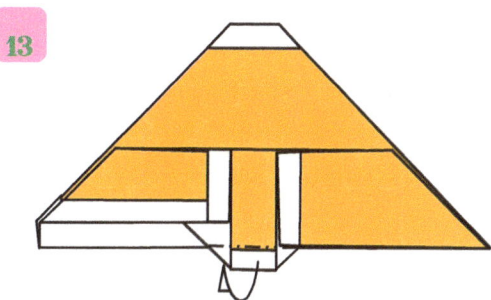

13

Tuck inside.

14

Repeat steps 10–13 behind.

Clownfish **61**

15

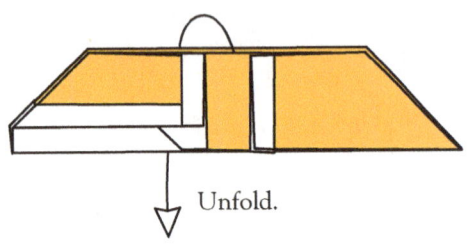

Unfold.

16

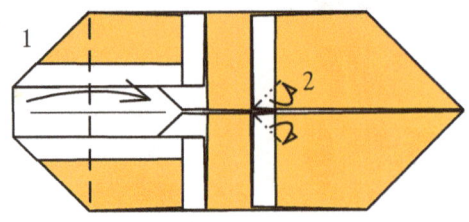

1. Fold to the right.
2. Fold behind.

17

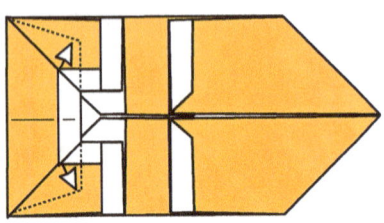

Spread the top layer.

18

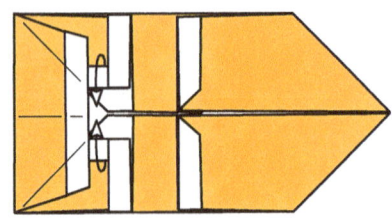

Unlock the white strips.

19

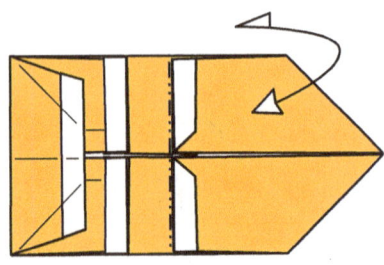

Fold and unfold.

20

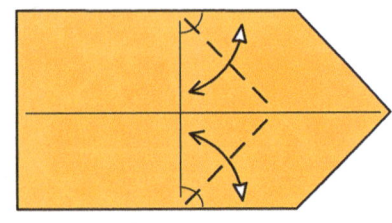

Fold and unfold.

21

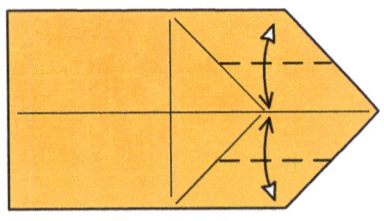

Fold to the center and unfold.

22

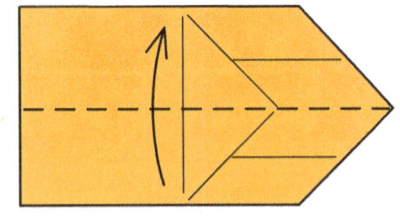

23

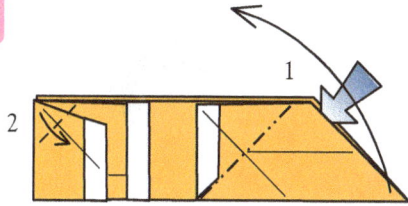

1. Reverse-fold.
2. Repeat behind.

24

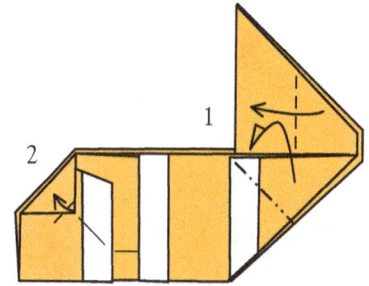

1. Reverse-fold.
2. Fold the eye.
Repeat behind.

25

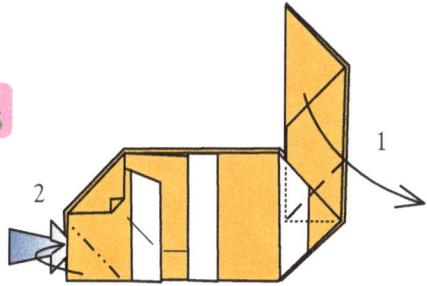

1. Fold all the layers.
2. Reverse-fold.

26

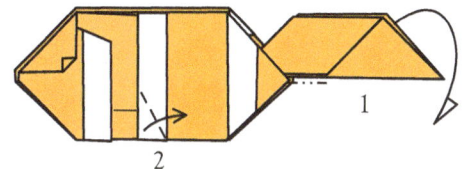

1. Fold the hidden layer down.
2. Repeat behind.

27

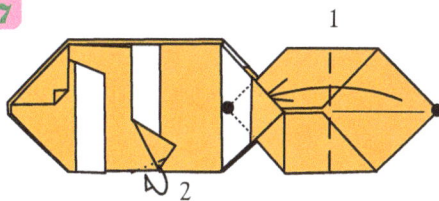

1. Tuck inside.
2. Repeat behind.

28

Make reverse folds.

29

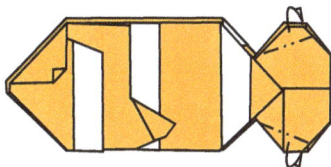

Fold inside, repeat behind.

30

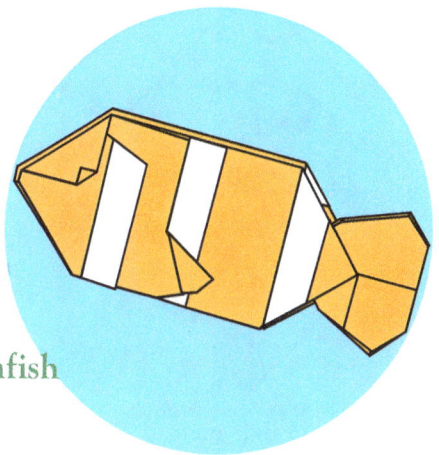

Clownfish

Queen Angelfish

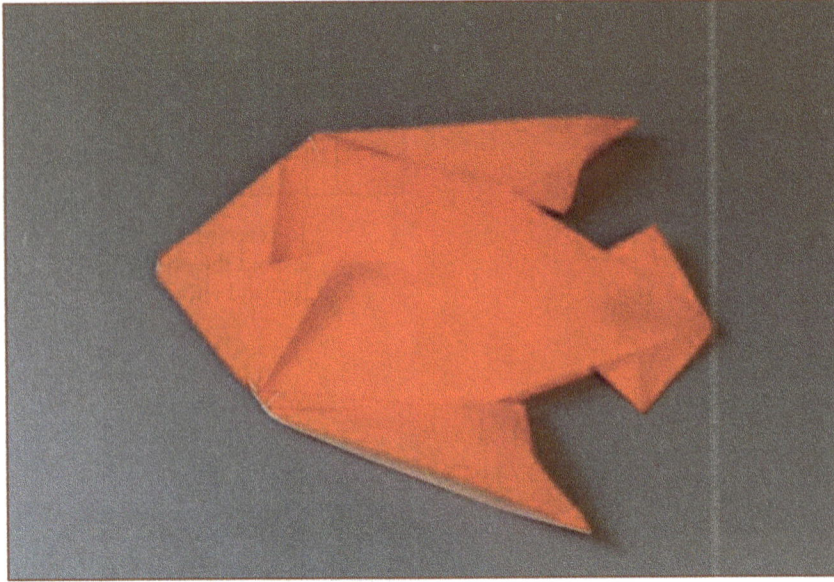

The Queen Angelfish swims in the reefs of the western Atlantic waters, including the Gulf of Mexico, Florida, and The Bahamas. The dark blue spot on its head resembles a crown, giving the fish its name. This colorful fish is vibrant yellow, blue, and orange. It grows to 18 inches and feeds on sponges, jellyfish, plankton, and algae.

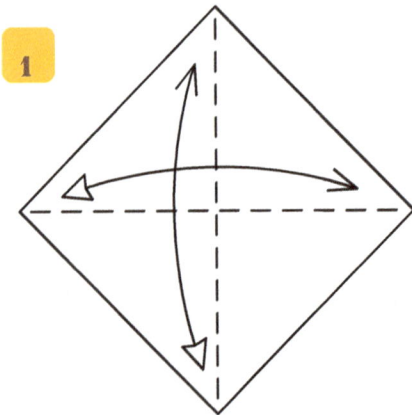

1
Fold and unfold.

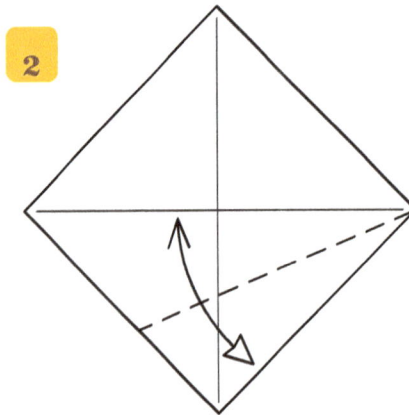

2
Fold to the center and unfold.

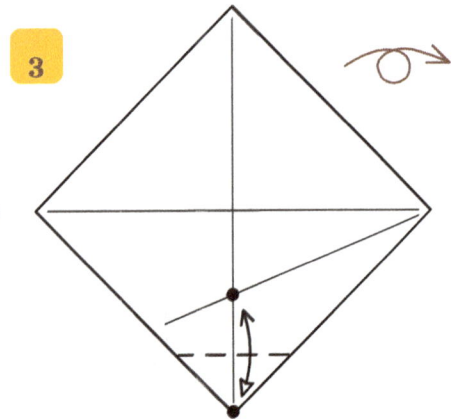

3
Fold and unfold.

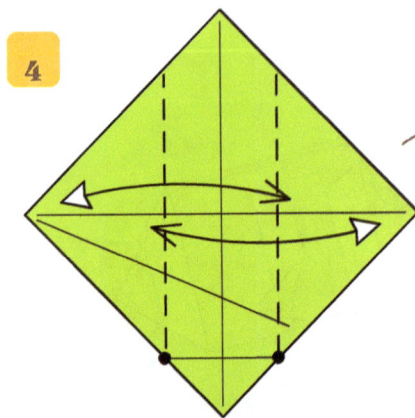

4
Fold and unfold.

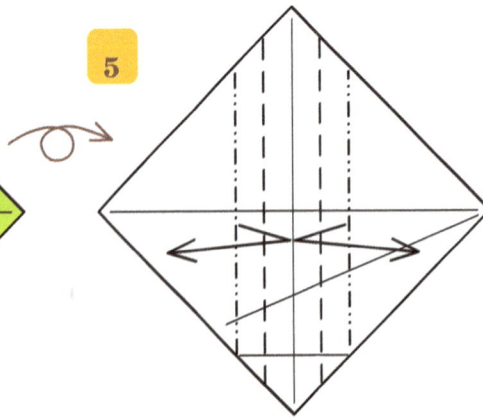

5
Mountain-fold along the creases for these pleat folds.

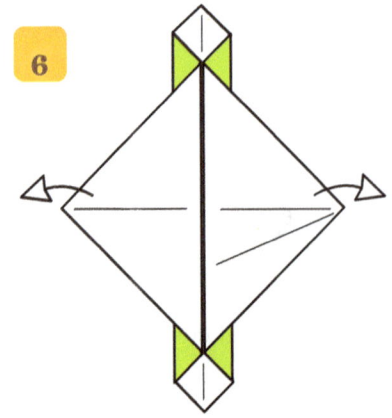

6
Unfold.

7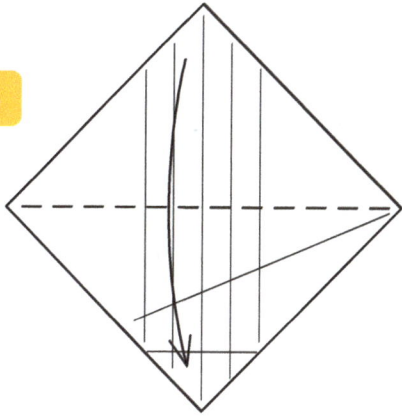

8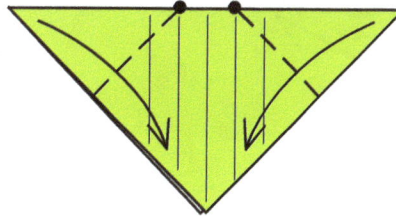

9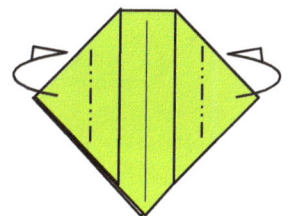

Fold along
hidden creases.

10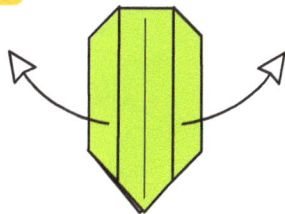

Unfold.

11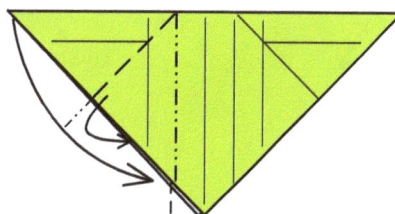

Crimp-fold.

12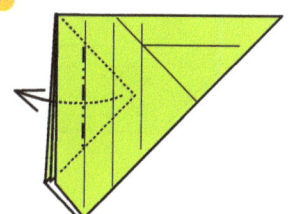

Reverse-fold along the
creases. Repeat behind.

13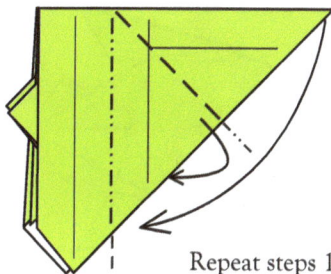

Repeat steps 11–12
on the right.

14

Fold to the
center.

15

Fold behind
and swing out.

16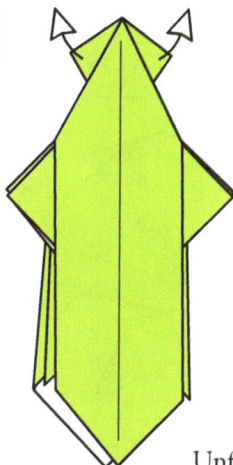

Unfold.

17

Sink and rotate 90°.

18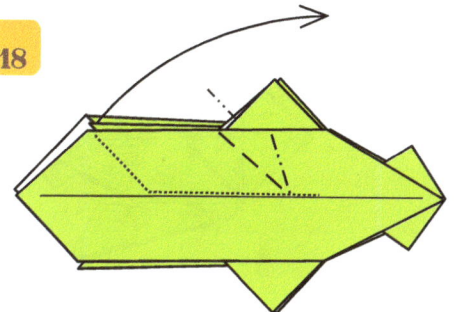

Squash-fold the inner flap.

19

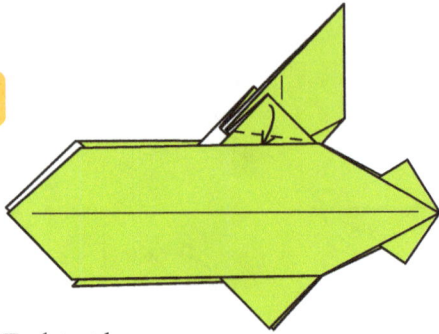

Tuck inside, repeat
behind. Rotate 180°.

20

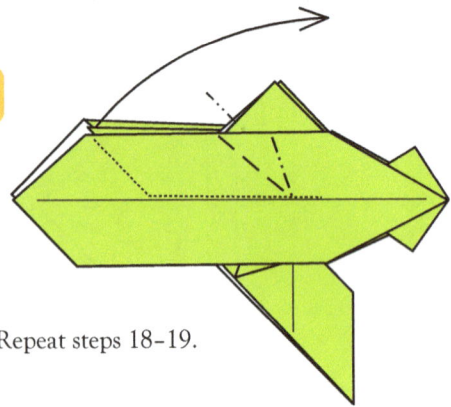

Repeat steps 18–19.

21

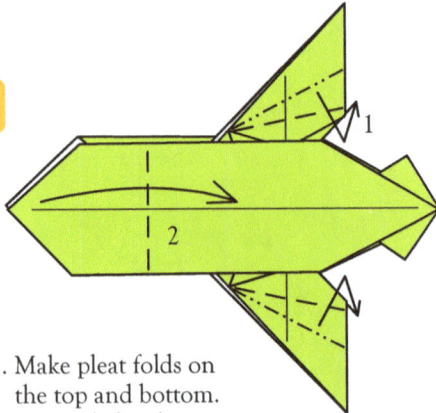

1. Make pleat folds on
   the top and bottom.
2. Repeat behind.

22

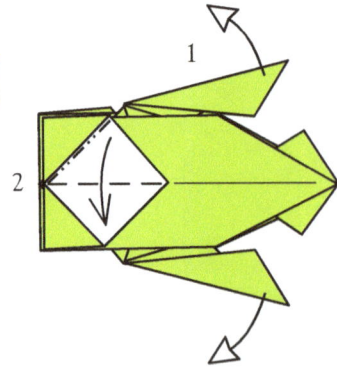

1. Unfold on the top and bottom.
2. Squash-fold, repeat behind.

23

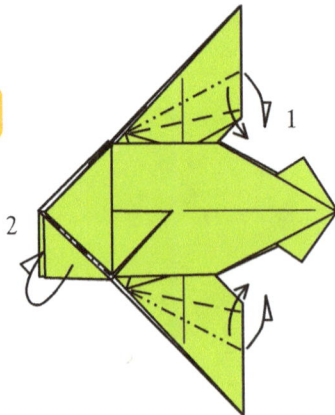

1. Make outside reverse folds.
2. Fold inside. Do not repeat behind.

24

Tuck into the top pocket.

25

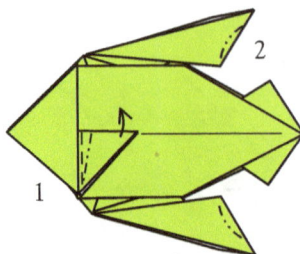

1. Pleat-fold, repeat behind.
2. Shape the fins.

26

Queen Angelfish

Four Stripe Damselfish

The Four Stripe Damselfish is also known as a Blacktail Damselfish or Black Humbug. Found in Indonesia, New Guinea, and the Great Barrier Reef of Australia, this small fish grows to about 3 inches. It feeds on algae, shrimp, and other small fish. As fun home aquarium pets, they are peaceful when young but become territorial and aggressive as adults.

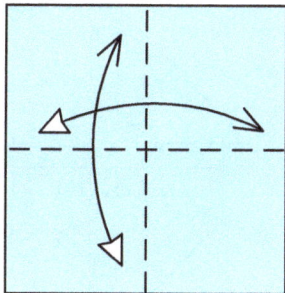

Fold and unfold.

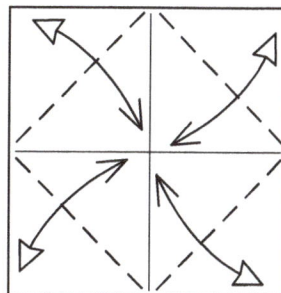

Fold to the center and unfold.

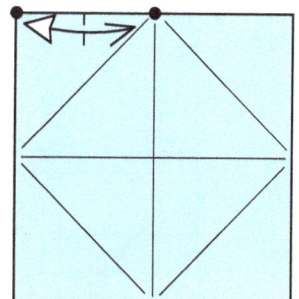

Fold and unfold on the top.

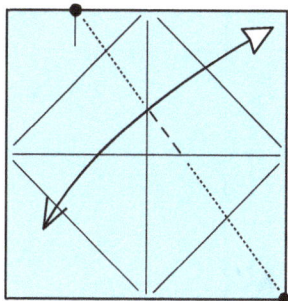

Fold and unfold in the center.

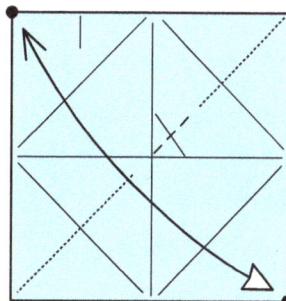

Fold and unfold at the intersection.

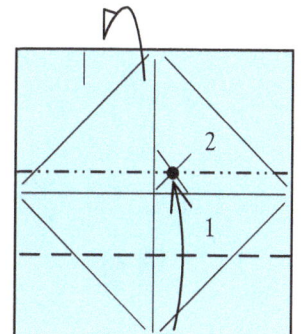

7

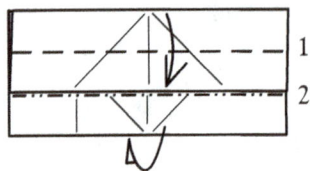

1
2

8

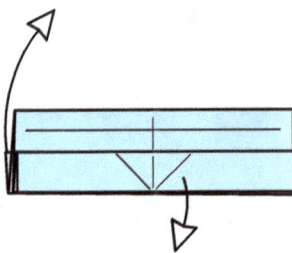

Unfold.

9

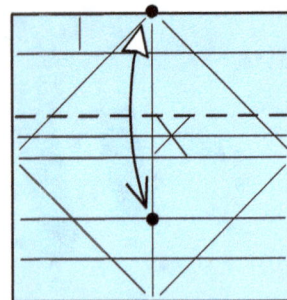

Fold and unfold.

10

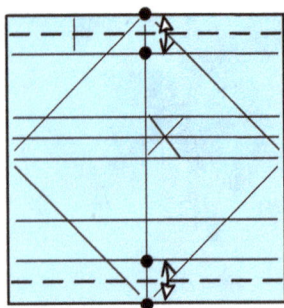

Fold and unfold.

11

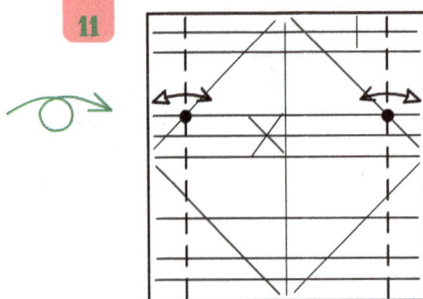

Fold and unfold.

12

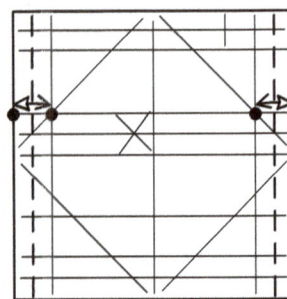

Fold and unfold.

13

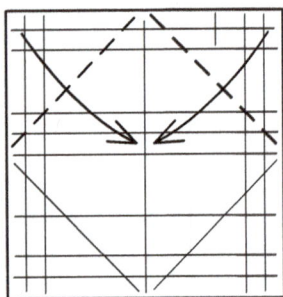

Fold along the
creases. Rotate 90°.

14

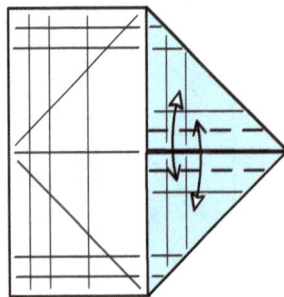

Fold and unfold both
layers along the creases.

15

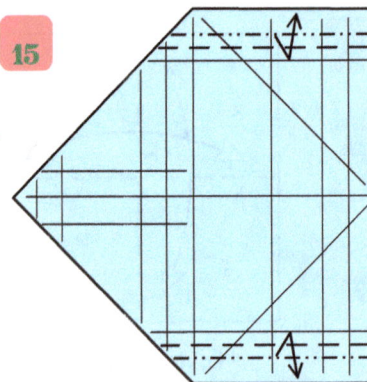

Mountain-fold along the
creases for these pleat folds.

16

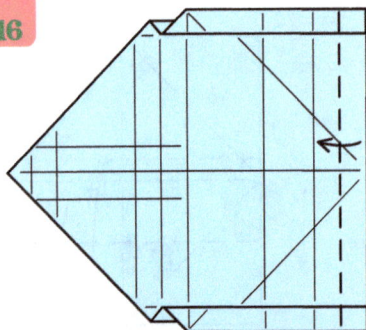

Fold along the crease.

17

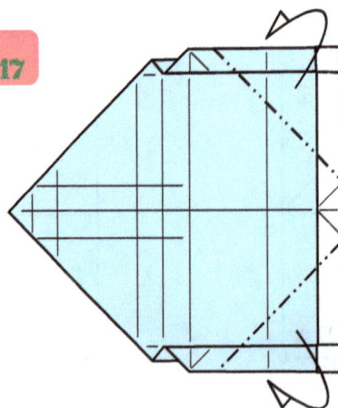

Fold along the creases.

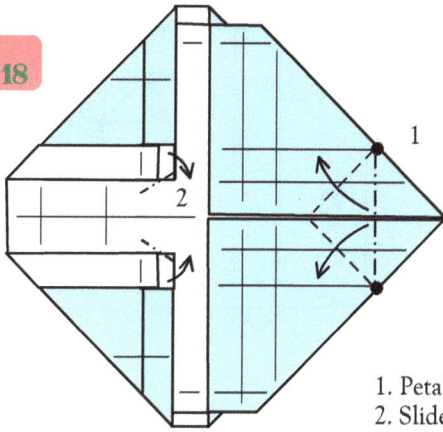

18

1. Petal-fold.
2. Slide the ends.

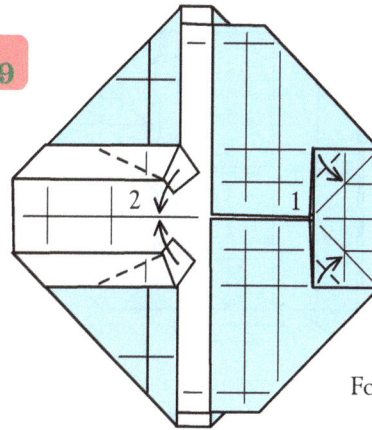

19

Fold in order.

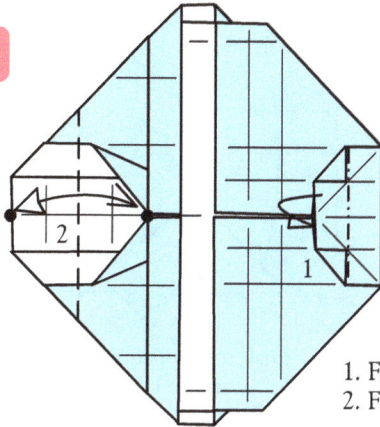

20

1. Fold inside.
2. Fold and unfold.

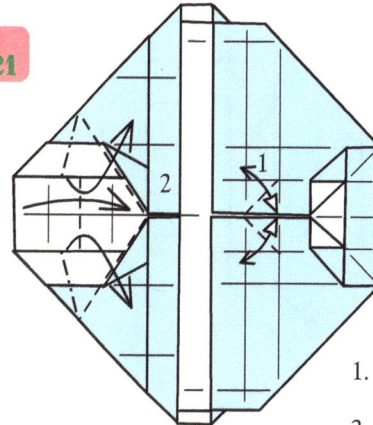

21

1. Fold and unfold
   both layers.
2. Petal-fold.

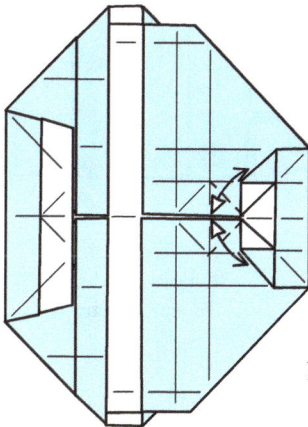

22

Fold and unfold.

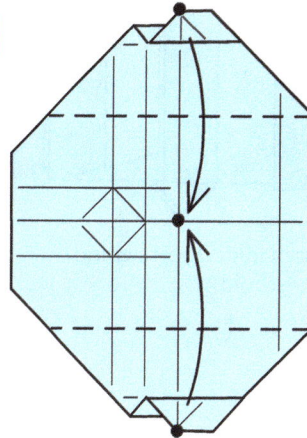

23

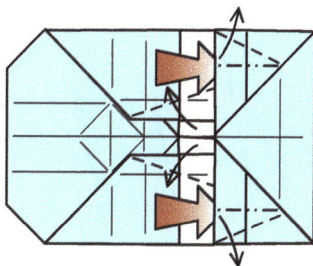

24

Make squash folds.

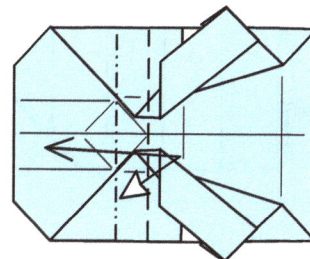

25

Pleat-fold and unfold
along the creases.

Damselfish **69**

26

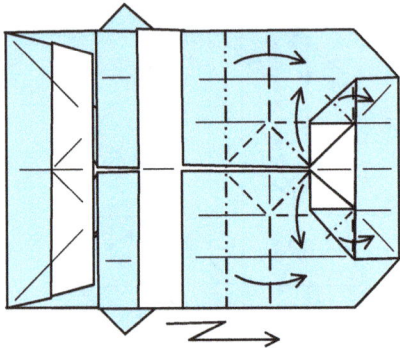

This is a combination of
pleat and squash folds.

27

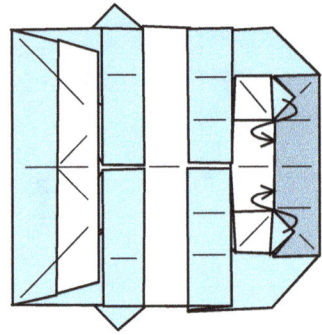

Tuck the small triangles
under the dark rectangle.

28

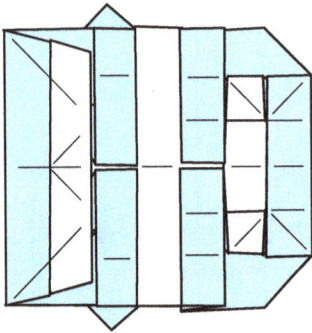

29

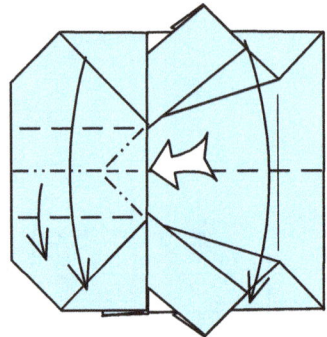

Push in to make pleat
folds on the left while
folding in half.

30

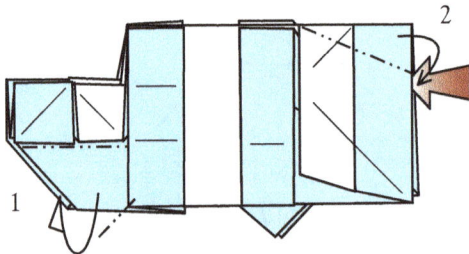

1. Squash-fold, repeat behind.
2. Reverse-fold.

31

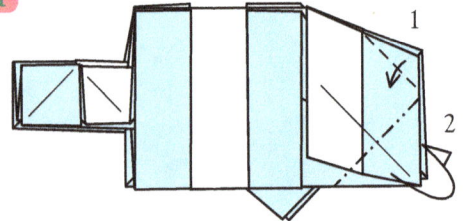

1. Valley-fold.
2. Fold inside.
Repeat behind.

32

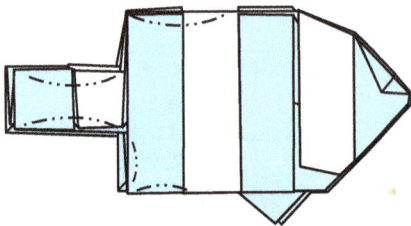

Shape the fish, repeat behind.

33

Damselfish

Third Movement

Minuet of Deltahedra with a
Trio of Duo-Colored Octahedra

The Minuet takes us on a cosmic journey as we explore triangular worlds. Deltahedra are polyhedra whose sides are equilateral triangles. There are eight convex Deltahedra (convex means any line connecting the vertices are on or inside the solid). Beautiful on their own, these Deltahedra complement the birds, fish, and invertebrates. Birds can perch on them and the sea creatures can swim or hide around them, providing an elegant background.

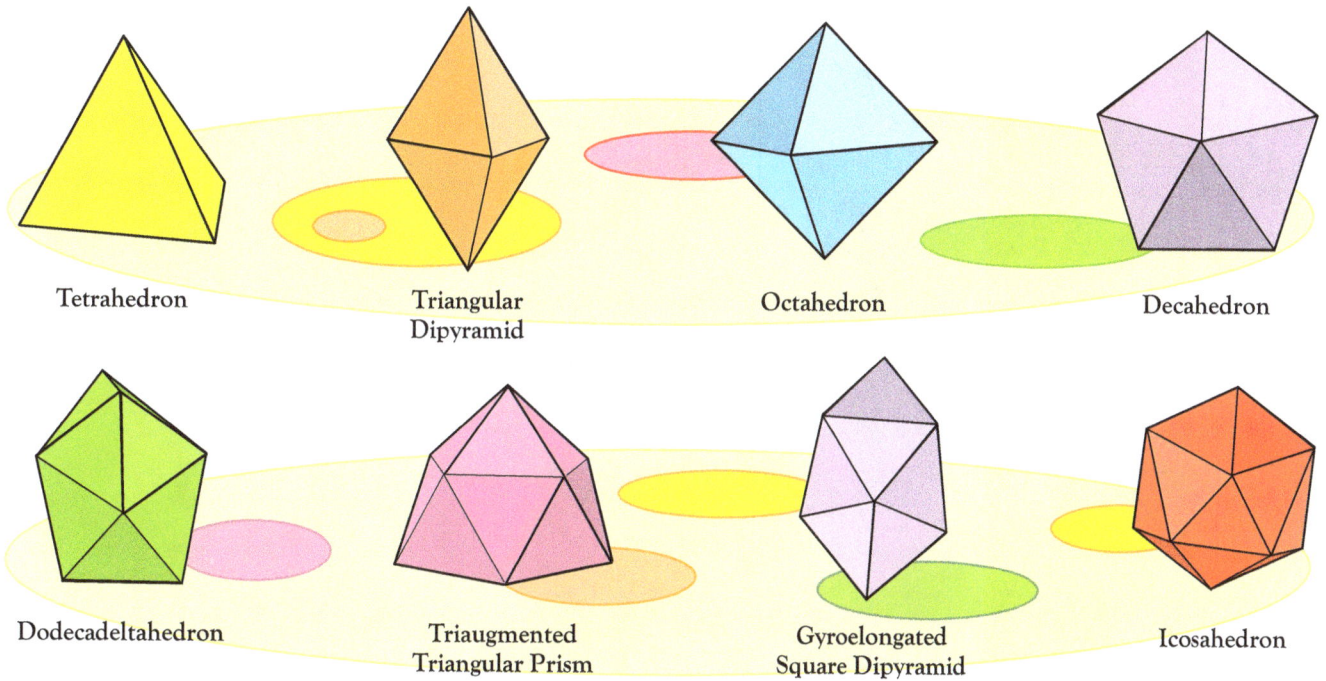

Tetrahedron

Triangular
Dipyramid

Octahedron

Decahedron

Dodecadeltahedron

Triaugmented
Triangular Prism

Gyroelongated
Square Dipyramid

Icosahedron

Tetrahedron

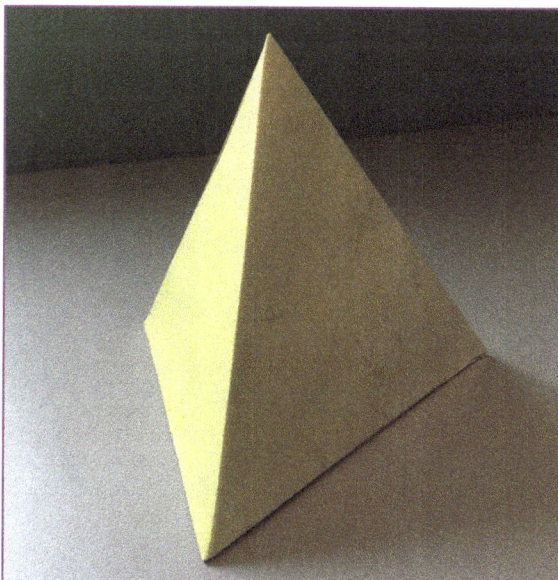

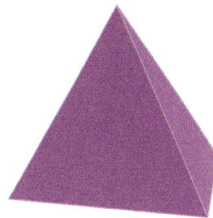

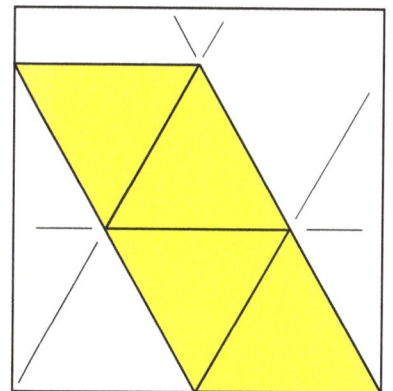

The first deltahedron is the Tetrahedron. This is one of the five Platonic Solids. Plato believed the tetrahedron represented fire because of its sharpness and simplicity. The diagram above shows the unfolded square, showing the crease pattern. The four triangular faces of the model are shown in yellow.

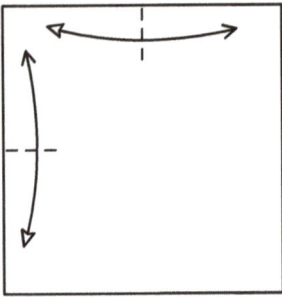

1 Fold and unfold.

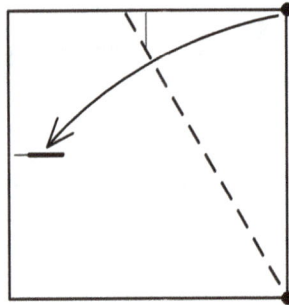

2 Bring the top corner to the line.

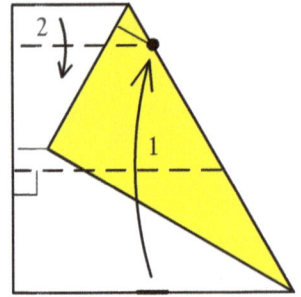

3 1. Bring the bottom edge to the dot.
2. Fold down.

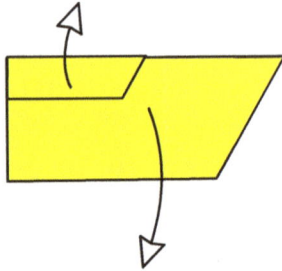

4 Unfold.

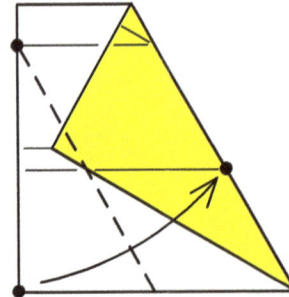

5 Bring the bottom dot to the right dot.

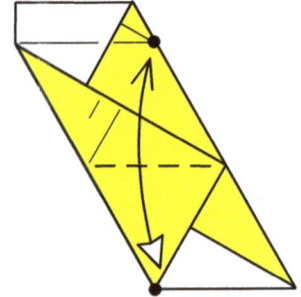

6 Fold and unfold.

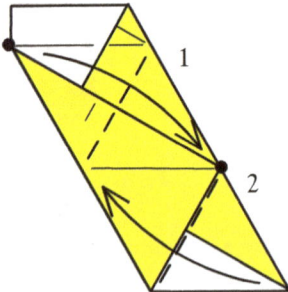

7 1. The dots will meet.
2. Fold along the edge.

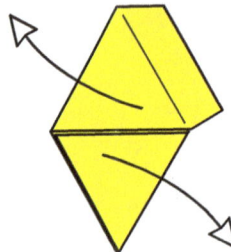

8 Unfold.

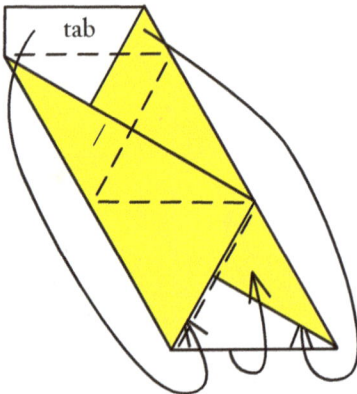

9 The left and right sides of the tab tuck into two pockets. Fold along the creases and tuck the tab inside the pockets.

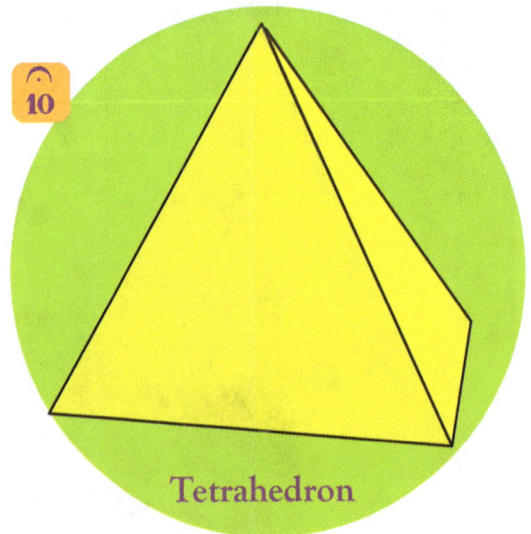

10 Tetrahedron

Triangular Dipyramid

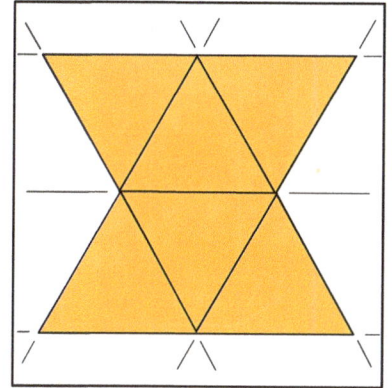

The six faces of this triangular dipyramid are all equilateral triangles. This diamond can be constructed by joining two tetrahedra at their base. The crease pattern shows even and odd symmetry. Even symmetry means the image is the same when reflected around a center line. Odd symmetry means the image is the same when rotate 180°.

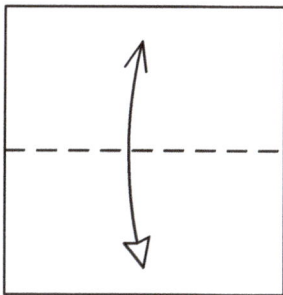

1

Fold and unfold.

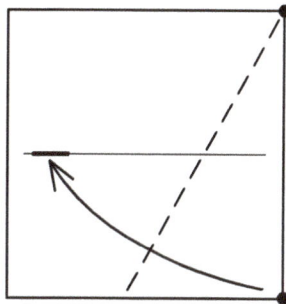

2

Bring the corner to the line.

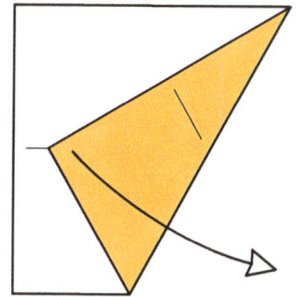

3

Unfold.

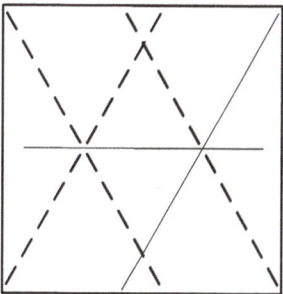

4

Fold and unfold three more times.

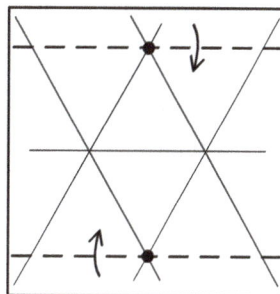

5

Rotate 90°.

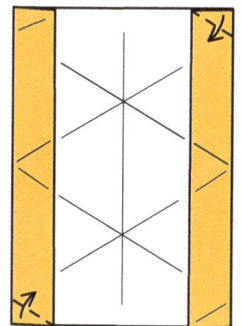

6

Fold along the creases.

7

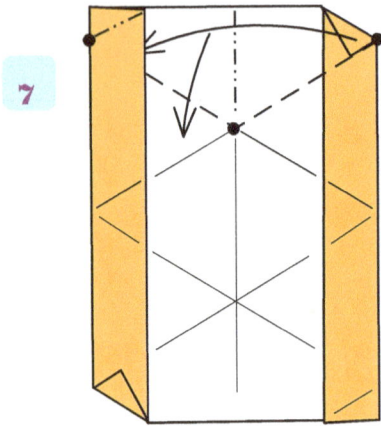

Push in at the center dot. Tuck the right side into the layers on the left so the dots meet. Rotate 180°.

8

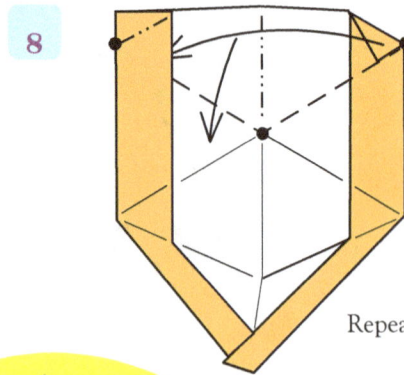

Repeat step 7.

9

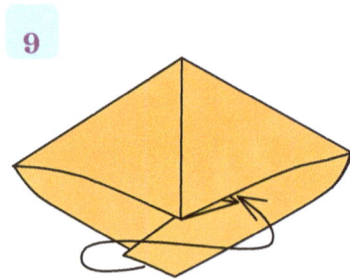

Interlock the tabs and rotate.

10

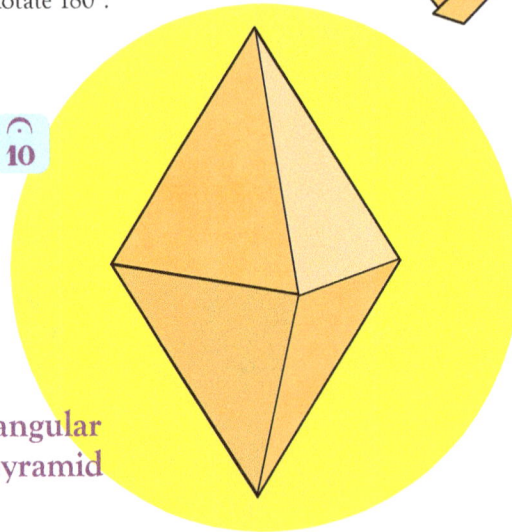

Triangular Dipyramid

Four Deltahedra:
Top row–Tetrahedron, Triangular Dipyramid
Bottom row–Decahedron, Octahedron

Octahedron

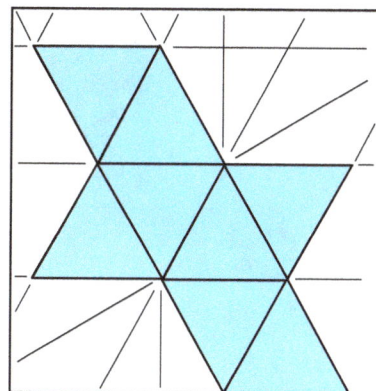

The octahedron is composed of eight equilateral triangles. It can be used as a base to create more polyhedra. According to Plato, the octahedron represented air because it appears to be suspended.

The crease pattern shows a band of six triangles going through the center and two triangles on the left and right. There is a tab at the top and the rest has odd symmetry.

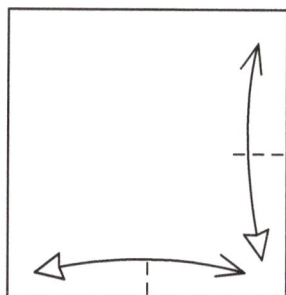

Fold and unfold
on the edge.

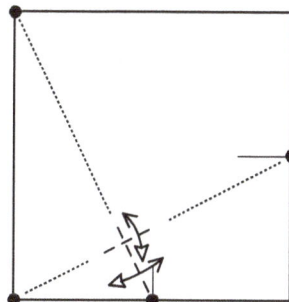

Fold and unfold.

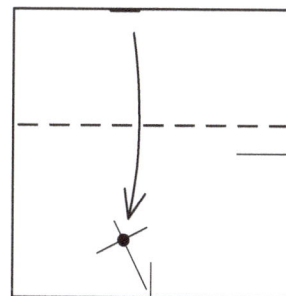

Bring the edge
to the dot.

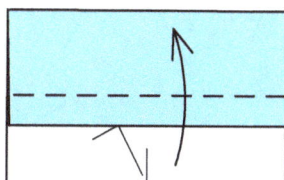

Fold in half.

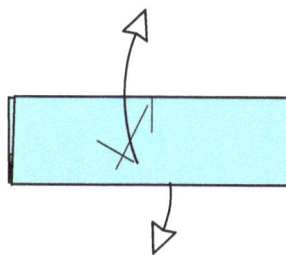

Unfold.

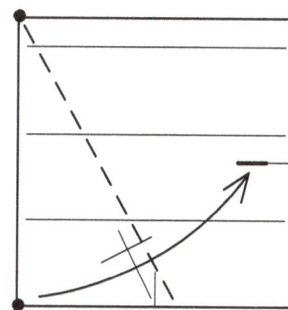

Bring the corner
to the line.

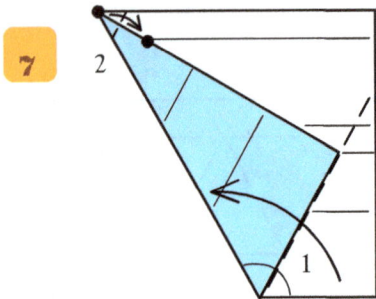

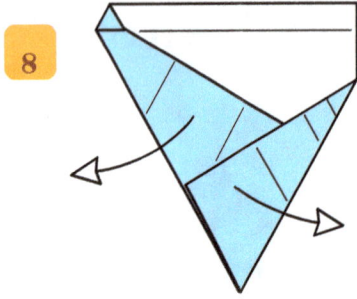

7

8

Unfold.

9

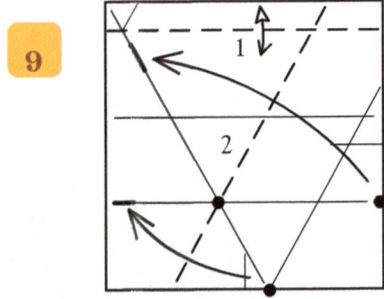

1. Fold and unfold
   along the crease.
2. The dots and lines
   will meet.

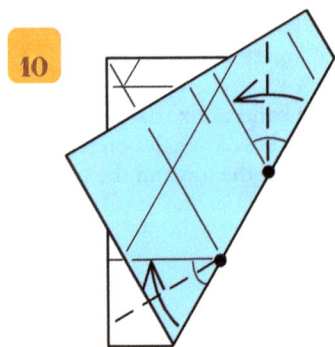

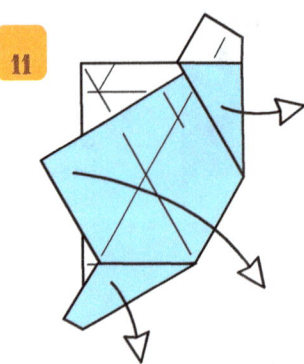

10

11

Unfold.

12

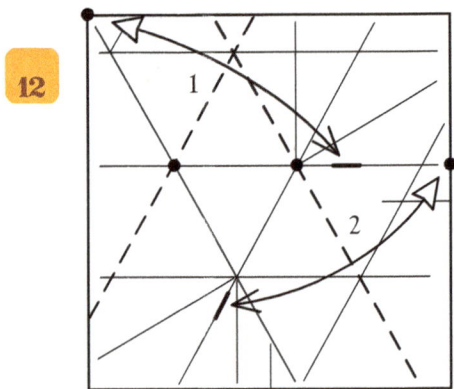

1. Fold and unfold.
2. Fold and unfold.
Rotate 180°.

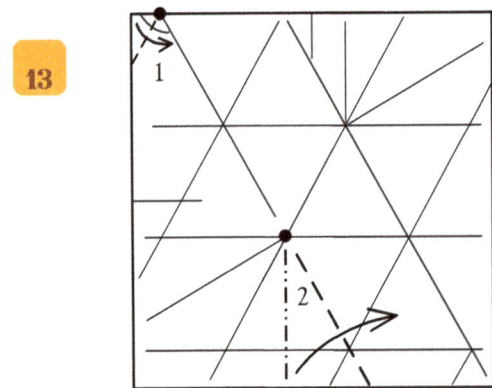

13

1. Fold to the line.
2. Push in at the dot.

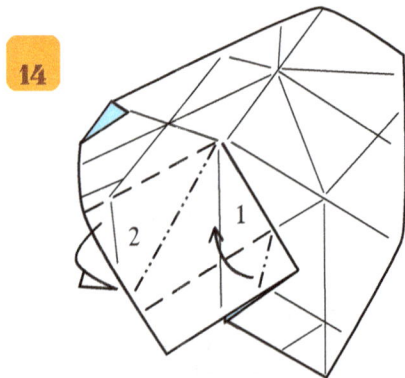

14

1. Squash-fold.
2. Fold along the creases.

15

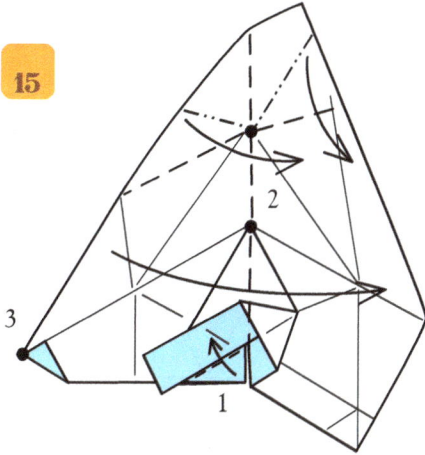

1. Fold on top.
2. Fold along the creases, push in at the dots, and flatten.
3. Rotate the left dot to the front and top.

16

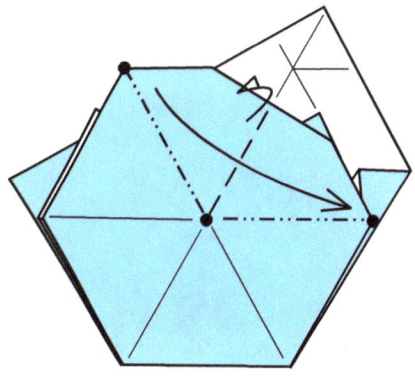

Puff out at the center dot.
The other dots will meet.

17

Fold and unfold along the crease.

18

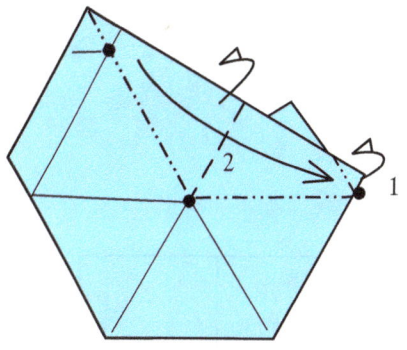

1. Wrap around.
2. Puff out at the center dot.
   The other dots will meet.
Rotate the center dot to the bottom.

19

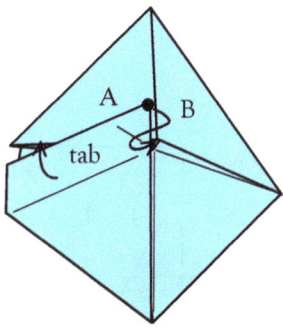

Begin by tucking the dot into the lower part of B, and continue by tucking the tab into the pocket of A.

20

Octahedron

Decahedron

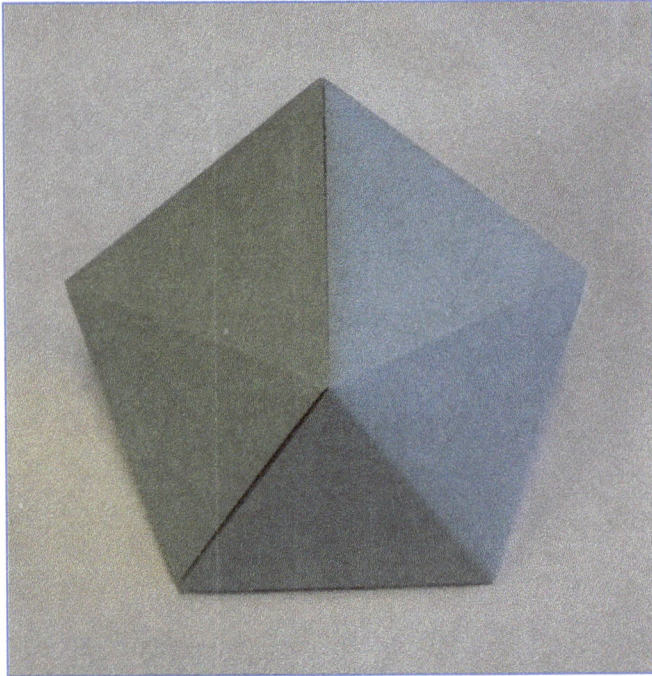

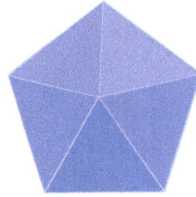

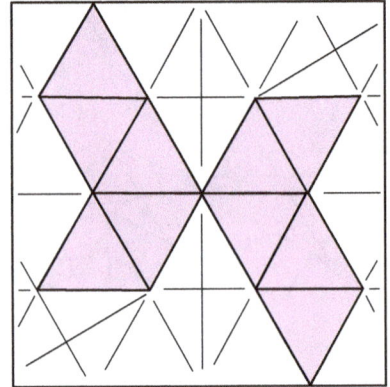

All the sides of this pentagonal diamond are equilateral triangles. The layout shows is has odd symmetry. This shape resembles a flying saucer.

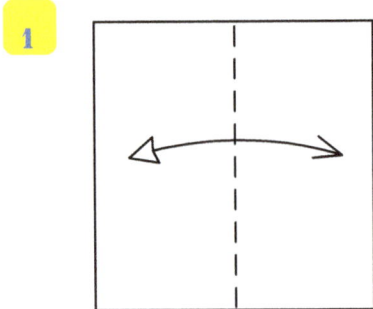

1

Fold and unfold.

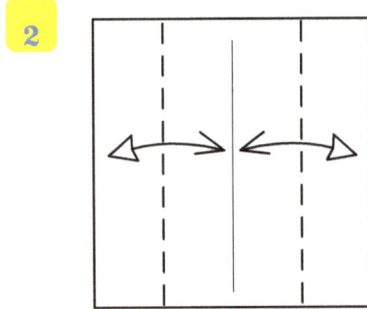

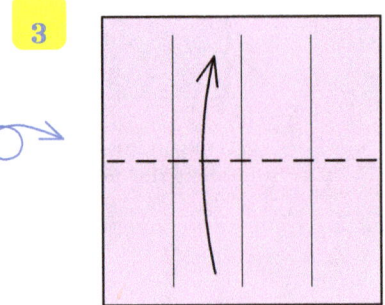

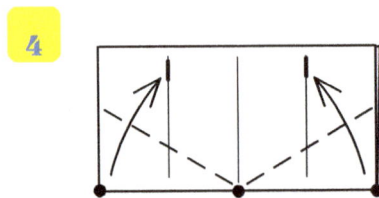

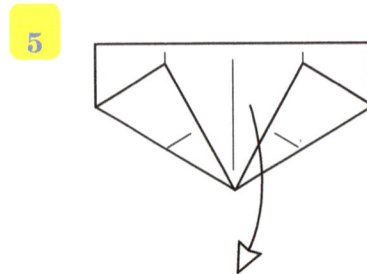

2

Fold and unfold.

3

4

5

Unfold and rotate 90°.

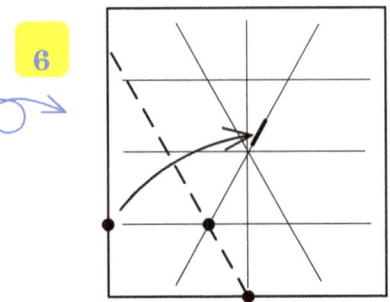

6

Fold and unfold.

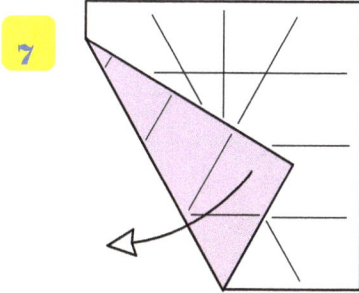

7

Unfold.

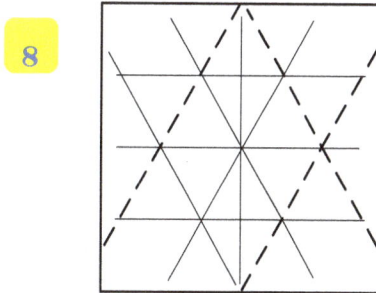

8

Fold and unfold.

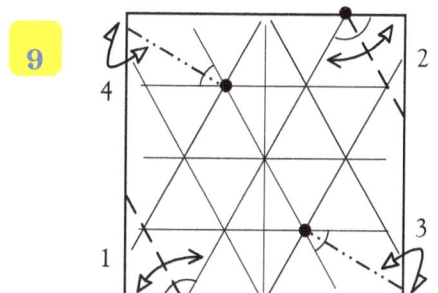

9

Fold and unfold.

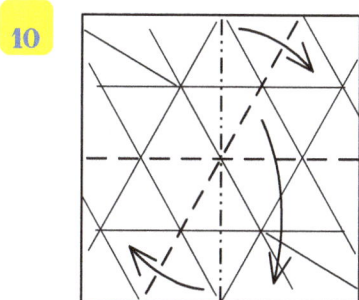

10

Fold along the creases and flatten.

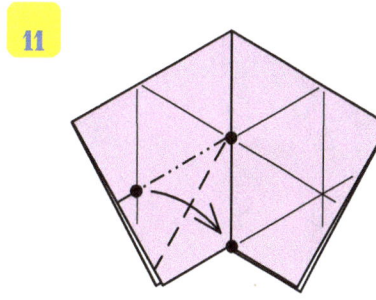

11

Puff out at the upper dot. Turn over and repeat.

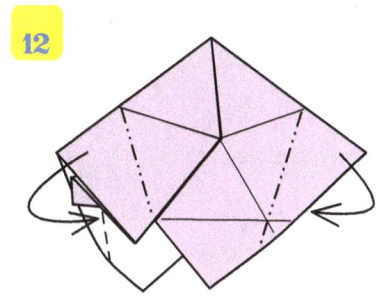

12

Fold along the creases for these reverse folds. Rotate 180°.

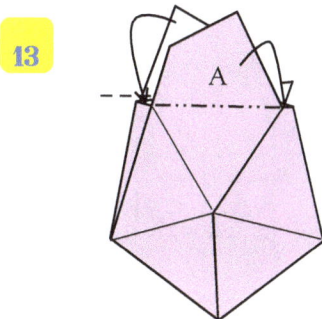

13

Tuck A into the small pocket on the right. Turn over and repeat.

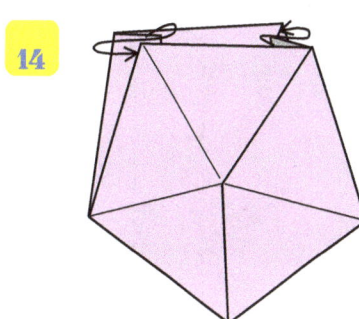

14

Tuck the small tabs into the pockets.

15

Decahedron

Dodecadeltahedron

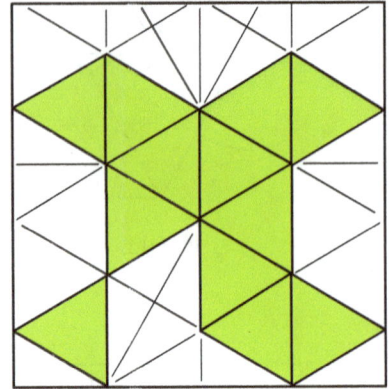

The twelve-sided dodecadeltahedron can also be called the Siamese Dodecahedron or Snub Disphenoid. The layout shows this design almost has even symmetry along the central vertical line.

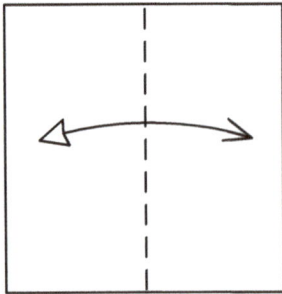

1

Fold and unfold.

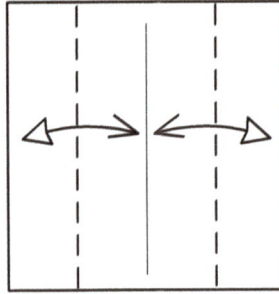

2

Fold and unfold.

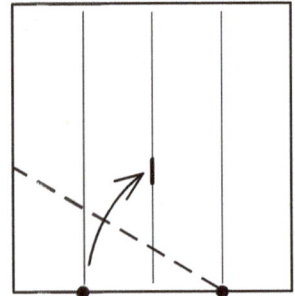

3

Bring the left dot to the line.

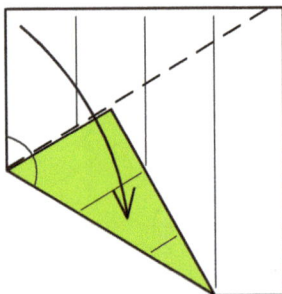

4

The valley line does not meet the top corner.

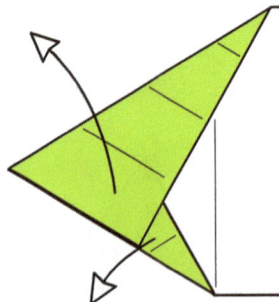

5

Unfold.

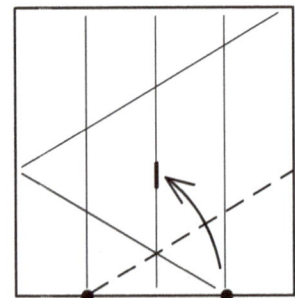

6

Repeat steps 3–5 on the right.

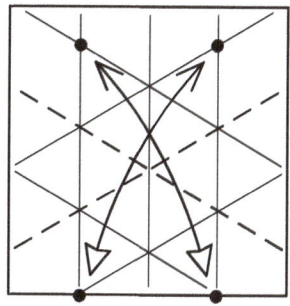

7

Fold and unfold.

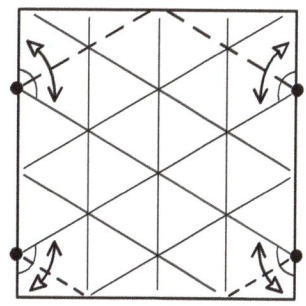

8

Fold and unfold.

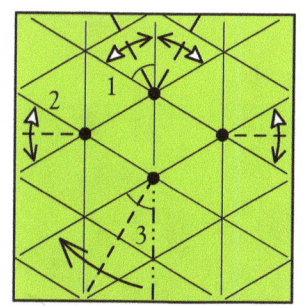

9

1. Fold and unfold at the top.
2. Fold and unfold on the left and right.
3. Puff out at the dot.

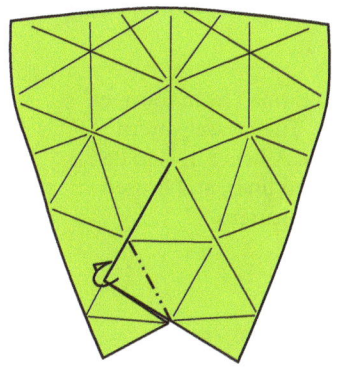

10

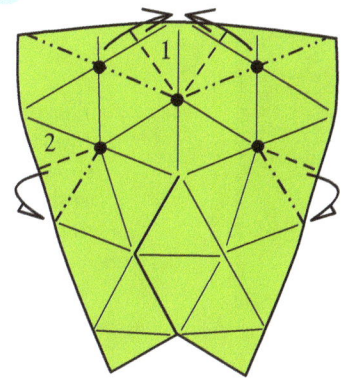

11

1. Puff out at the lower dot, the other dots will meet.
2. Puff out at the dots on the left and right.

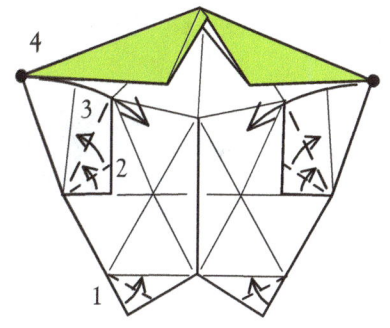

12

1. Fold to the line.
2. Fold to the line.
3. Continue folding the flap along the crease.
4. The corner will come down and cover the fold in part 3.
Repeat on the right.

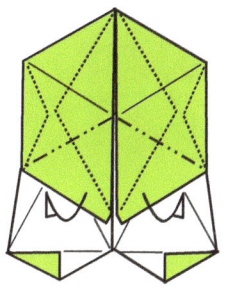

13

Fold behind and cover the hidden flaps.

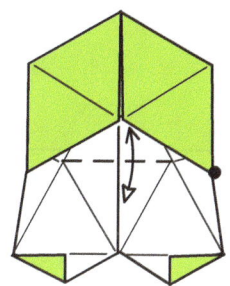

14

Fold and unfold along the crease. Rotate the dot to the top and center.

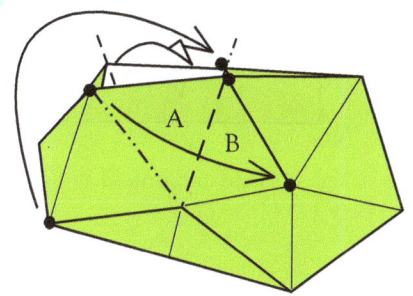

15

Triangle A will cover B so two dots will meet. Repeat behind at the same time so three dots (on the left and two at the top) meet.

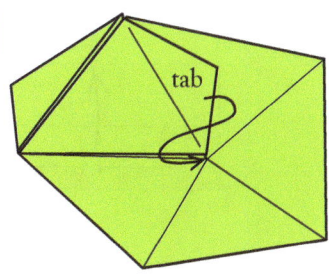

16

Tuck the tab into the pocket. Repeat behind. Rotate.

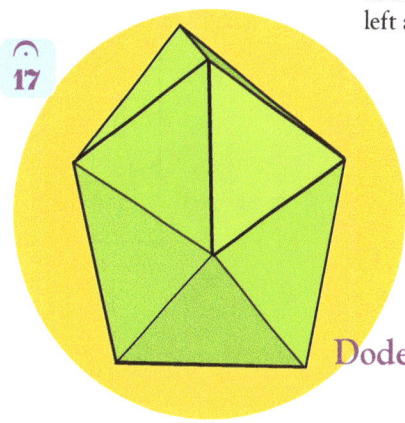

17

Dodecadeltahedron

Triaugmented Triangular Prism

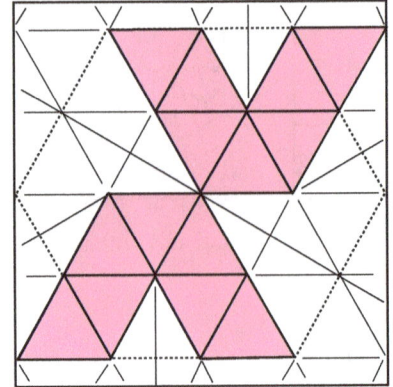

This deltahedron is formed from fourteen equilateral triangles. The crease pattern shows odd symmetry. A hexagon is folded, as shown by the dotted lines, and is used to generate the crease pattern.

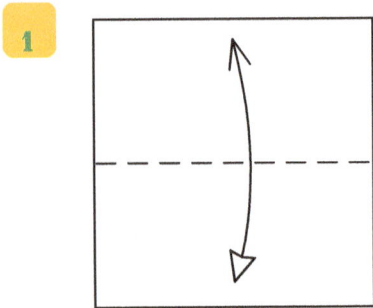

1

Fold and unfold.

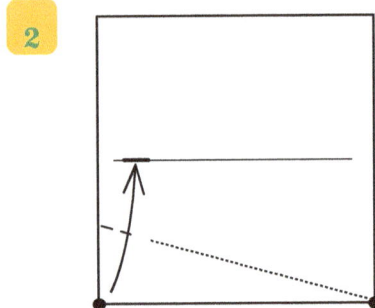

2

Bring the corner to the line and crease on the left.

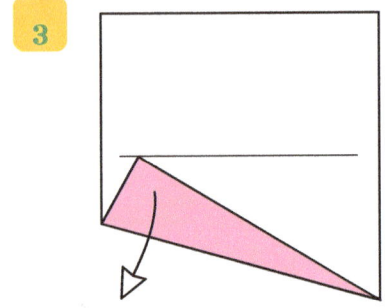

3

Unfold.

4

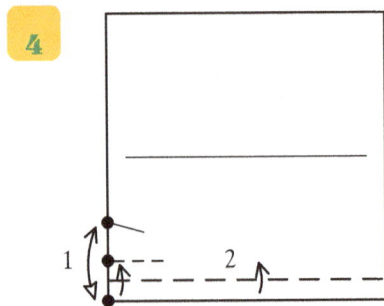

1. Fold and unfold on the left.
2. Fold to the dot.
Rotate 180°.

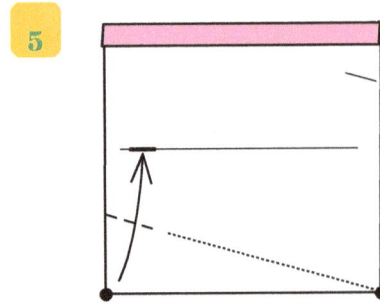

5

Repeat steps 2–5.

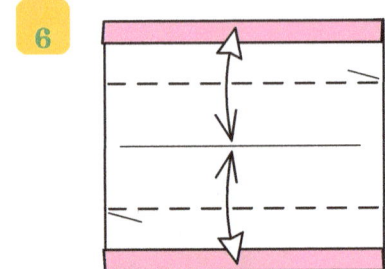

6

Fold to the center and unfold.

7

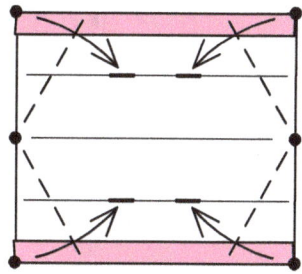

Bring the corners to the lines.

8

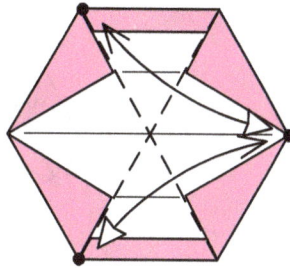

This is a regular hexagon. Fold and unfold.

9

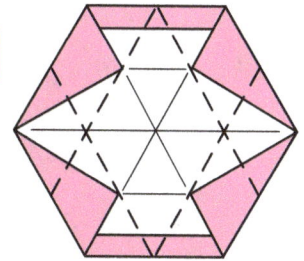

Fold to the center and unfold, on four sides.

10

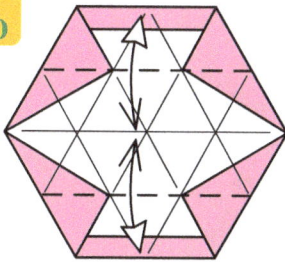

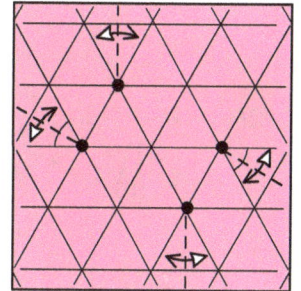

Fold and unfold along partially hidden creases.

11

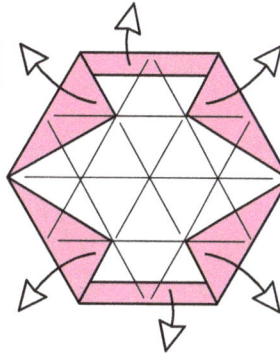

Unfold everything.

12

Fold and unfold.

13

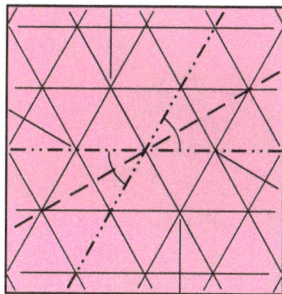

Fold and unfold to bisect the angles. Mountain-fold along the creases.

14

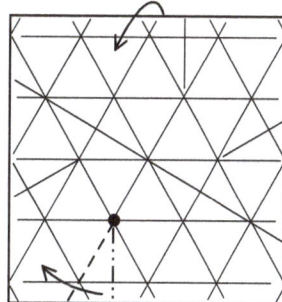

Push in at the dot.

15

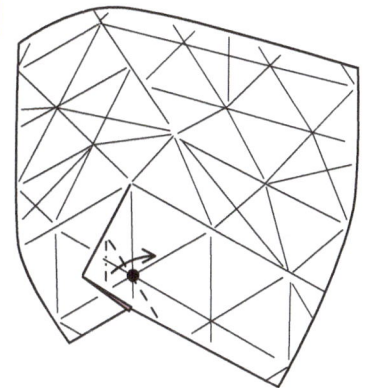

Squash-fold through the dot.

16

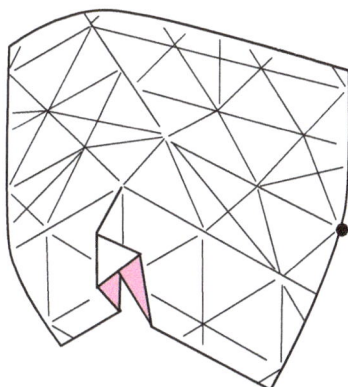

Rotate 180° and repeat steps 14–15. Rotate to view the outside so the dot is at the center and top.

17

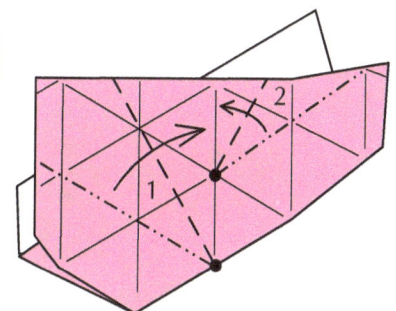

Fold along the creases and puff out at the dots. Turn over and repeat.

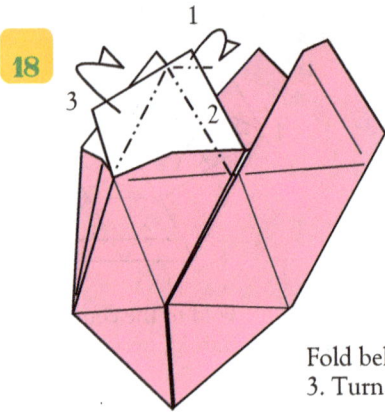

18 Fold behind at 1, 2, and 3. Turn over and repeat.

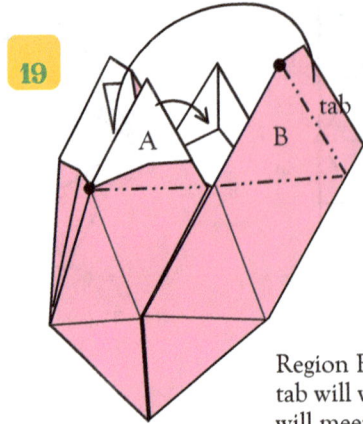

19 Region B will cover A and the tab will wrap around A. The dots will meet. Turn over and repeat.

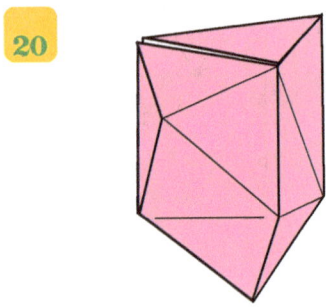

20 Rotate the top to the bottom.

21 **Triaugmented Triangular Prism**

Four Deltahedra:
Top row–Dodecadeltahedron, Triaugmented Triangular Prism
Bottom row–Icosahedron, Gyroelongated Square Dipyramid

Gyroelongated Square Dipyramid

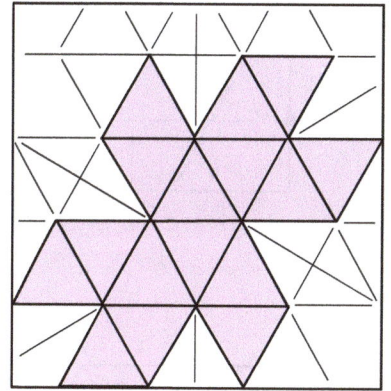

This Gyroelongated Square Dipyramid is a deltahedron with 16 sides. It can also be called a hexadecahedron, hexa for 6 and deca for 10. This forms an egg shaped polyhedron. The crease pattern shows a tab on top, and the layout has odd symmetry.

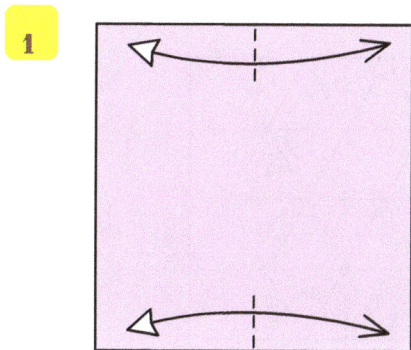

1

Fold and unfold on the top and bottom.

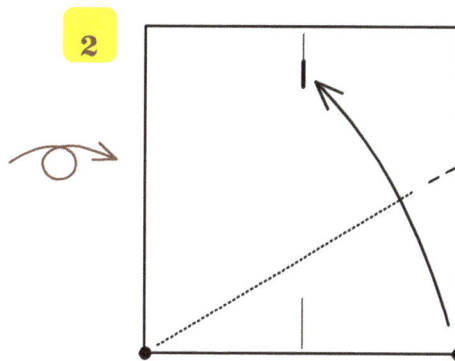

2

Bring the corner to the line and crease on the right.

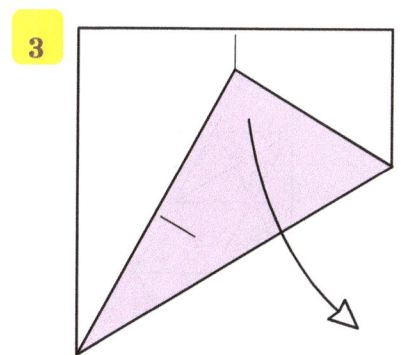

3

Unfold.

4

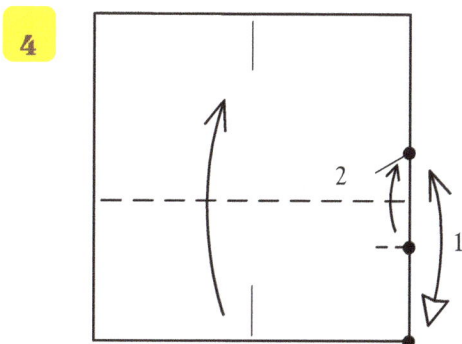

1. Fold and unfold on the right.
2. Fold up.

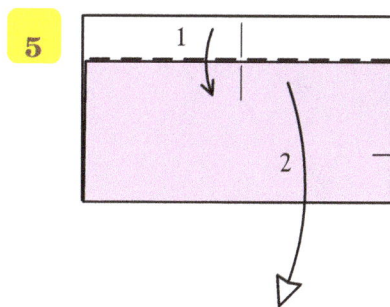

5

1. Fold along the edge.
2. Unfold.

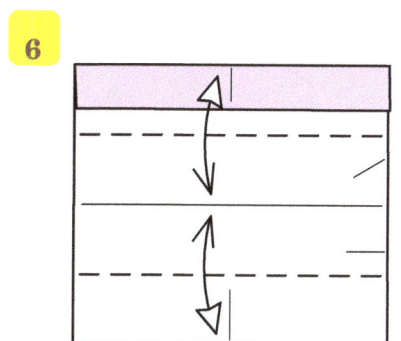

6

Fold to the center and unfold.

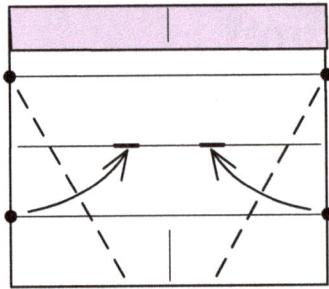

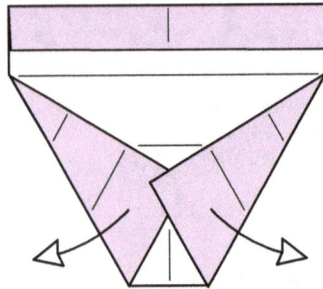

Unfold.

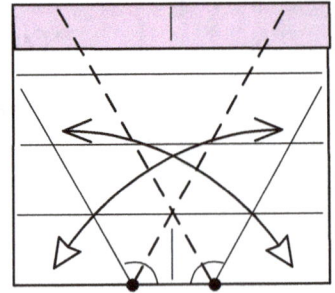

Fold and unfold.
Rotate 180°.

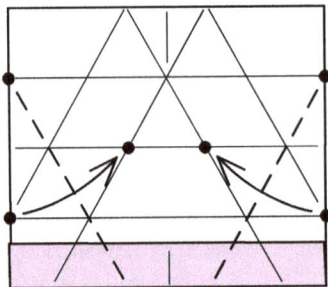

Repeat steps 7–9.

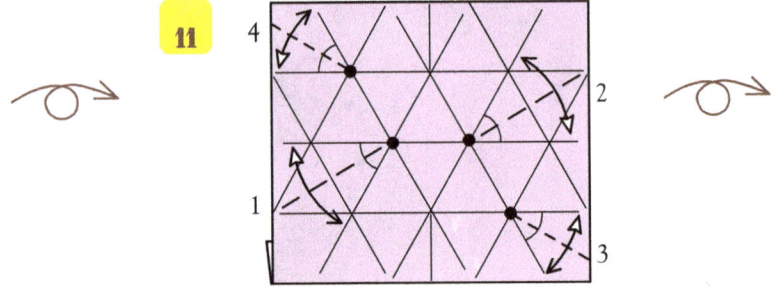

Fold and unfold.

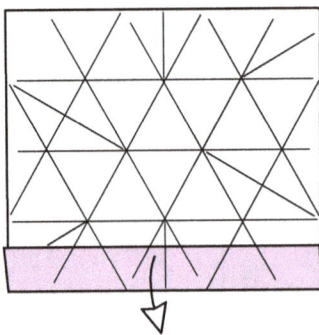

Unfold.

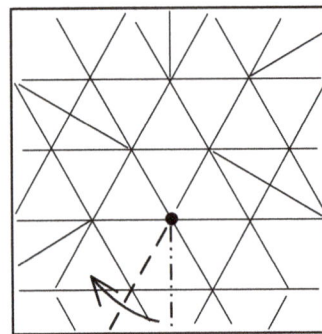

Push in at the dot.

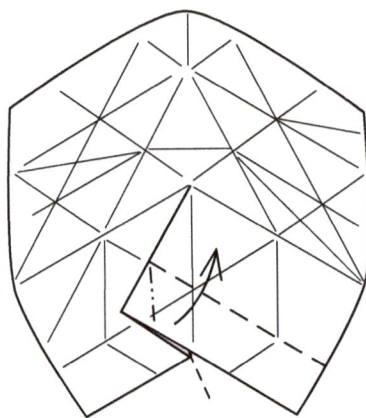

Squash-fold.

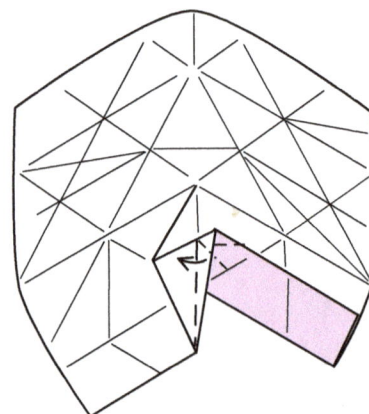

Make a thin squash fold.

16

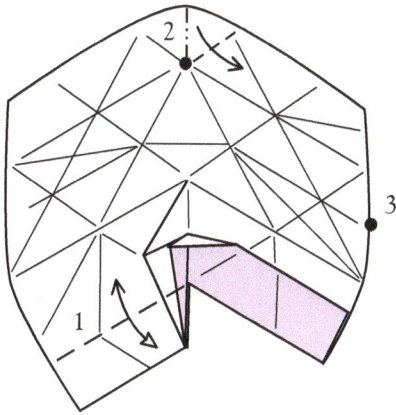

1. Fold and unfold along the crease.
2. Push in at the dot.
3. Rotate the dot to the front and top.

17

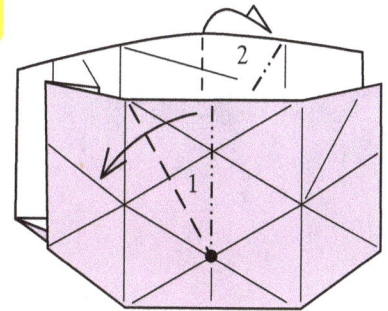

1. Puff out at the dot.
2. Turn over and repeat.

18

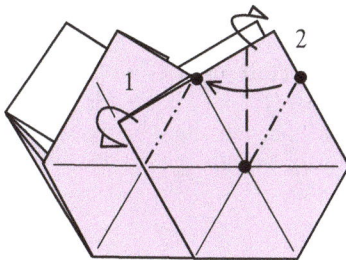

1. Fold behind and repeat behind.
2. Puff out at the lower dot.
   Repeat behind, but note
   the flap is longer.

19

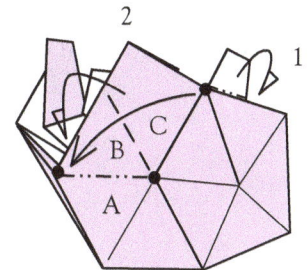

1. Fold behind.
   (Do not repeat behind.)
2. Puff out at the center dot.
   Flatten B and C behind A.
   Turn over and repeat.
Rotate the center dot to the right.

20

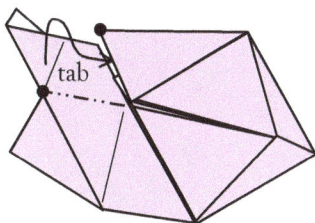

Tuck the tab into the
pocket so the dots meet.

21

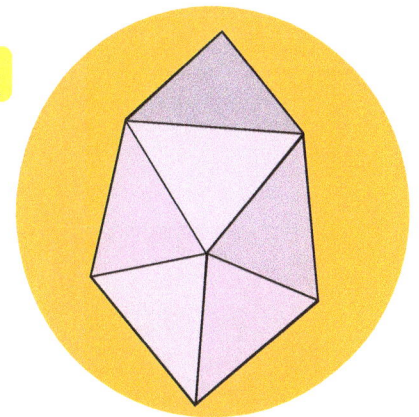

Gyroelongated
Square Dipyramid

Icosahedron

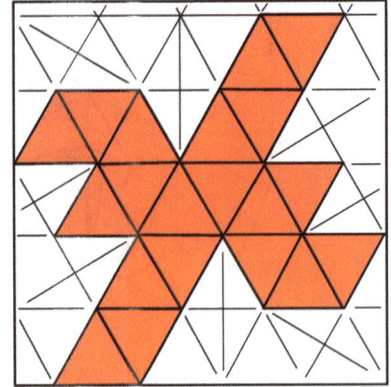

The Icosahedron is composed of 20 equilateral triangles. Plato attributed this model to water because of its ability to roll.

This is my largest version. The thin strip at the top shows some of the tab. Thus the tab is a bit small. When folded from larger paper (10" x 10") it holds well enough and is clean and large. The tab might be too small for smaller paper. Outside of the tab, the model shows odd symmetry.

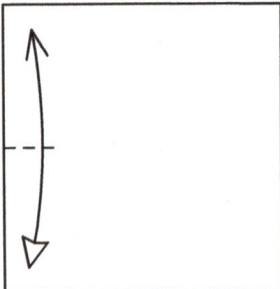

1

Fold and unfold
on the left.

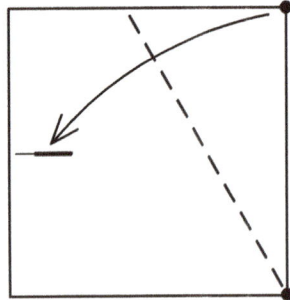

2

Bring the top
corner to the line.

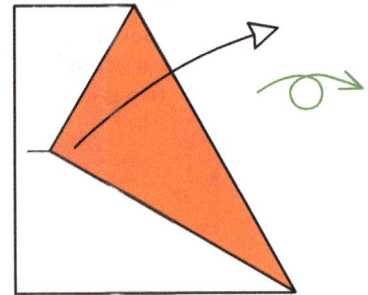

3

Unfold.

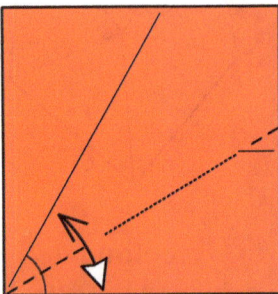

4

Fold and unfold on
the left and right.

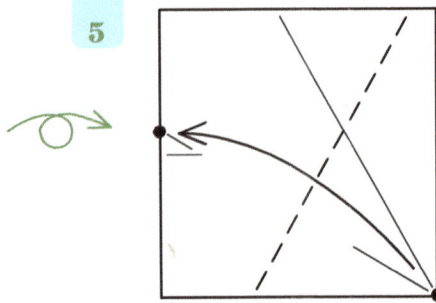

5

The dots will meet.

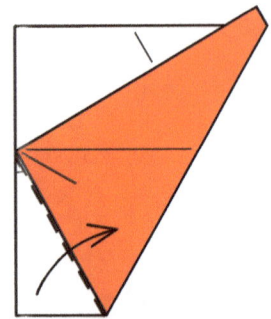

6

7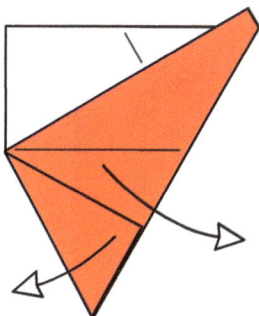

Unfold.

8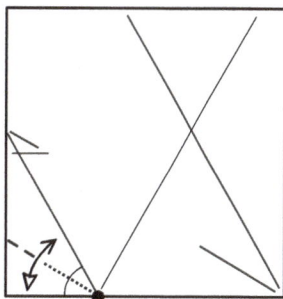

Fold and unfold
on the left.

9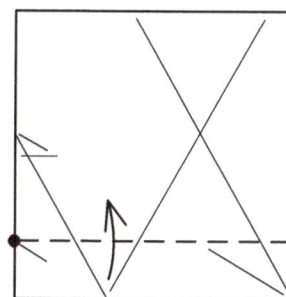

10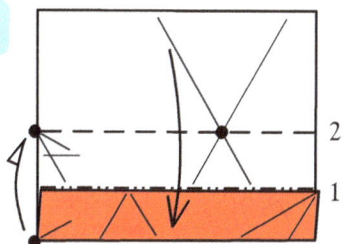

11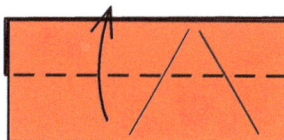

Fold along the
hidden edge.

12

Fold along the
hidden edge.

13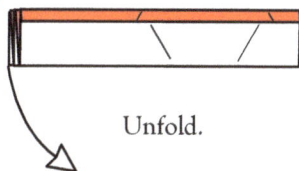

Unfold.

14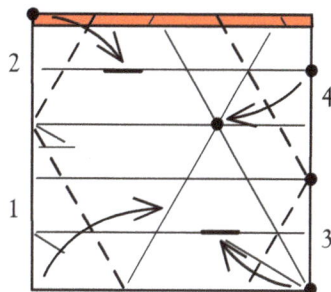

1. Fold along the crease.
2, 3, 4. Fold in order.

15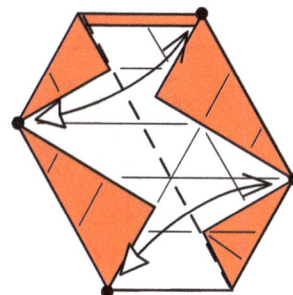

Fold and unfold.

16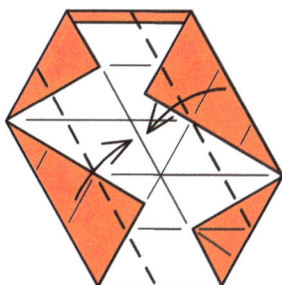

Fold to the center.

17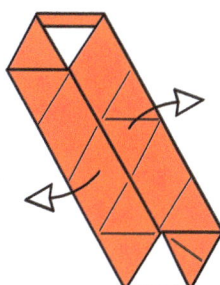

Unfold.

18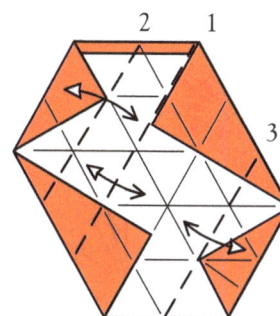

Fold and unfold.

19

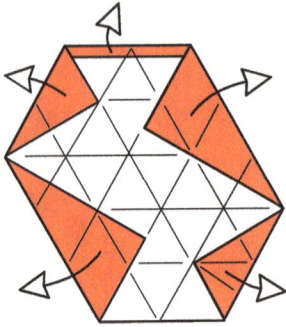

Unfold.

20

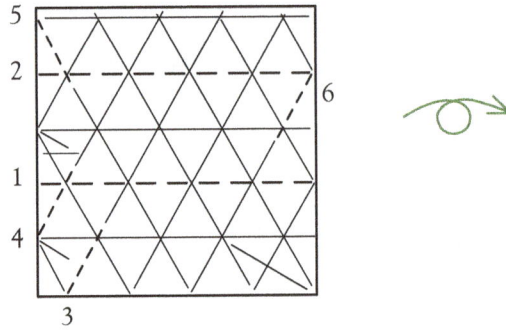

1, 2. Fold and unfold along
    the creases.
3, 4, 5, 6. Fold and unfold
    to extend the creases.

21

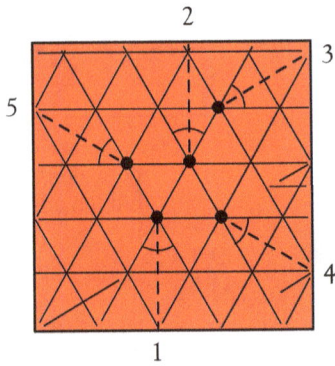

Fold and unfold.

22

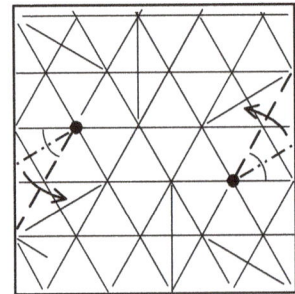

Push in at the dots.

23

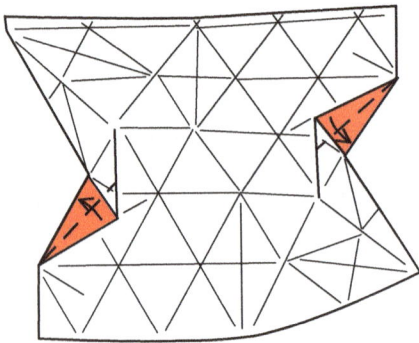

This is 3D.

24

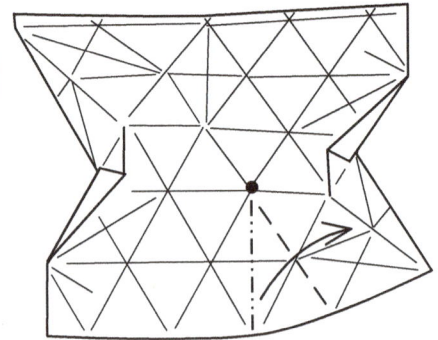

Push in at the dot.

25

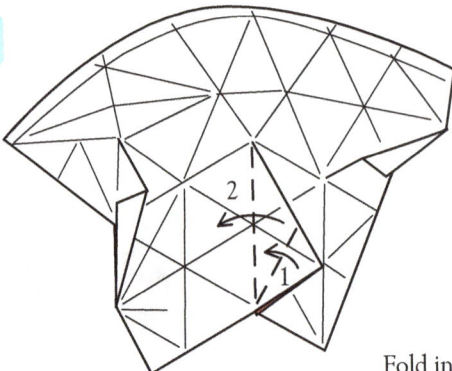

Fold in order.
Rotate 180°.

26

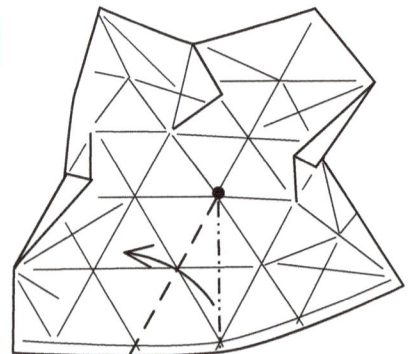

Push in at the dot.

27

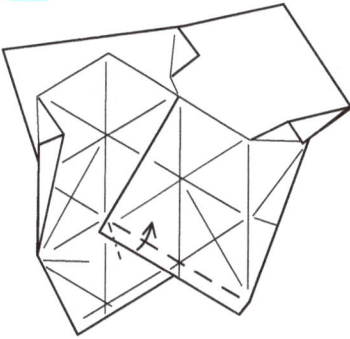

Squash-fold.

28

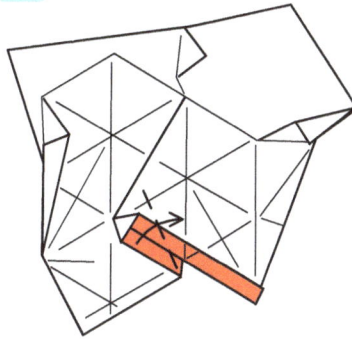

29

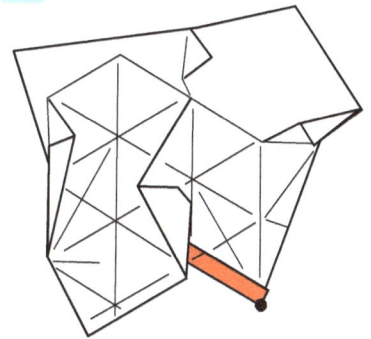

Rotate to view the
outside so the dot is
at the top and center.

30

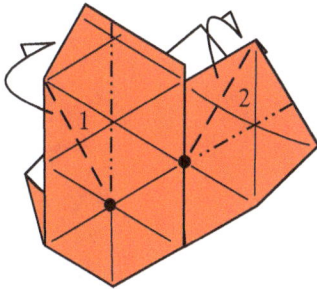

Fold in order. Puff out at the
dots. Turn over and repeat.

31

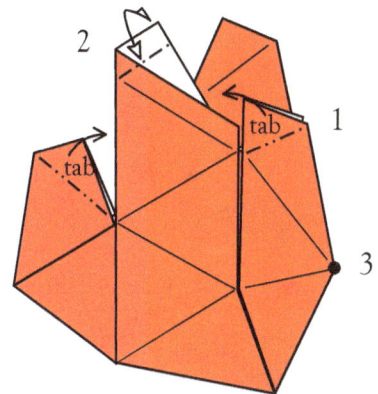

1. Fold the tabs down just a little bit.
   They will soon be covered.
2. Fold and unfold along the crease.
3. Rotate the dot to the center.

32

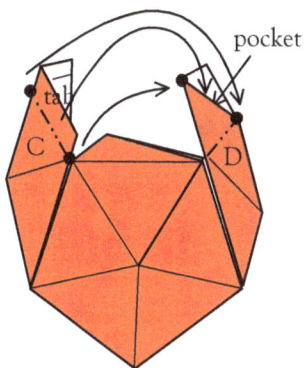

Tuck the tab into the pocket.
The pairs of dots will meet and
triangle C will be next to D.

33

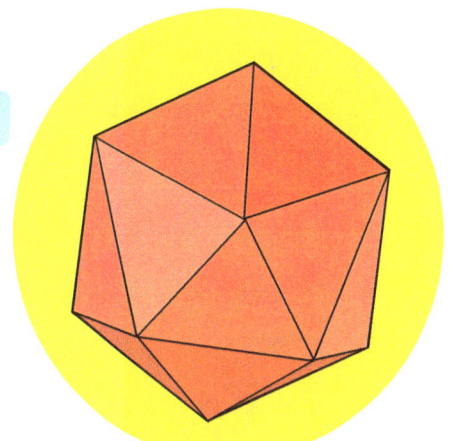

Icosahedron

Trio of Duo-Colored Octahedra

The journey through outer space takes us to three unusual worlds. This Trio of Duo-Colored Octahedra shows a dazzling display of colorful effects. There are several arrangements of the eight triangles in a plane to form an Octahedron. The layouts will be shown for each model.

Banded Octahedron

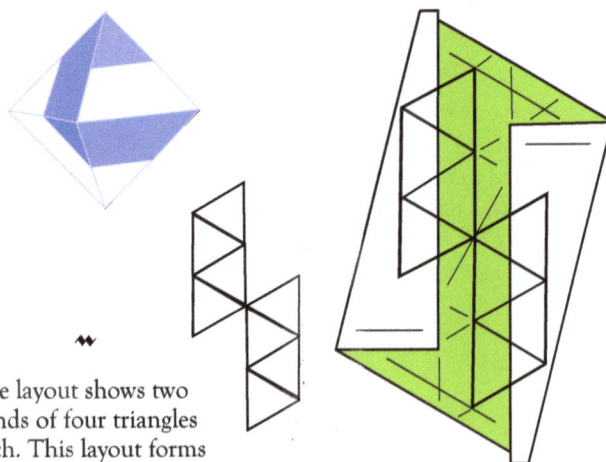

The layout shows two bands of four triangles each. This layout forms an octahedron. Odd symmetry is used.

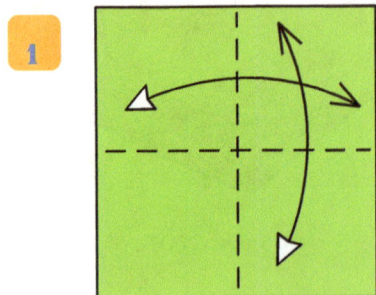

Fold and unfold.

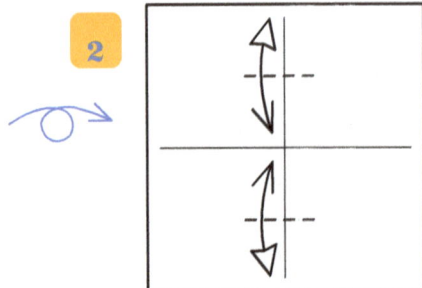

Fold and unfold. Crease lightly.

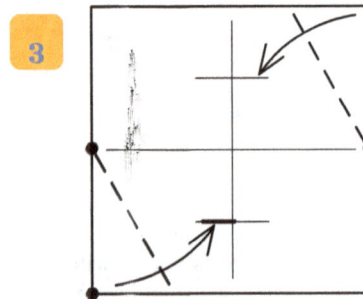

Bring the corners to the lines.

4

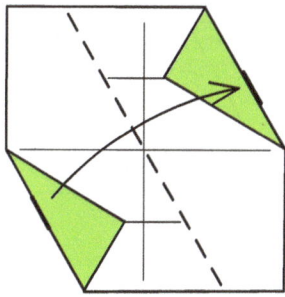

5

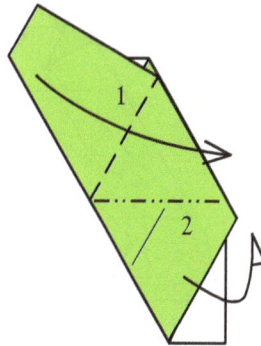

1. Fold along the crease.
2. Fold along a hidden crease.

6

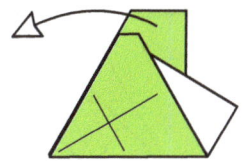

Unfold.

7

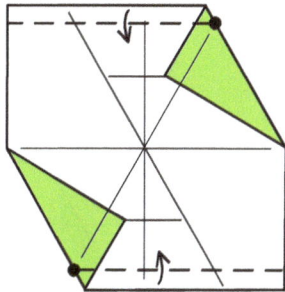

8

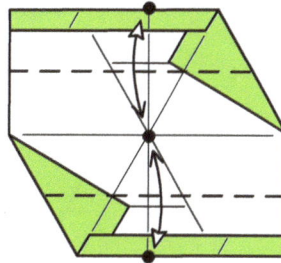

Fold and unfold.

9

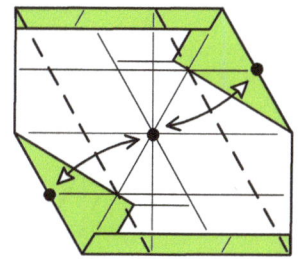

Fold and unfold.

10

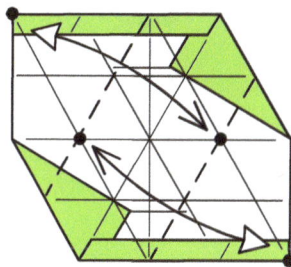

Fold and unfold.

11

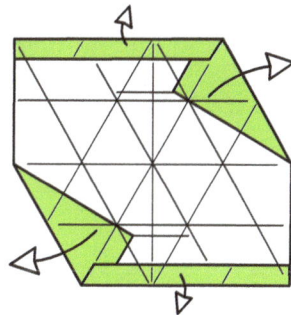

Unfold.

12

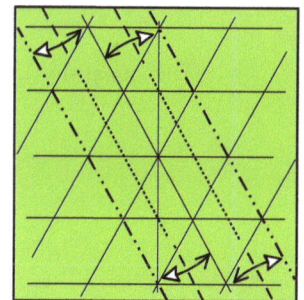

Fold and unfold.

13

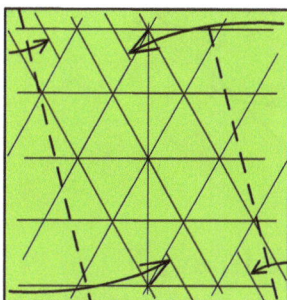

Fold the edges to
the crease marks.

14

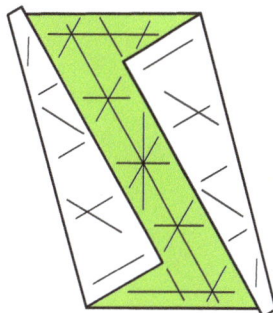

15

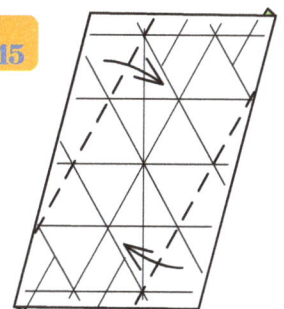

Fold along
the creases.

Banded Octahedron **93**

16

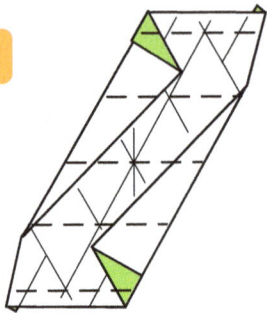

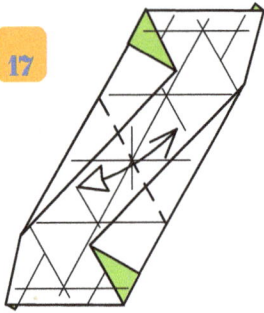

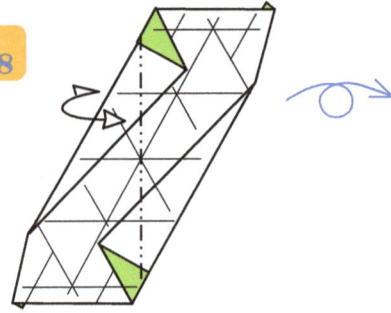

Fold and unfold.

17

Fold and unfold.

18

Fold and unfold.

19

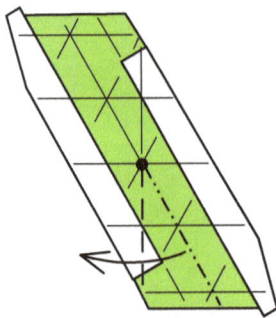

Puff out at the dot.

20

Fold and unfold along
the creases. Rotate 180°.

21

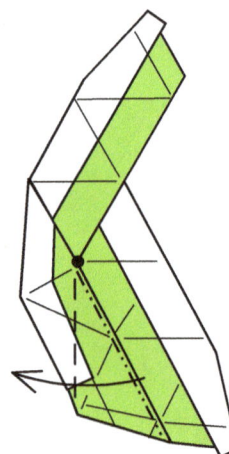

Repeat steps 19–20.

22

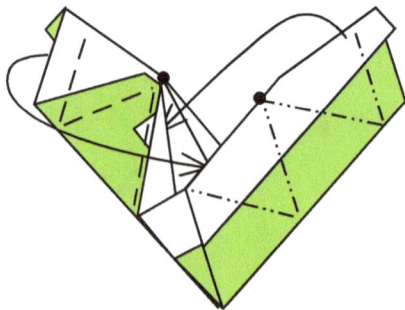

Tuck inside. The dots will meet.

23

Banded Octahedron

Magic Octahedron

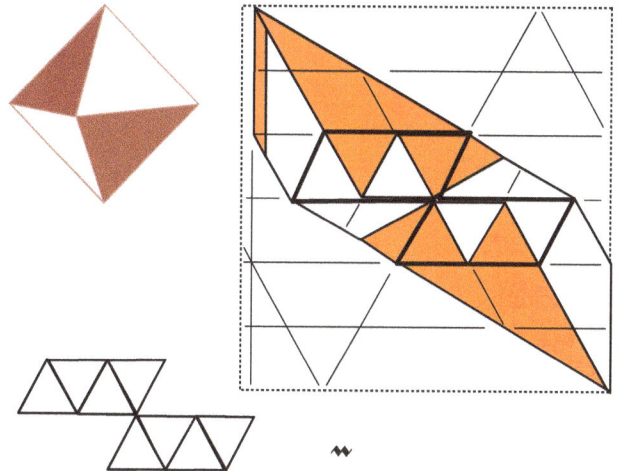

The colors of the faces alternate between a color and white. Odd symmetry is used. Not only is this a magical model because of the alternating color pattern, but also because this complex structure can be accomplished in only 24 steps.

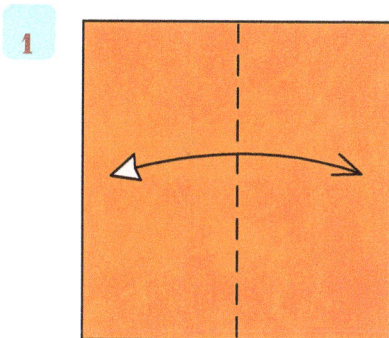

1

Fold and unfold.

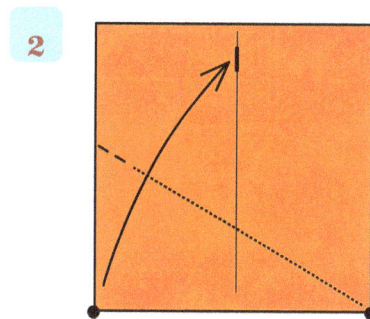

2

Bring the left dot to the line. Crease on the left.

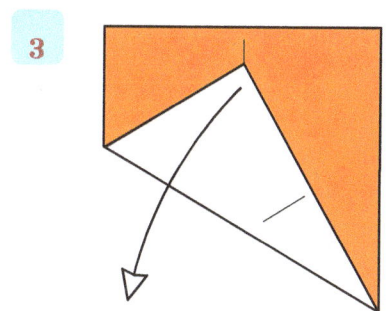

3

Unfold.

4

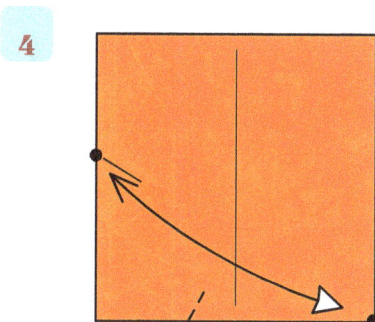

Fold and unfold at the bottom.

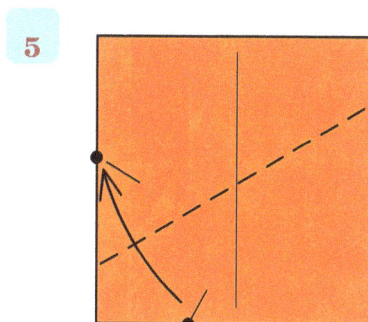

5

The dots will meet.

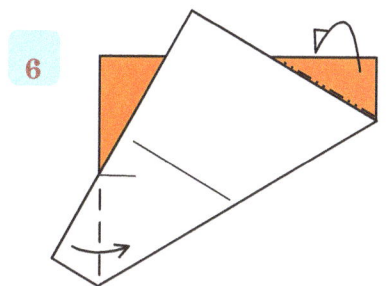

6

7

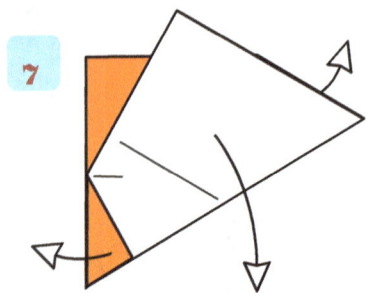

Unfold everything and rotate 90°.

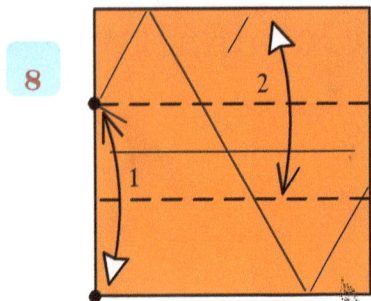

8

1

2

Fold and unfold.

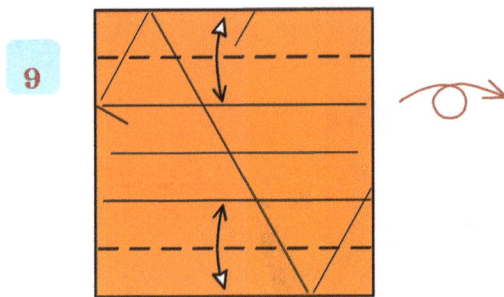

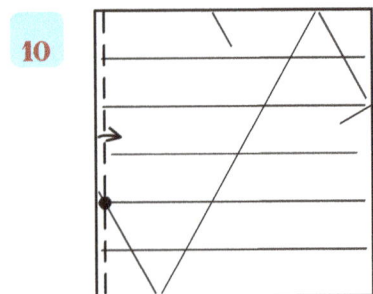

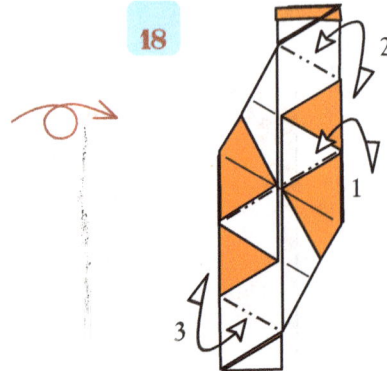

9

Fold and unfold.

10

Fold a thin strip at the dot.

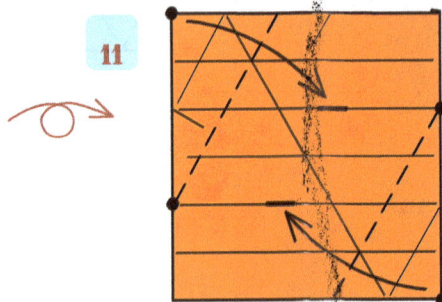

11

Bring the corners to the lines.

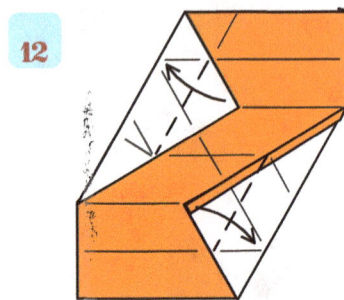

12

Fold along the creases.

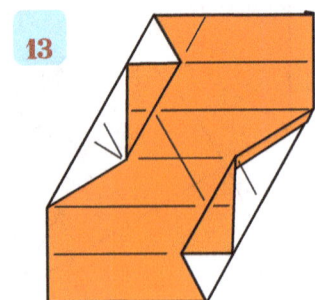

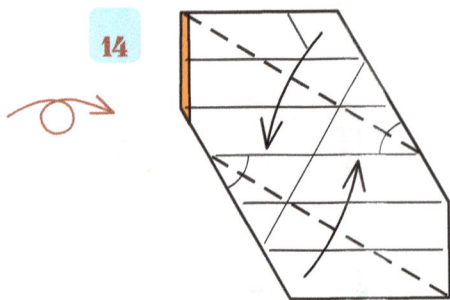

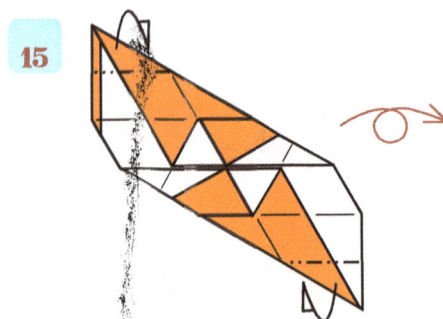

13

14

15

Fold along the creases. Rotate 90°.

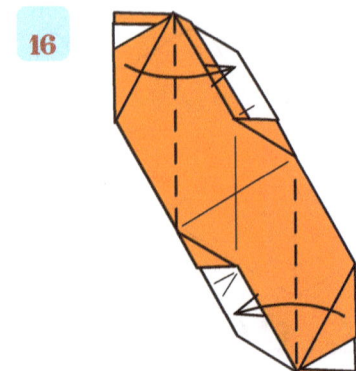

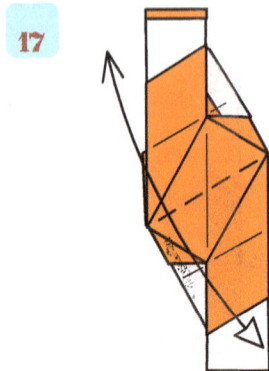

16

17

Fold and unfold.

18

2

1

3

Fold and unfold.

19

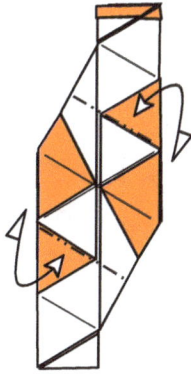

Fold and unfold.

20

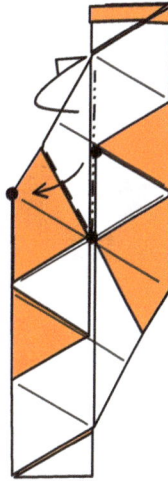

Puff out at the
lower dot.

21

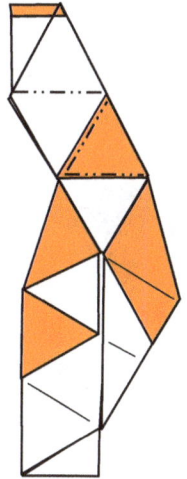

Fold and unfold along
the edges. Rotate 180°.

22

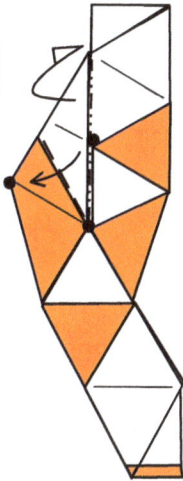

Repeat steps
20–21.

23

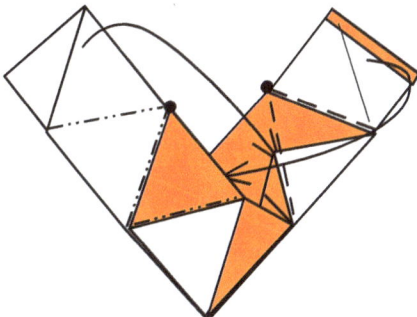

Tuck inside. The
dots will meet.

24

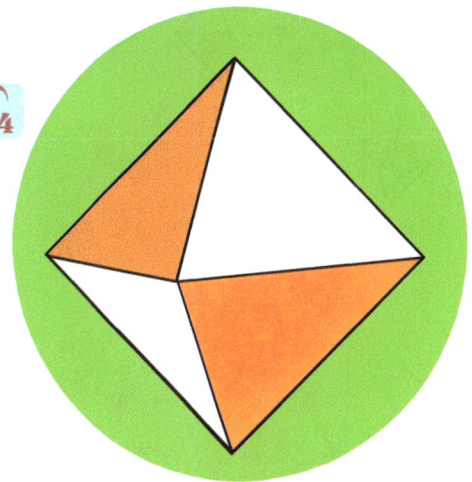

Magic Octahedron

Spinning Octahedron

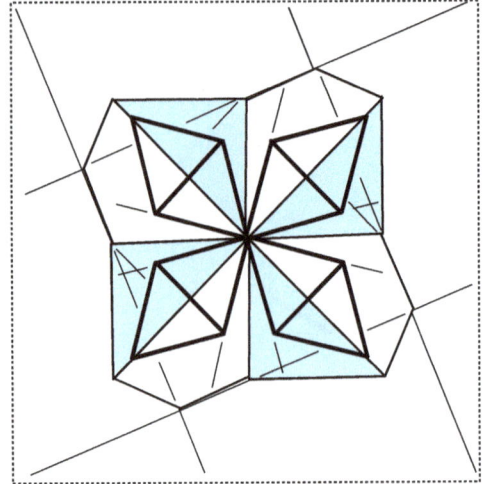

This Spinning Octahedron has two colors on each face. The color pattern is made from the base in step 15, which is then formed into an octahedron. Square symmetry is used and the model closes with a four-way twist lock. The two photos show different points of view.

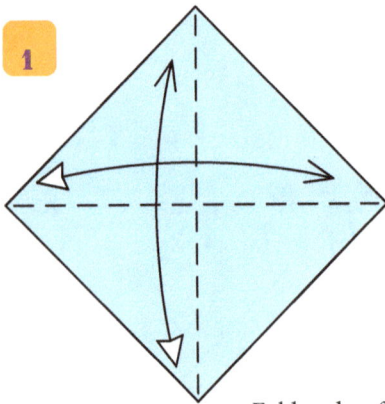

1

Fold and unfold.

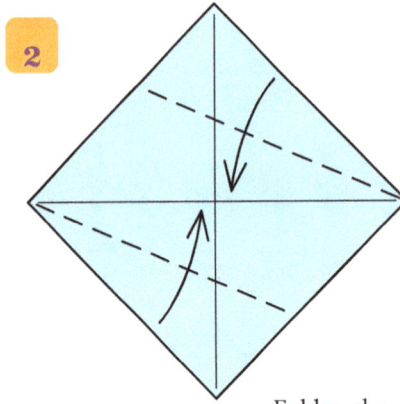

2

Fold to the center.

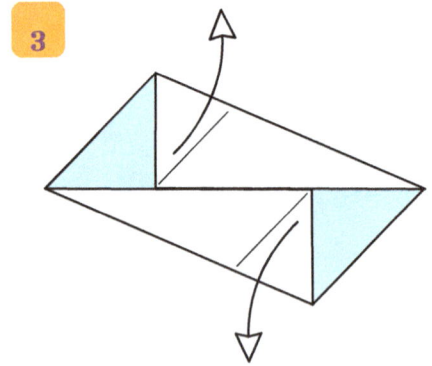

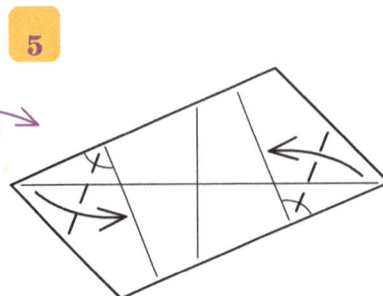

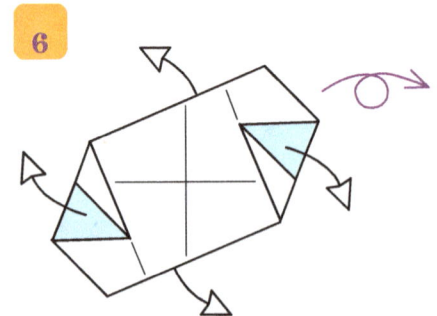

3

Unfold and rotate 90°.

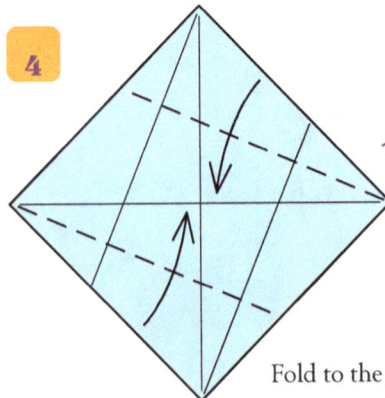

4

Fold to the center.

5

6

Unfold everything and rotate 90°.

7

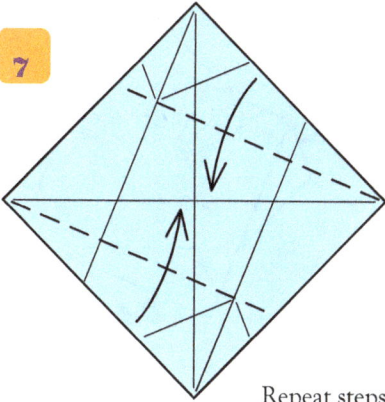

Repeat steps 4–6.
Rotate 45°.

8

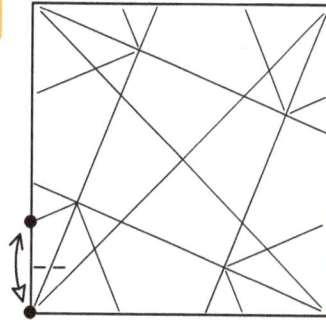

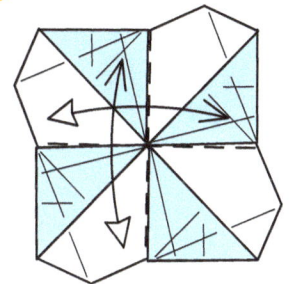

Fold and unfold
on the left.

9

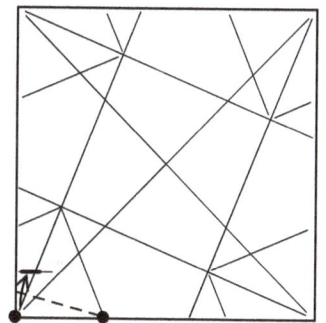

Bring the dot
to the crease.

10

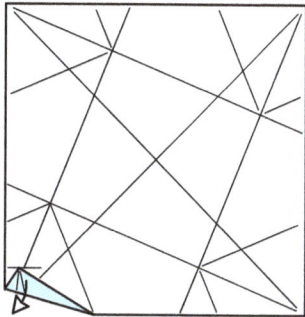

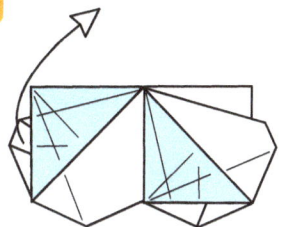

Unfold and rotate 90°.

11

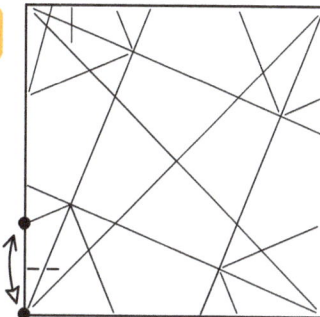

Repeat steps 8–10 three
times. Rotate 45°.

12

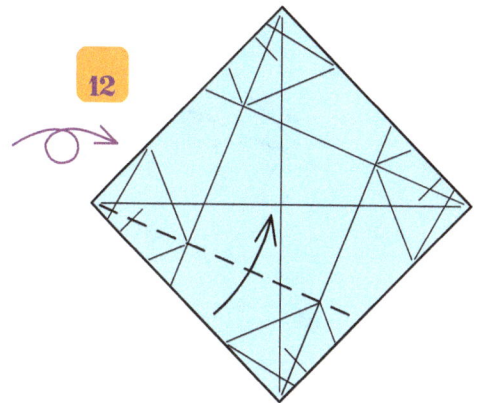

Fold along the crease.

13

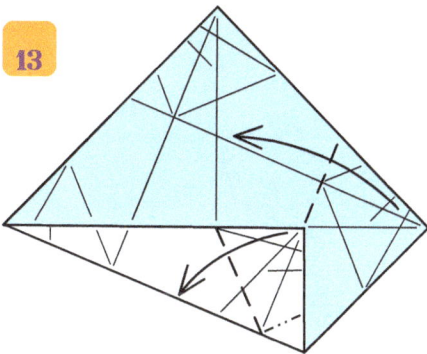

Squash-fold along the
creases. Rotate 90°.

14

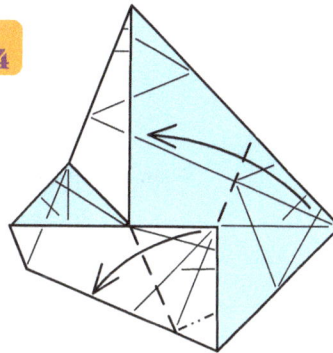

Repeat all around.
Rotate 45°.

15

Fold and unfold.

16

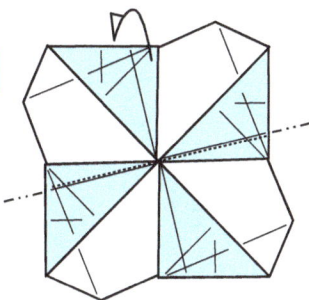

Fold behind. Do not
fold the top layers.

17

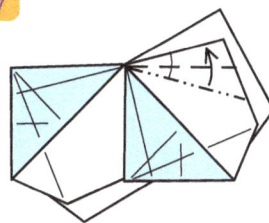

Valley-fold along the crease.
Turn over and repeat.

18

Unfold and rotate 90°.

19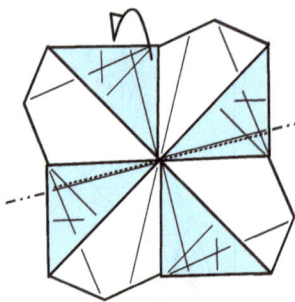

Repeat steps 16–18.
Rotate 45°.

20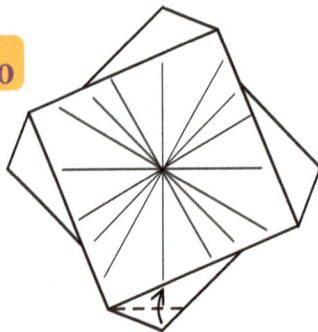

21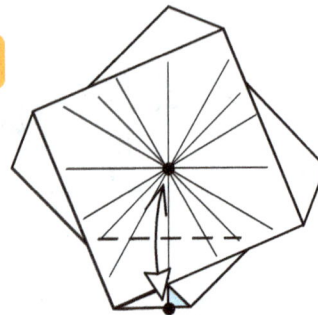

Fold and unfold.

22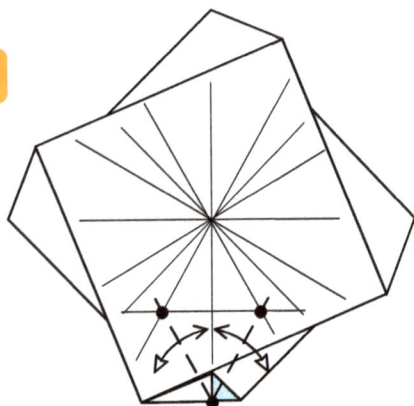

Fold and unfold.

23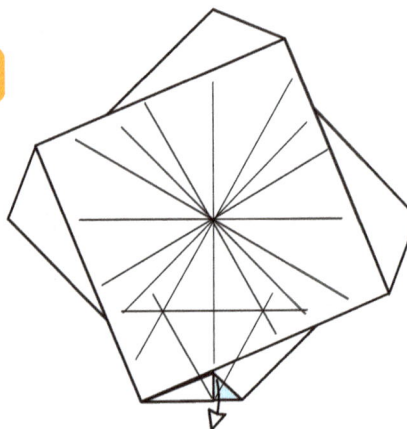

Unfold and rotate 90°.

24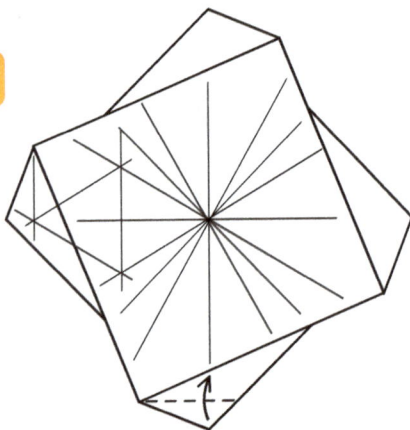

Repeat steps 20–23
three times.

25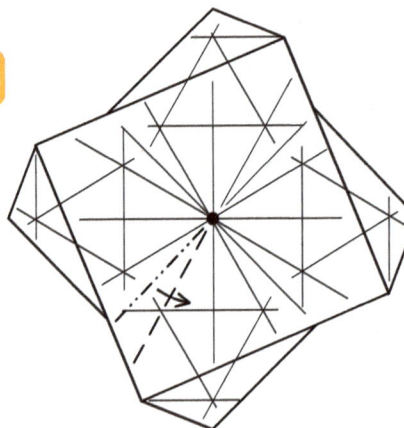

Fold along the creases
and push in at the dot.

26

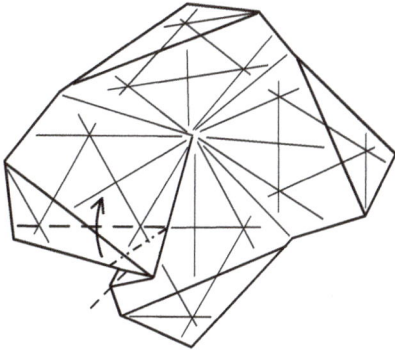

Squash-fold. Valley-fold along the crease.

27

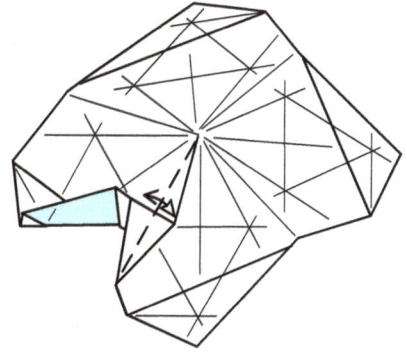

Fold and unfold. Rotate 90°.

28

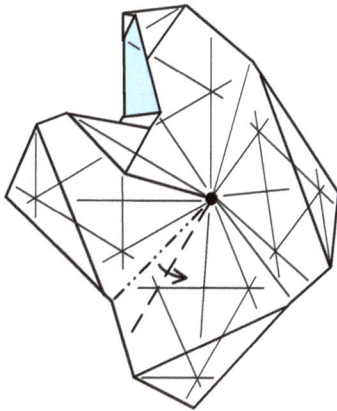

Repeat steps 25–27 three times. Rotate to view the outside. The dot will go to the bottom.

29

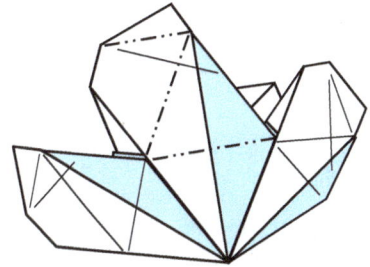

Fold and unfold along the creases. Rotate 90° and repeat three times.

30

tab 2

tab 1

A

B

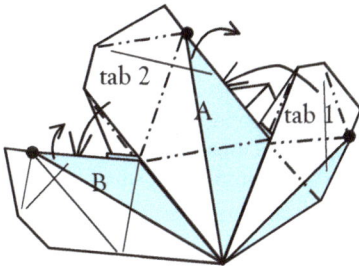

The model closes with a four-way twist lock. A will cover tab 1 and B will cover tab 2. The dots will meet at the top.

Typically, for a four-way twist lock, an easy method is to first put three sides in place. Then unfold, put another set of three side in place, and then tuck the fourth one in.

31

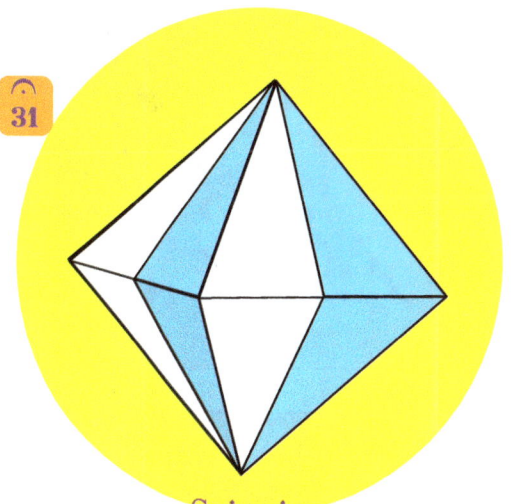

Spinning Octahedron

You can spin the octahedron like a top. It spins best if the bottom vertex is from the center of the original square.

Fourth Movement

Allegro: Deep Melodies from the Sea Invertebrates

Back to the waters we go, to explore the multitudes of Sea Invertebrates. From the shores to coral reefs, and to even greater depths, they could have many arms, tentacles, or live in shells. Some glow in the dark, others can camouflage with incredible patterns. Some are unchanged from millions of years ago. Let's journey deep into the oceans to enjoy the Deep Melodies from the Sea Invertebrates.

Starfish

Starfish usually have five arms but some have up to 40 arms. There are 2000 species of this star-shaped echinoderm. At the ends of each arm is a small red eye, though they do not see much detail. Starfish are found on the seabed in waters around the world. They have tough skin which acts as armor and can regenerate damaged arms. They feed on clams, snails, mussels, small fish, and algae.

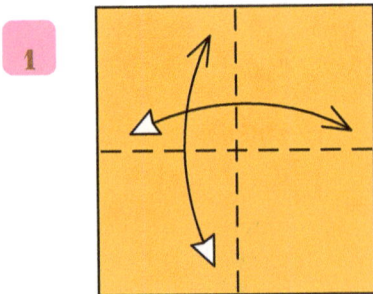

1 Fold and unfold.

2 Fold and unfold.

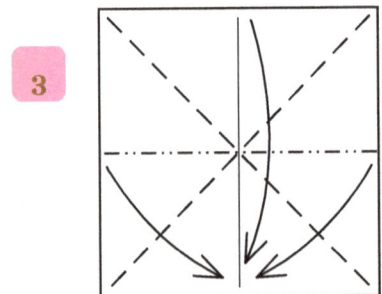

3 Fold along the creases to make a Waterbomb Base.

4 Fold and unfold.

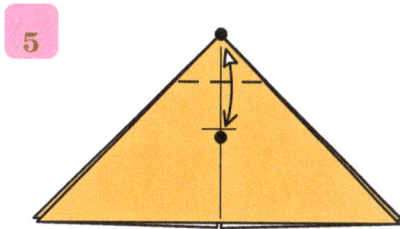

5 Fold and unfold slightly below the intersection.

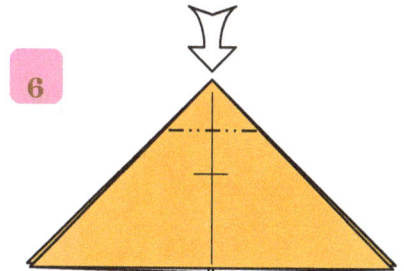

6 Sink.

7 Fold and unfold. Repeat behind.

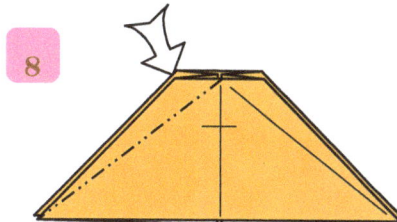

8 Sink.

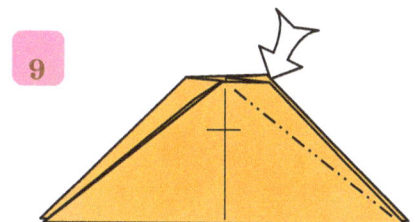

9 Sink three more times, on the right and behind.

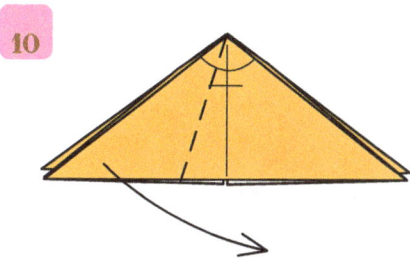

10 Fold at an angle of 1/3. Turn over and repeat.

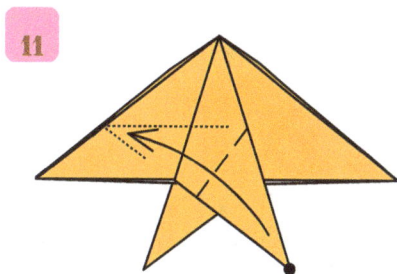

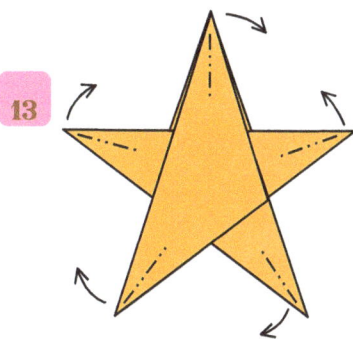

11 Bring the dot to the edge at the bold line, so the top of the flap is horizontal. Turn over and repeat.

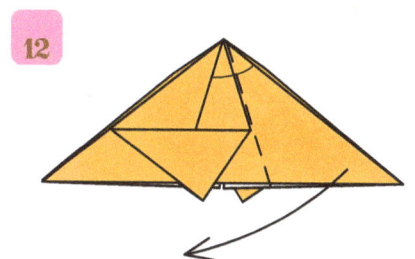

12 Turn over and repeat.

13 Shape the arms.

14 Starfish

Jellyfish

The Jellyfish we see as an umbrella shaped gelatinous body with dangling tentacles is the medusa form as part of its life cycle. The Jellyfish is not a fish, but is plankton that wanders with the current. About 95% water, the Jellyfish stings its prey of crustaceans and small fish. This prehistoric creature has been around oceans of the world for 500 million years. Warning, do not touch the tentacles while folding.

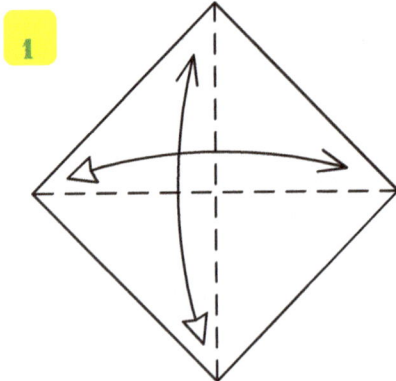

Fold and unfold.

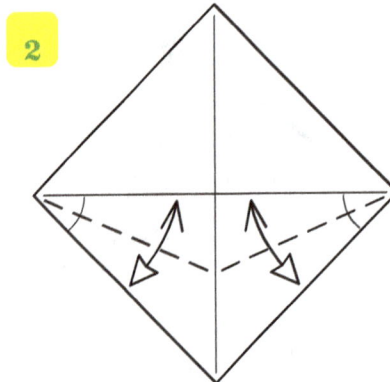

Fold and unfold.
Rotate 90°.

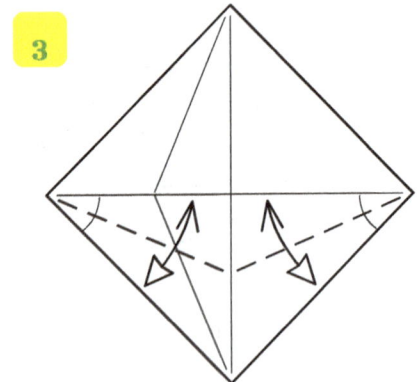

Repeat step 2 three times. Rotate 45°.

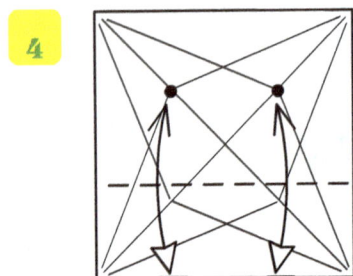

Fold and unfold.
Rotate 90°.

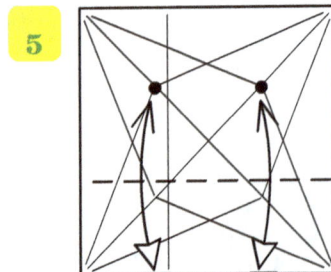

Repeat step 4 three times.

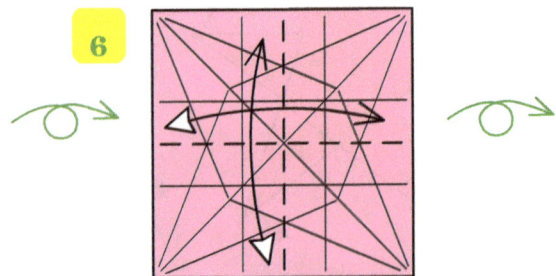

Fold and unfold.
Rotate 45°.

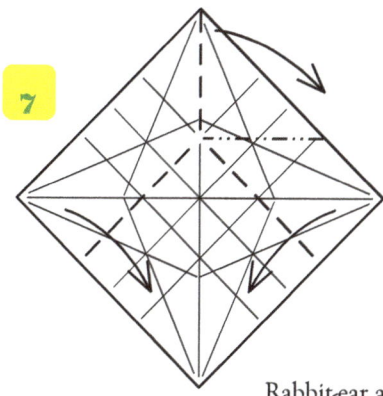

Rabbit-ear along
the creases.

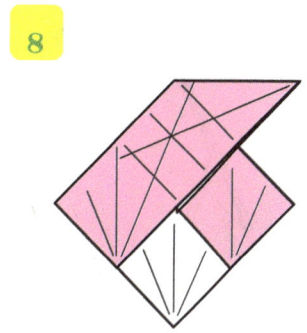

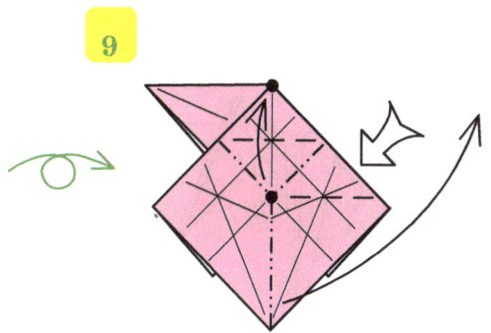

Puff out at the lower dot
and fold along the creases.

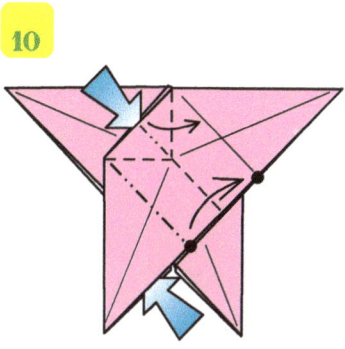

This is a combination
of squash folds.

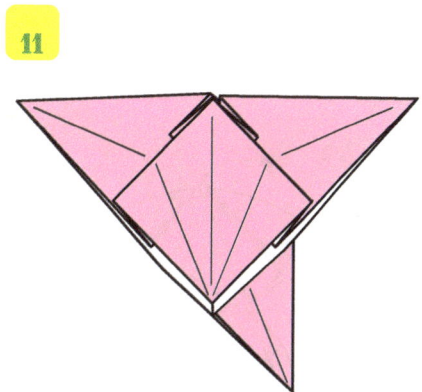

Repeat step 10 behind.

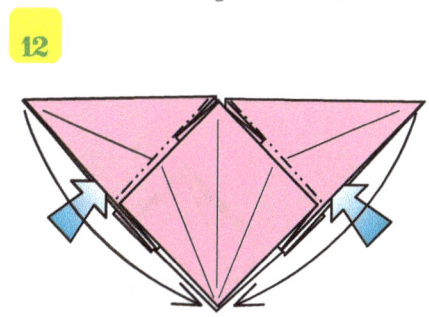

Make reverse folds.

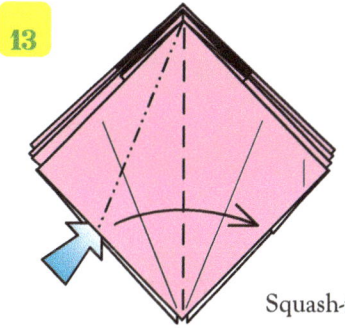

Squash-fold.

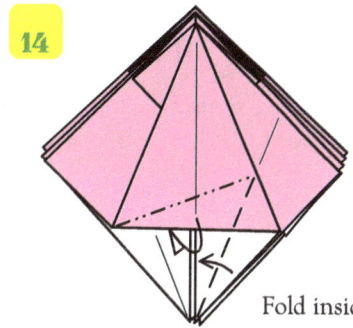

Fold inside.

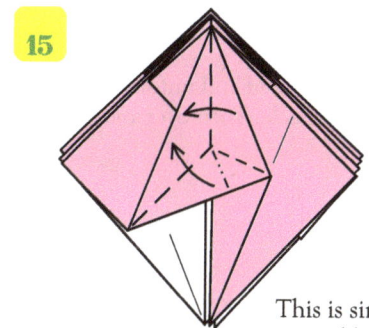

This is similar
to a rabbit ear.

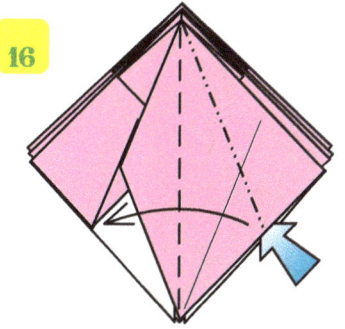

Repeat steps 13–15
on the right.

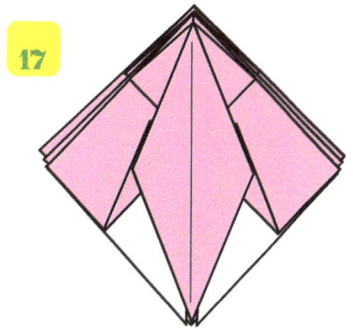

Repeat steps 13–16 three
times, on the back and sides.

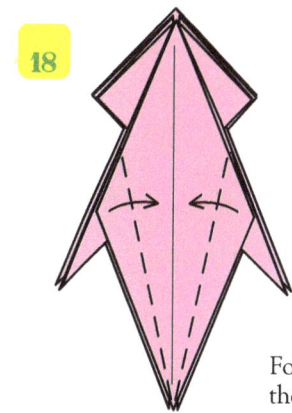

Fold toward
the center.
Repeat behind.

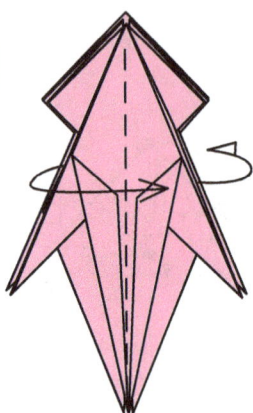

19

Fold half of the layers, repeat behind.

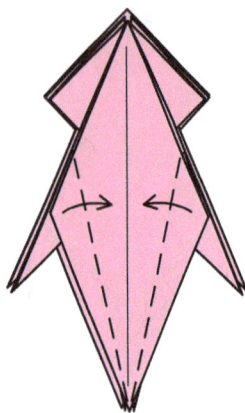

20

Fold toward the center. Repeat behind.

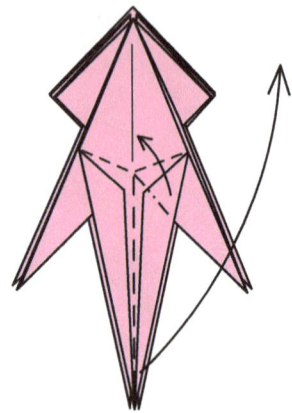

21

Rabbit-ear, repeat behind.

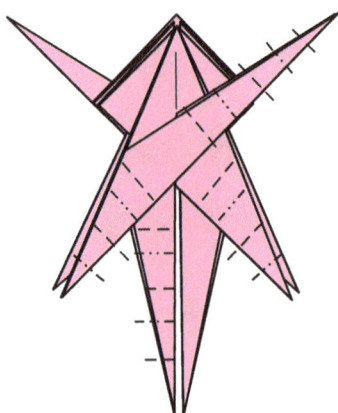

22

Pleat-fold and unfold each tentacle. Turn over and repeat.

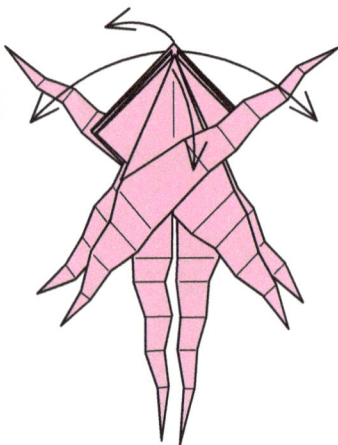

23

Spread the top.

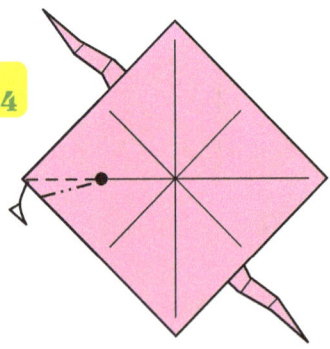

24

Puff out at the dot.

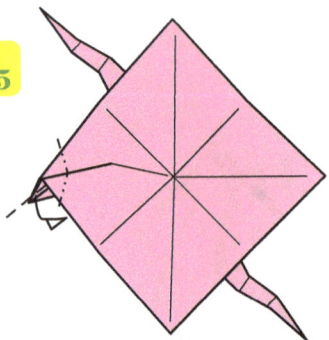

25

Fold behind.

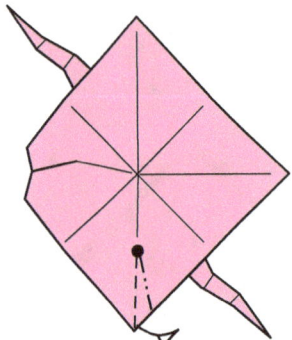

26

Repeat steps 24–25 three times.

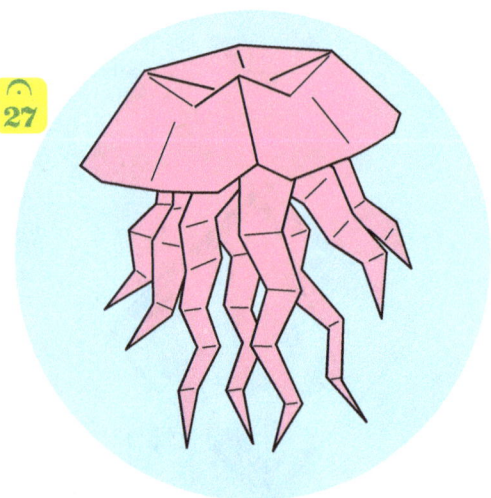

27

Jellyfish

Octopus

The Octopus really has two legs and six arms. They use
two for walking while the other six gather food. Their
arms contain chemoreceptors so they can taste what they
touch. They like to bring food to their den and stock
several meals there. Favorite meals include crustaceans,
mullusks, and fish. They can regenerate damaged arms
and can change their skin color to camouflage into the
background. For being a mullusk, they have extremely
fine vision and are exceptionally intelligent creatures.
Some have theorized that these cephalopods are aliens.

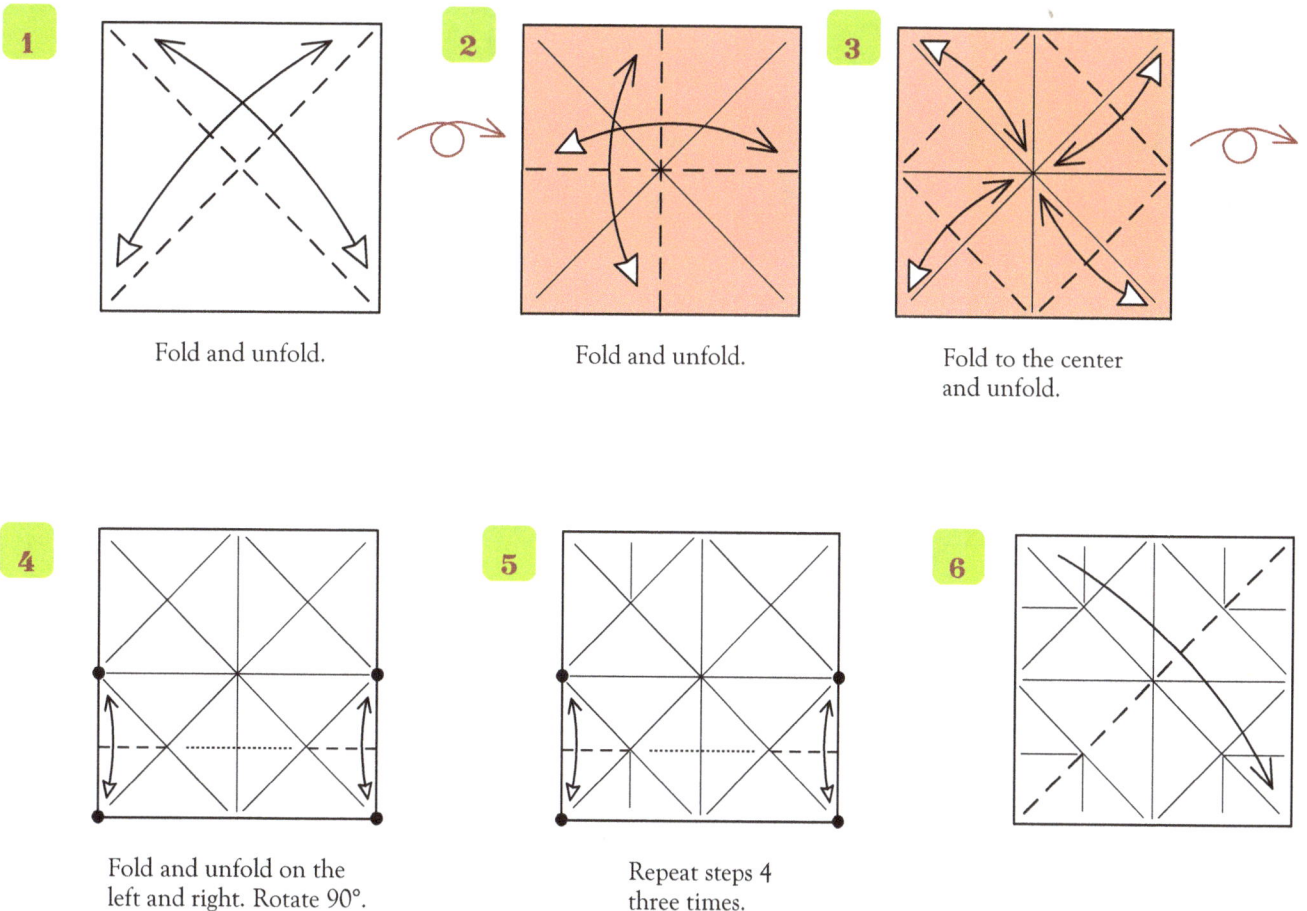

Fold and unfold.

Fold and unfold.

Fold to the center
and unfold.

Fold and unfold on the
left and right. Rotate 90°.

Repeat steps 4
three times.

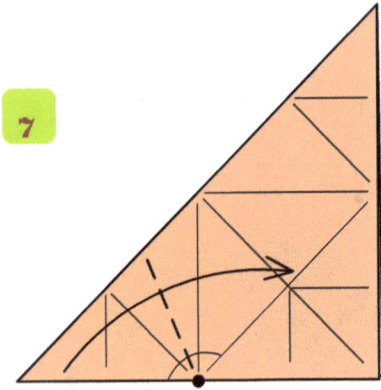

7

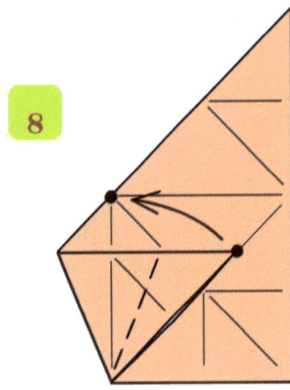

8

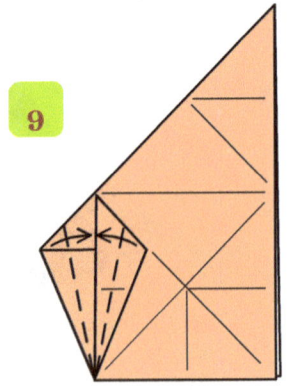

9

Fold to center.

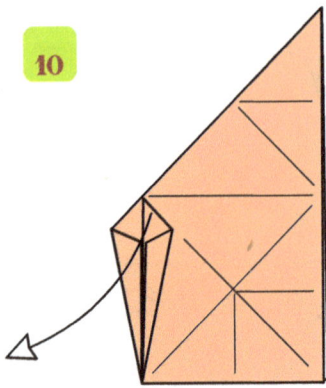

10

Unfold.

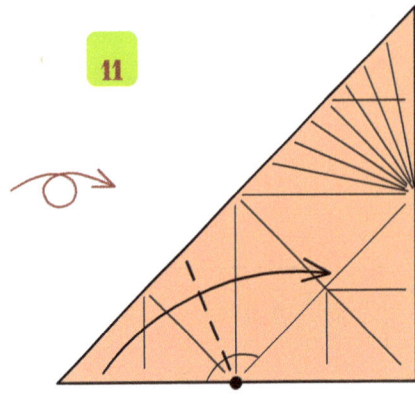

11

Repeat steps 7–10.

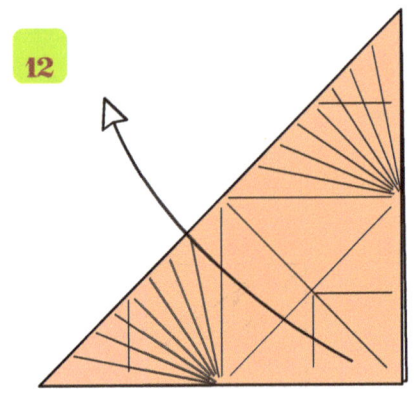

12

Unfold and rotate 90°.

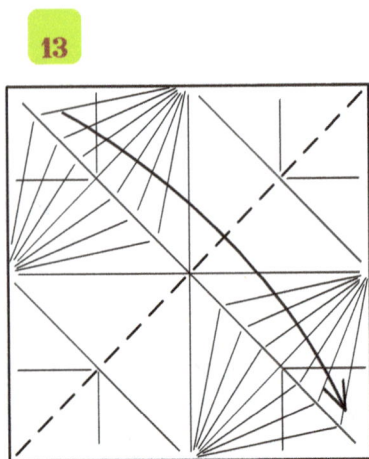

13

Repeat steps 6–12.

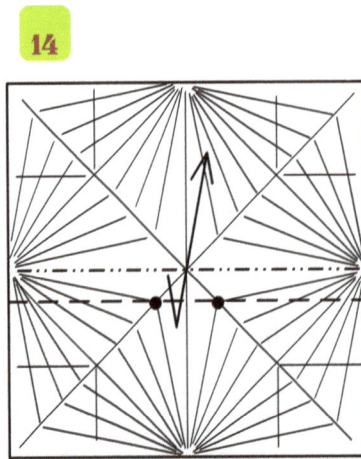

14

Mountain-fold along the crease for this pleat fold.

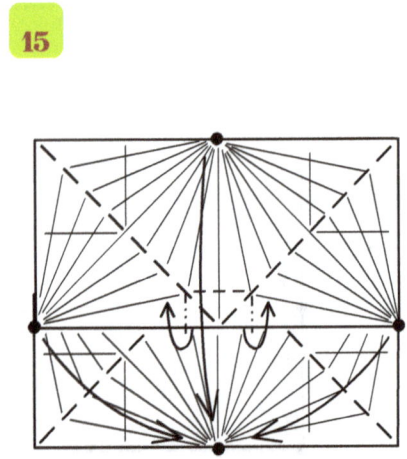

15

The dots will meet at the bottom.

108 *Origami Symphony No. 4*

16

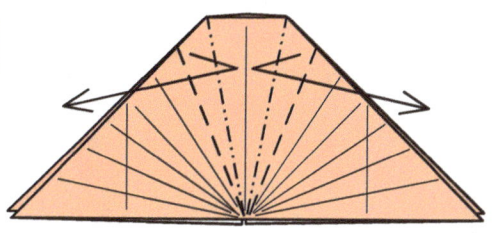

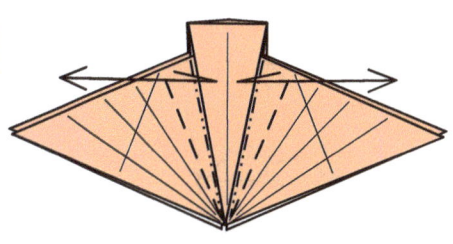

Make crimp folds along the
creases. Repeat behind.

17

Make crimp folds along the
creases. Repeat behind.

18

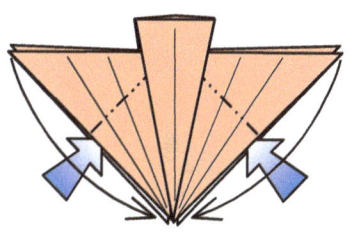

Make reverse folds along
the creases. Repeat behind.

19

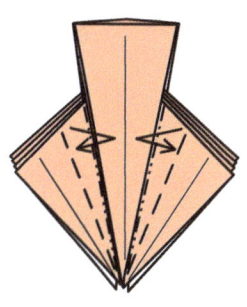

Make crimp folds along
the creases. Repeat three
times on each side.

20

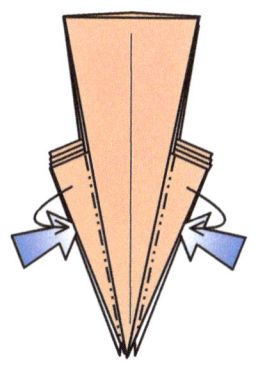

Make reverse folds along
the creases. Repeat three
times on each side.

21

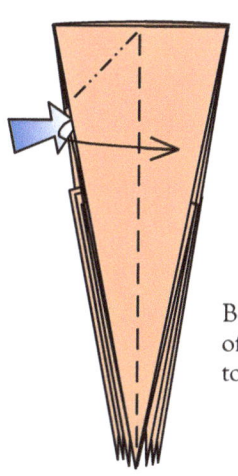

Begin this combination
of folds by folding the
top layer.

22

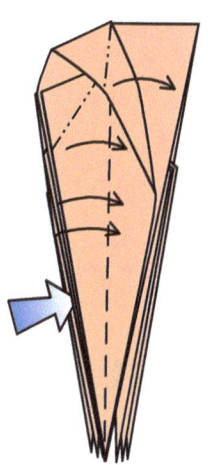

This is 3D. Fold the top flap to
the right and make four spread
squash folds. The diagram shows
mountain folds for the highest
two spread squash folds.

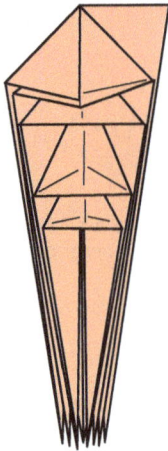

23

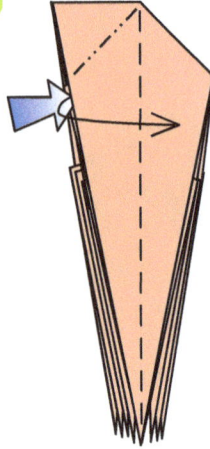

24

Repeat steps 21–22.

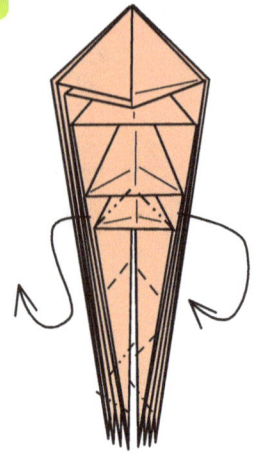

25

Shape the front legs
with reverse folds.

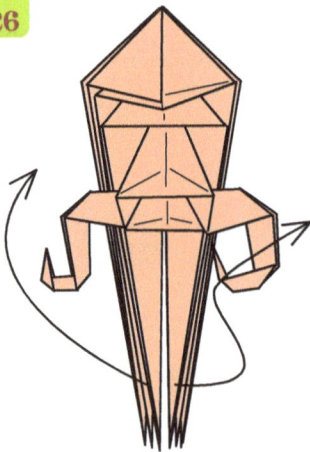

26

Shape the rest of the
legs with reverse folds.

27

Octopus

Squid

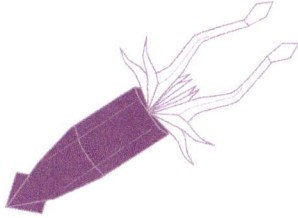

Squids are cephalopods with long bodies, eight arms, two long tentacles, and two large eyes. At ten inches wide, the Giant Squid has the largest eyes of all animals. While many Squid are two feet long, the Giant Squid can grow to 43 feet. There are over 300 species of this mullusk and some glow in the dark, especially in deep waters. They swim quickly as they sneak up to their prey, which they grab with their tentacles. Favorite prey include fish, shrimp, and crabs. Their body is enclosed in a protective mantle and they can camouflage into multiple colorful patterns. They can squirt black ink to escape from predators.

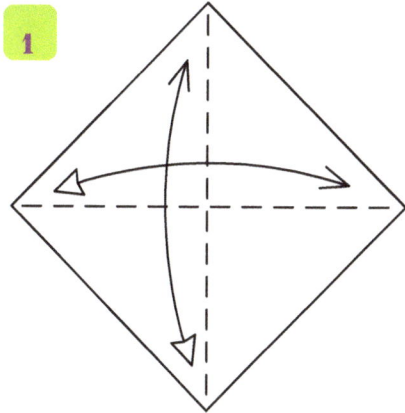

1

Fold and unfold.

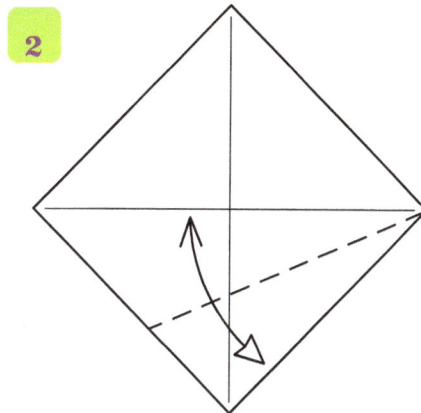

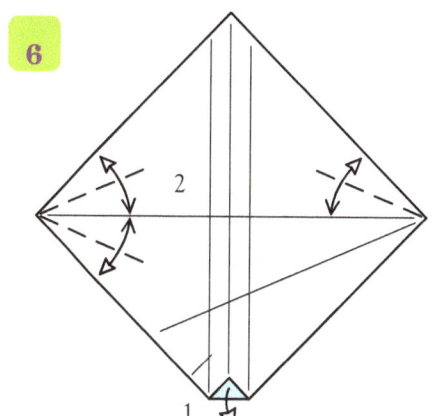

2

Fold to the center and unfold.

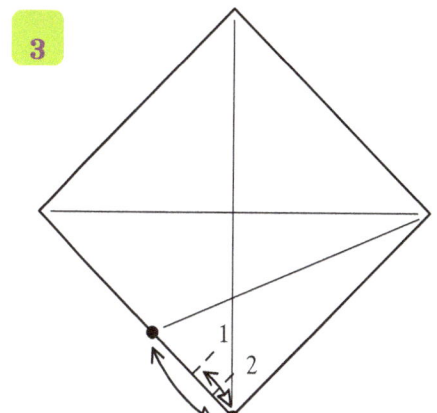

3

Fold and unfold on the edge.

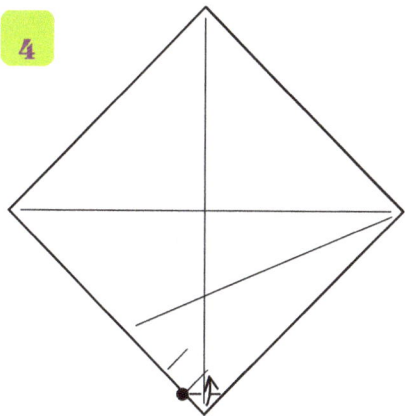

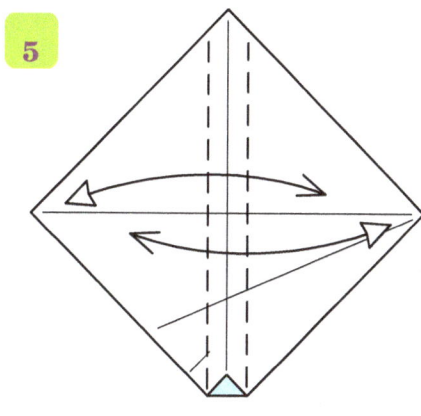

4

5

Fold and unfold.

6

1. Unfold.
2. Fold and unfold.

7

8

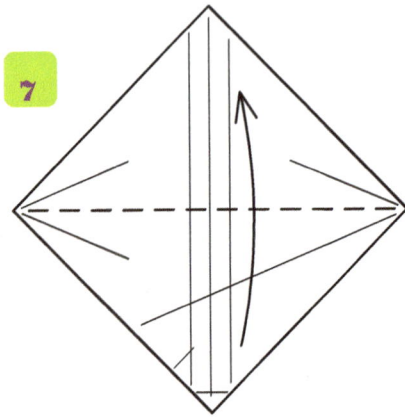

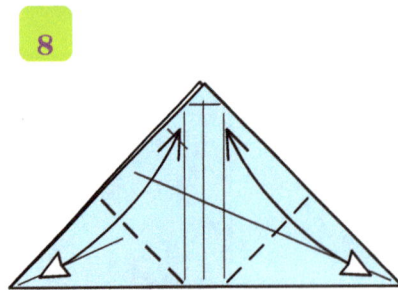

Fold and unfold.

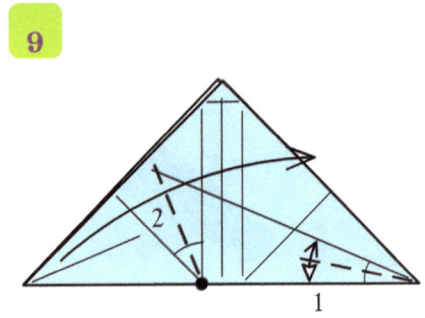

9

1. Fold and unfold.
2. Valley-fold.

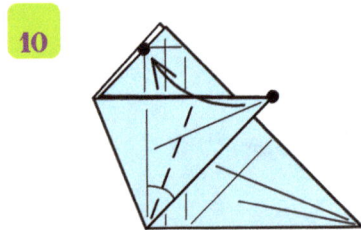

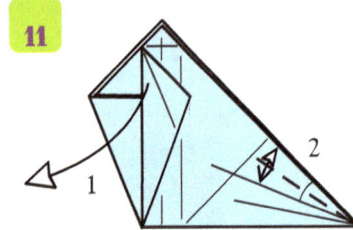

10

11

1. Unfold.
2. Fold and unfold
   both layers.

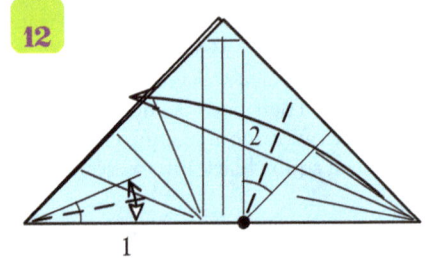

12

Repeat steps 9–11 in
the opposite direction.

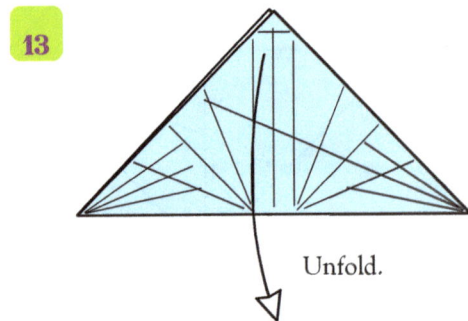

13

Unfold.

14

15

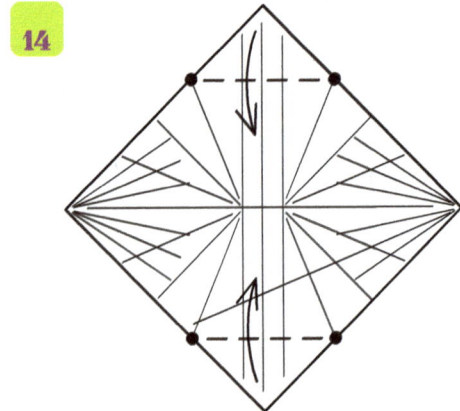

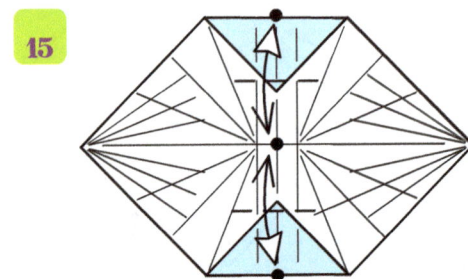

Fold to the center
and unfold.

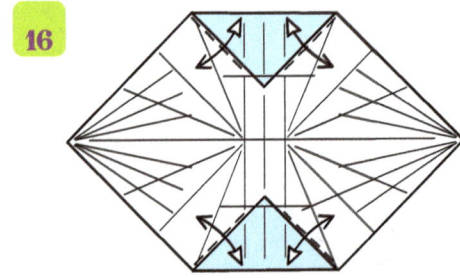

16

Fold and unfold.

17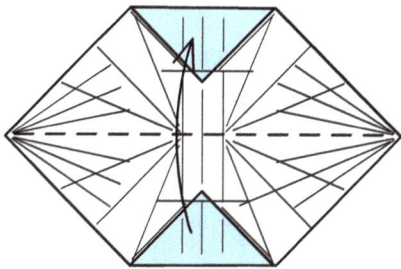

18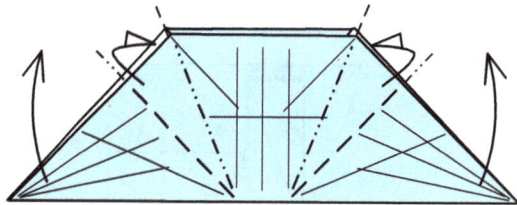

Fold along the creases
for these crimp folds.

19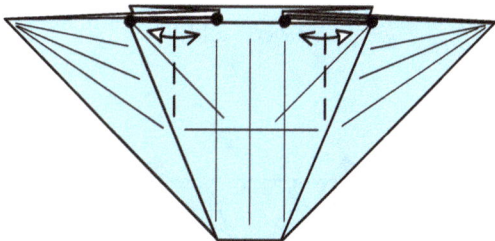

Fold and unfold.

20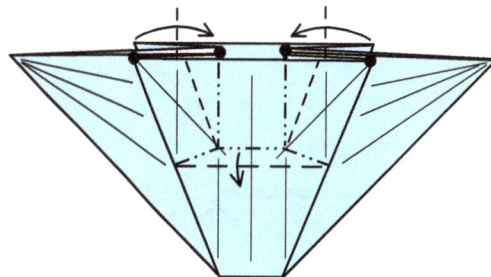

Fold along some
of the creases.

21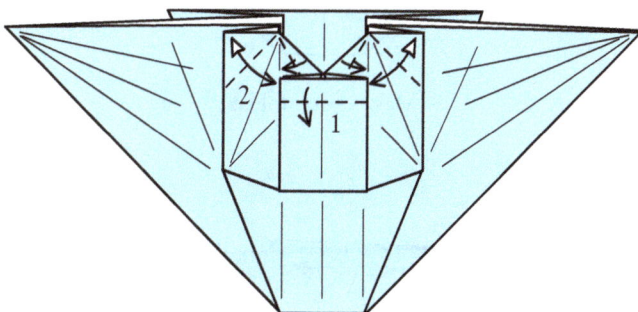

1. Petal-fold.
2. Fold and unfold.

22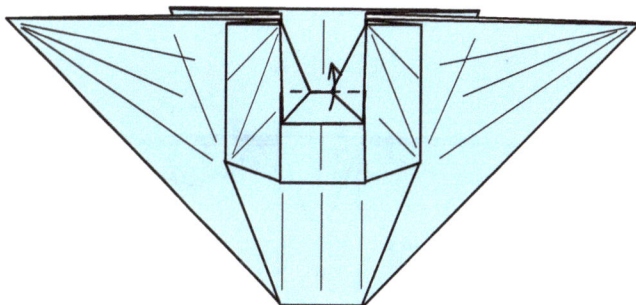

23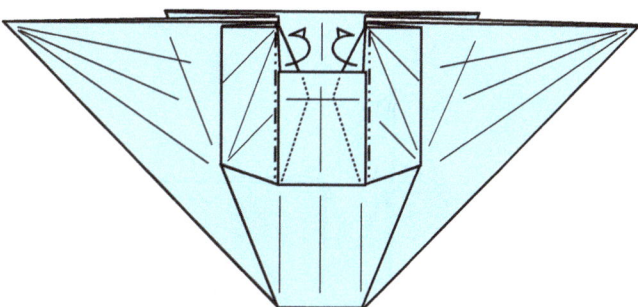

Fold inside.

24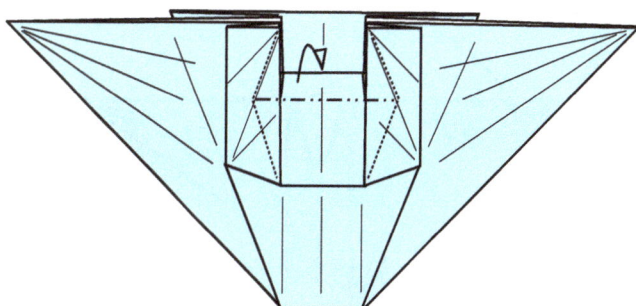

Fold inside.

25

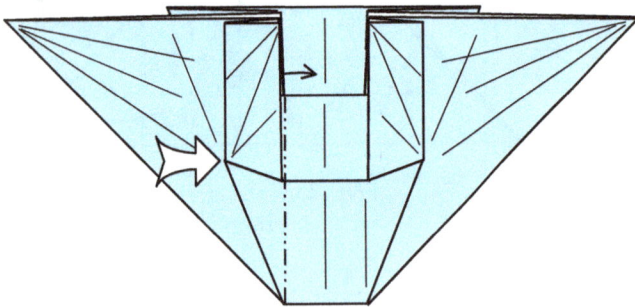

Sink.

26

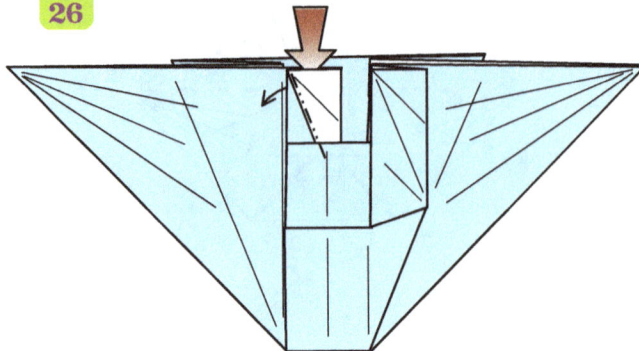

Reverse-fold.

27

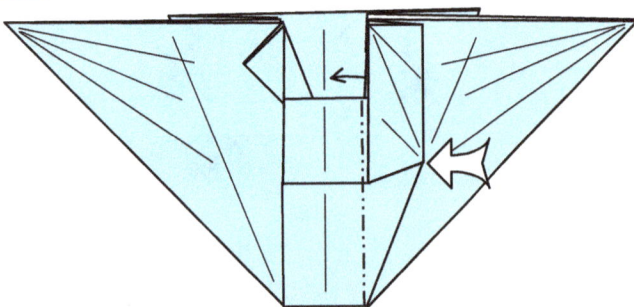

Repeat steps 25–26
on the right.

28

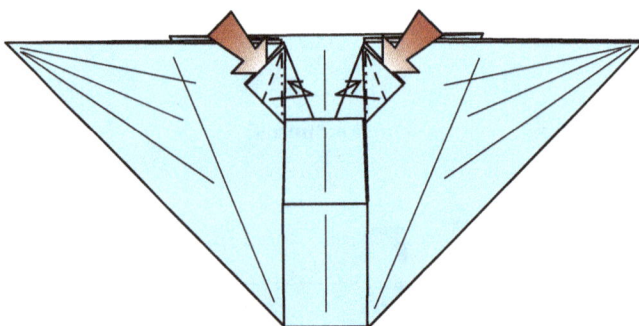

Make crimp folds.

29

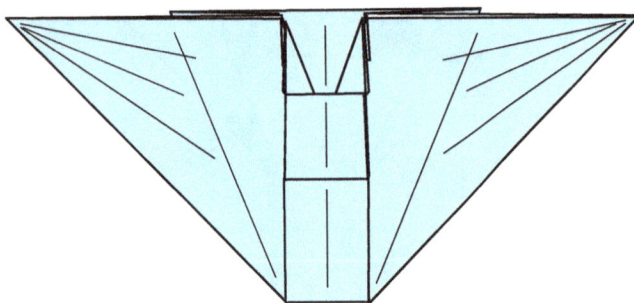

30

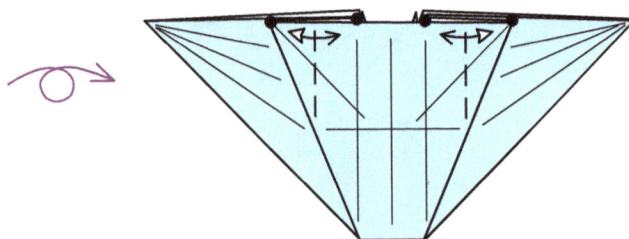

Repeat steps 19–28.

31

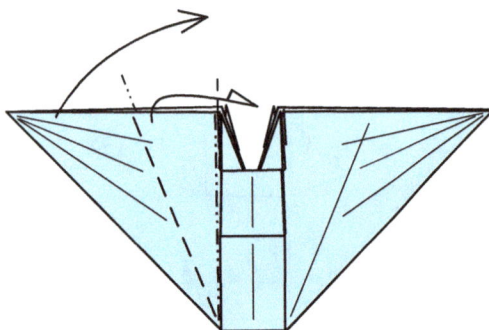

Crimp-fold.

32

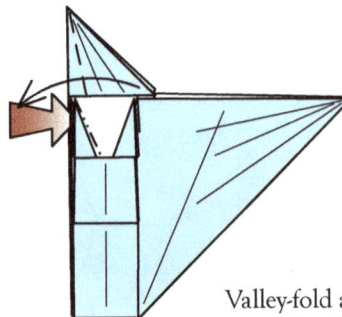

Valley-fold along the
crease for this reverse
fold. Repeat behind.

33

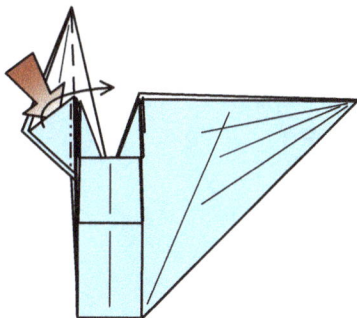

Valley-fold along the crease for this reverse fold. Repeat behind.

34

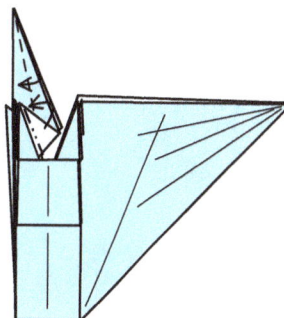

Valley-fold along the crease for this reverse fold. Repeat behind.

35

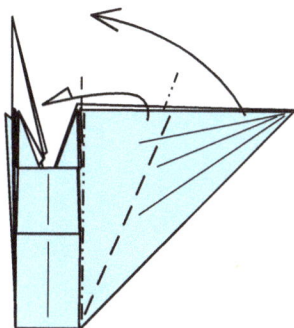

Repeat steps 31–34 on the right.

36

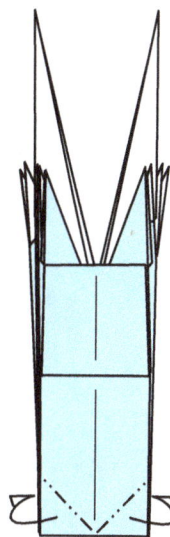

Fold to the center.

37

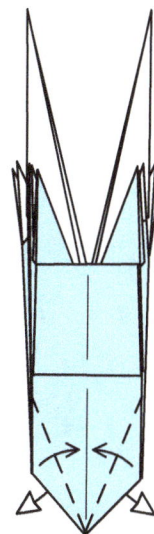

Fold to the center and swing out from behind.

38

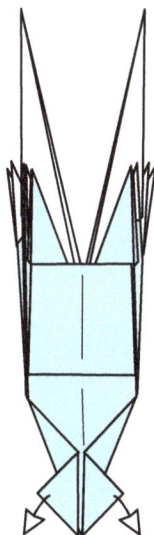

Unfold.

39

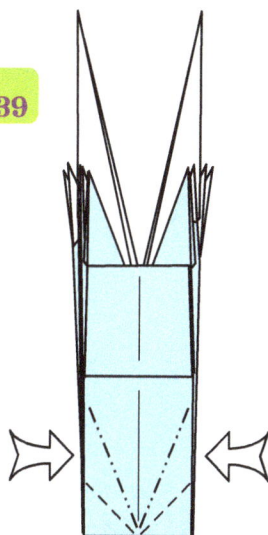

Sink in and out.

40

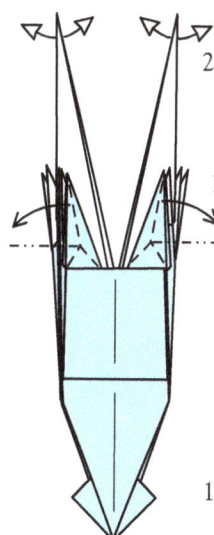

1. Rabbit-ear all the layers on the left and right. Repeat behind.
2. Spread at the tip.

41

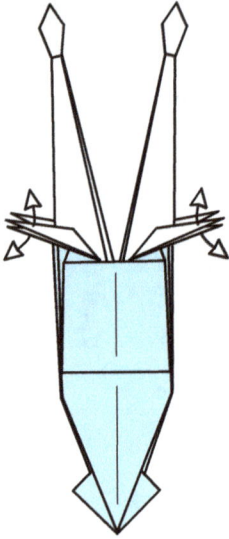

Spread the tentacles.
Repeat behind.

42

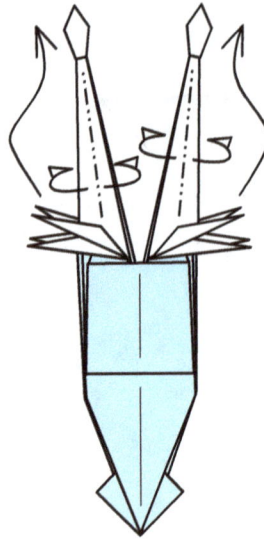

Curl the tentacles.

43

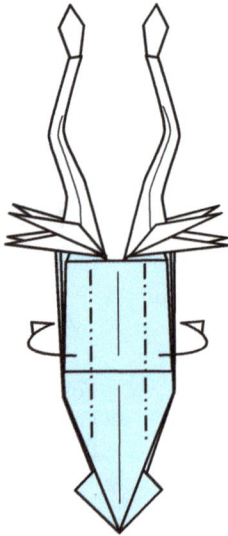

Shape the body
with soft folds.

44

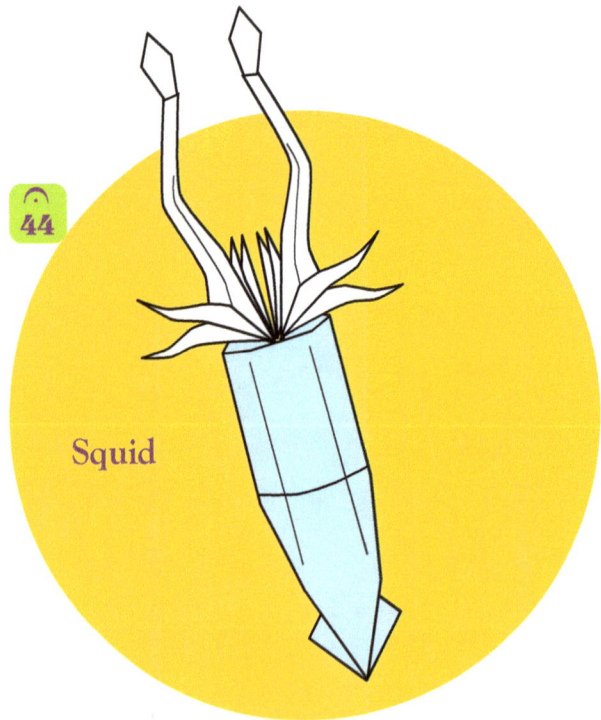

Squid

Nautilus

Unchanged for 500 million years, the Nautilus is a living fossil. As an 8 inch mullusk, it is the only cephalopod to live in a shell. The shell is chambered and spiral-shaped. While the young start with a few chambers, it grows more throughout its long life span of 20 years. The soft body stays inside only the outer-most chamber. The other chambers are sealed off and aid in buoyancy and for swimming, as it spends its life swimming backward. Its method of swimming is so efficient that it only needs to eat once a month, feeding on shrimp, fish, and other small crustaceans. It wraps its 40 or more tentacles around its prey, trapping it with a sticky substance.

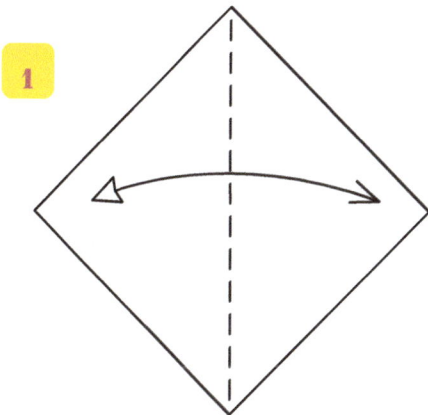

1

Fold and unfold.

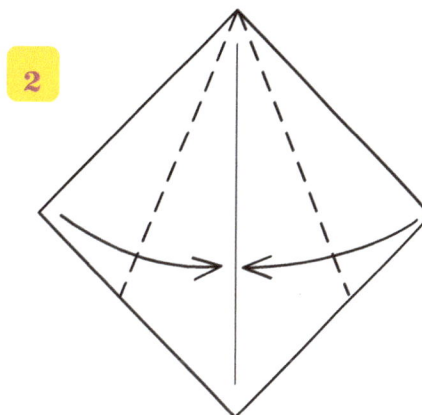

2

Fold to the center.

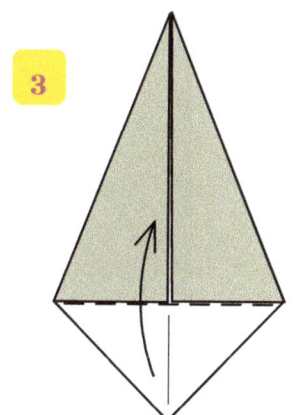

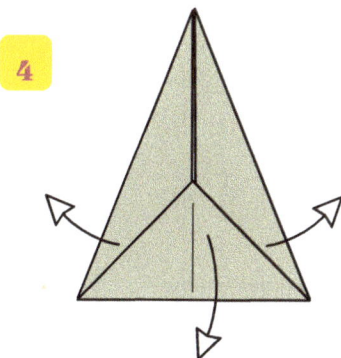

3

4

Unfold.

5

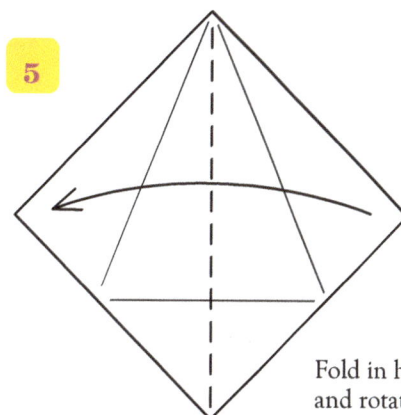

Fold in half
and rotate.

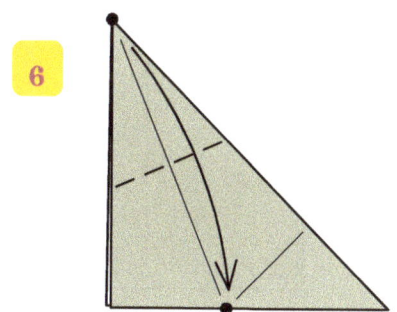

6

7

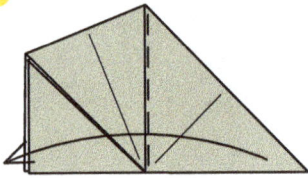

8

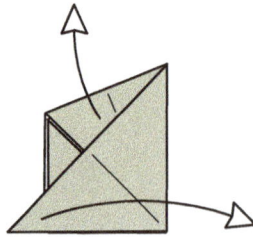

Unfold.

9

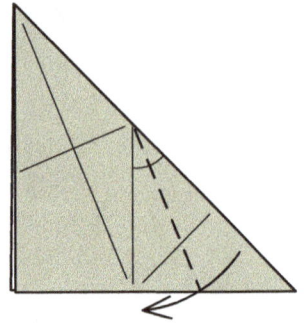

10

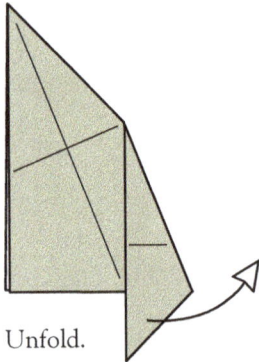

Unfold.

11

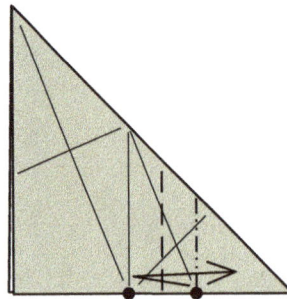

Pleat-fold.

12

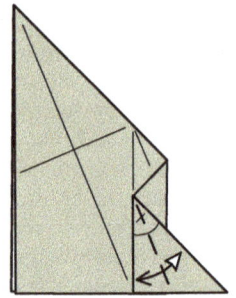

Fold and unfold.

13

Pleat-fold.

14

Unfold.

15

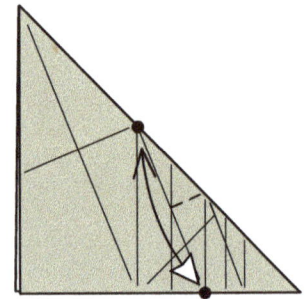

Fold and unfold.

16

Fold and unfold.

17

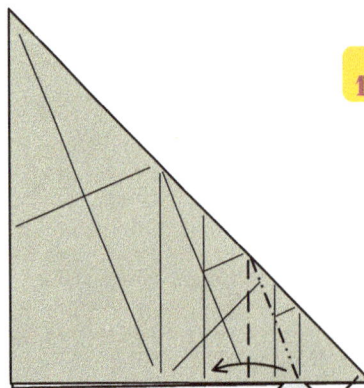

Squash-fold along
the creases.

18

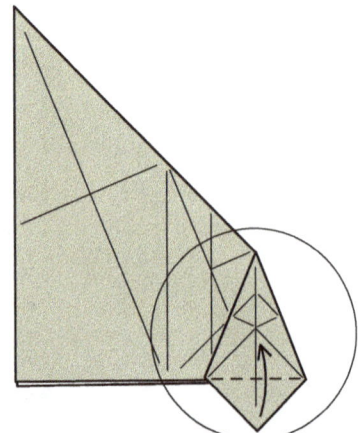

The view will be magnified
in the next step.

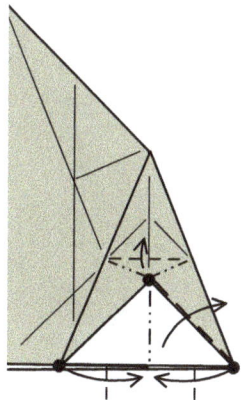

19

Lift up at the upper dot. The lower dots will meet.

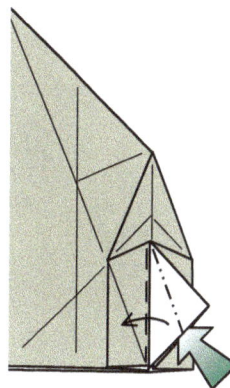

20

Squash-fold.

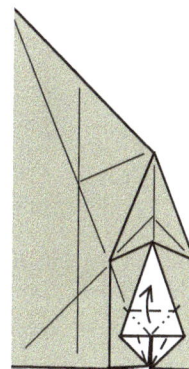

21

Petal-fold.

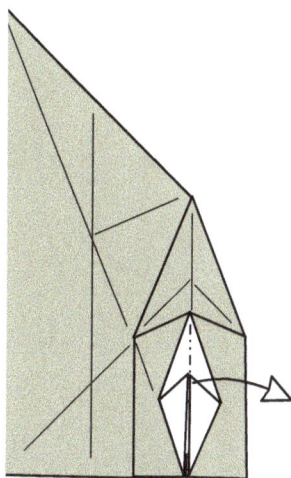

22

Unfold back to step 20.

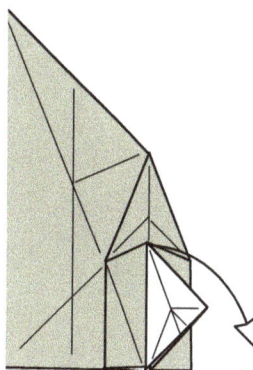

23

Unwrap the white paper.

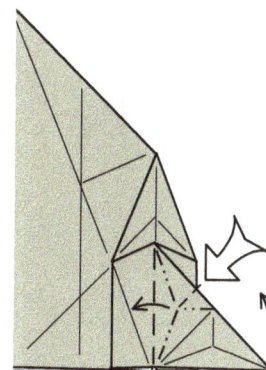

24

Fold along the creases.

25

Squash-fold.

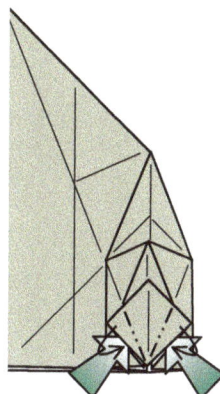

26

Make reverse folds.

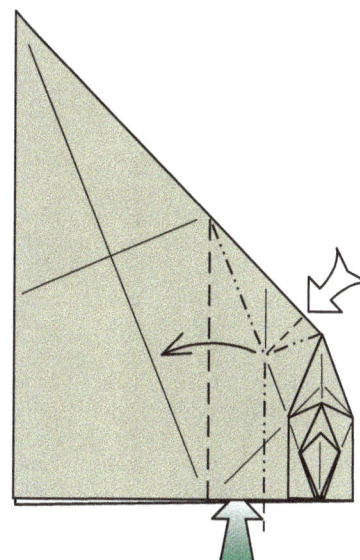

27

Fold along the creases.

28

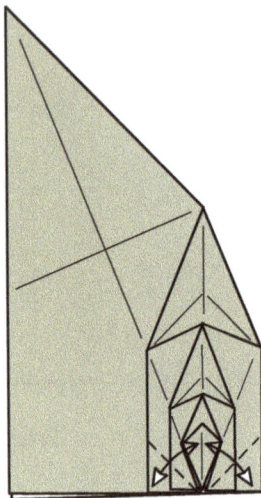

Fold and unfold
several layers.

29

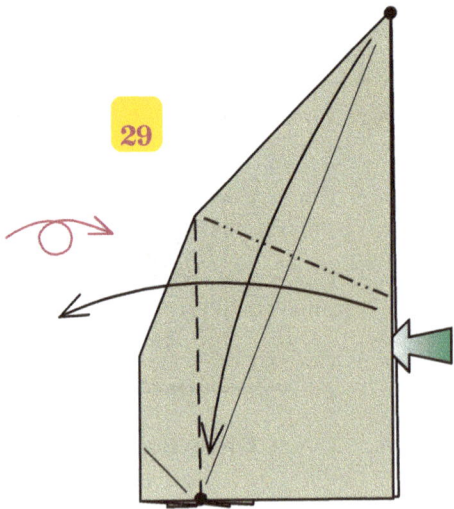

Squash-fold so
the dots meet.

30

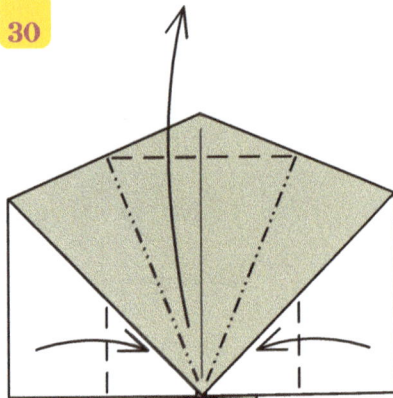

Petal-fold.

31

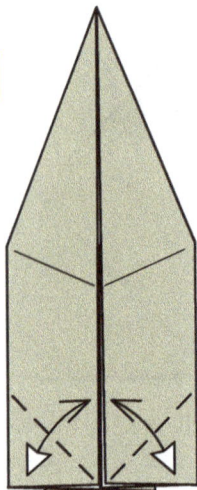

Fold and unfold.

32

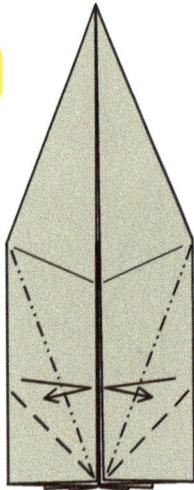

Make crimp folds.

33

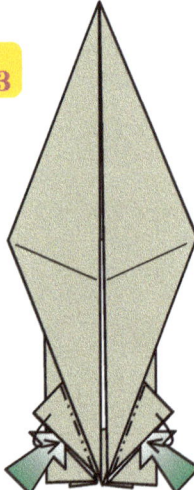

Make reverse folds.

34

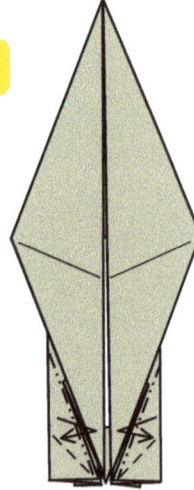

Make crimp folds.

35

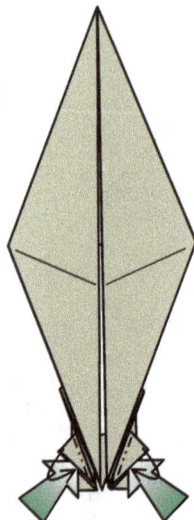

Make reverse folds.

36

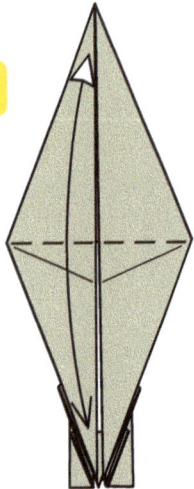

Fold and unfold.

37

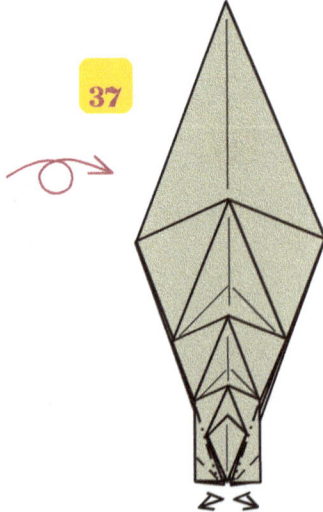

Make crimp folds.

38

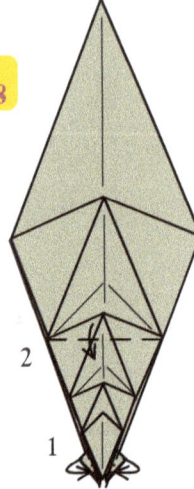

1. Make reverse folds.
2. Fold down.

39

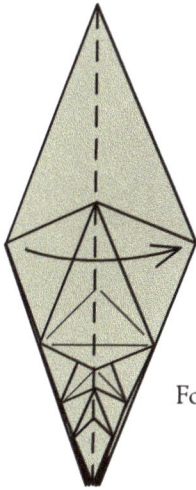

Fold in half.

40

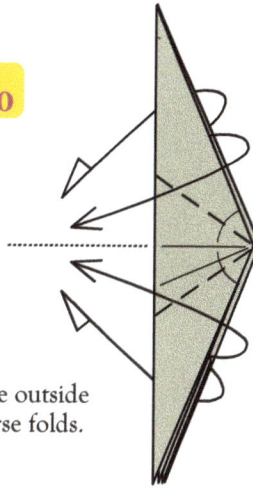

Make outside reverse folds.

41

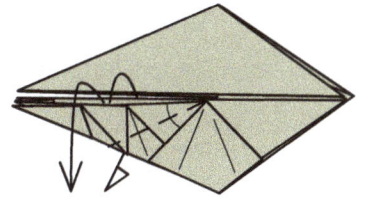

Outside-reverse-fold the tentacles.

42

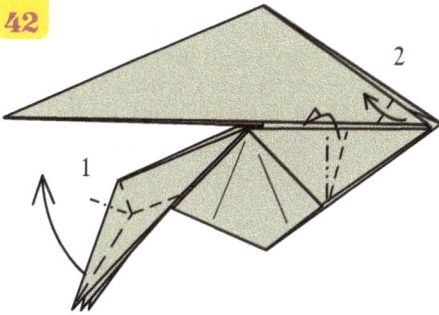

1. Rabbit-ear the top flap.
2. This is similar to a squash fold.
Repeat behind.

43

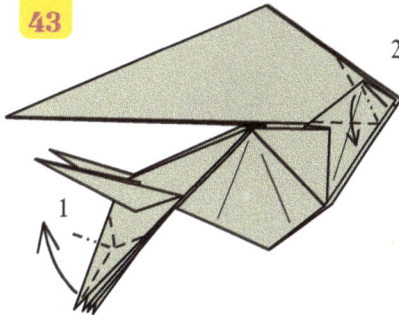

1. Rabbit-ear.
2. Squash-fold.
Repeat behind.

44

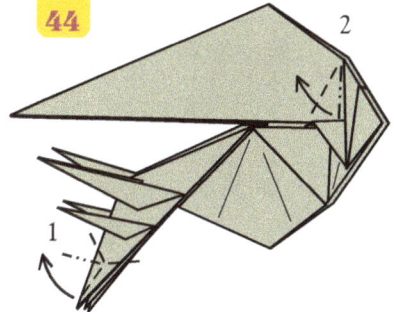

1. Rabbit-ear two flaps together.
2. Pull out.
Repeat behind.

45

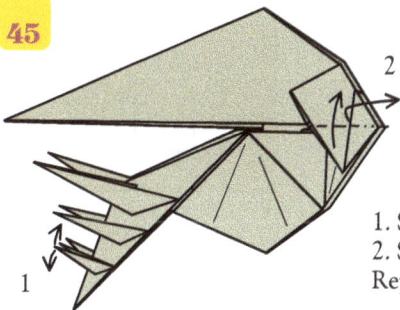

1. Spread the flaps.
2. Squash-fold.
Repeat behind.

46

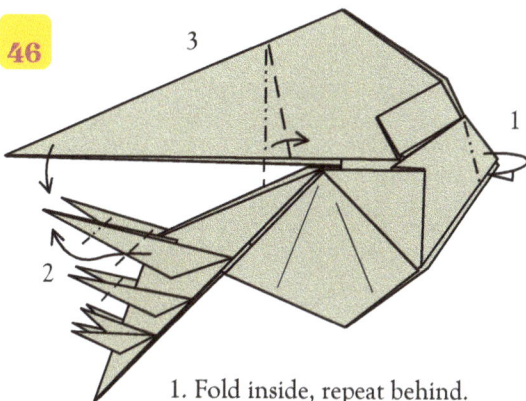

1. Fold inside, repeat behind.
2. Shape the tentacles, repeat behind.
3. Crimp-fold.

47

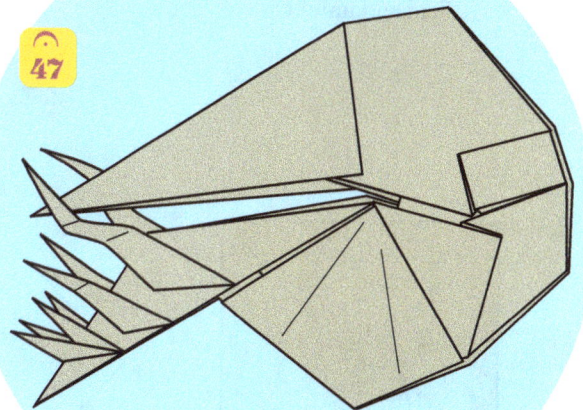

Nautilus

Crab

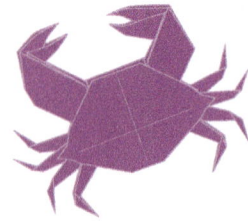

Crabs are found in shallow ocean waters and sea shores around the world. There are over 6000 species of this crustacean. Of their ten legs, two are claws used for catching prey. One claw is often larger than the other. They usually walk sideways with the other eight legs. Crabs hide in crevices waiting for prey to swim by, which they catch with their armored claws. They eat meat and plants.

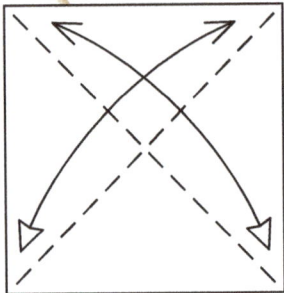

Fold and unfold.

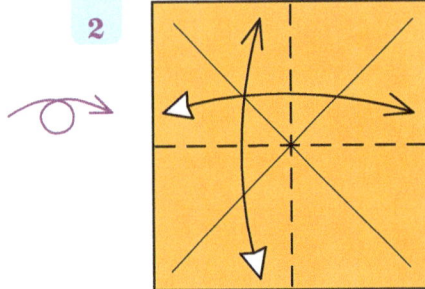

Fold and unfold.

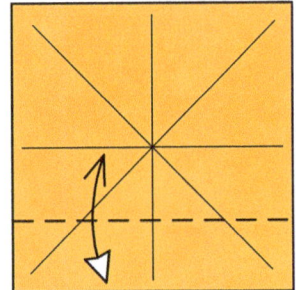

Fold and unfold.
Rotate 90°.

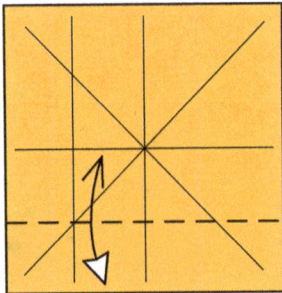

Repeat step 3 three times. Rotate 45°.

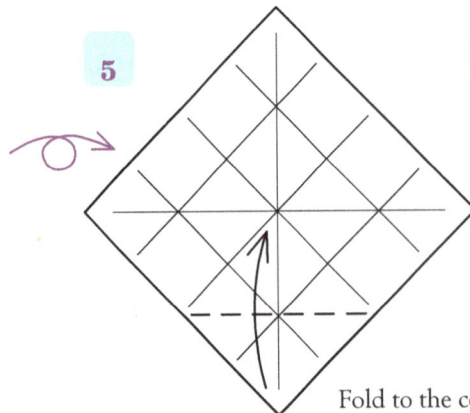

Fold to the center.

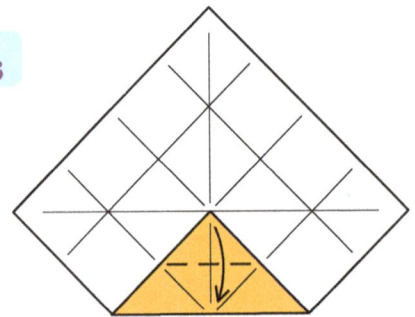

7

8

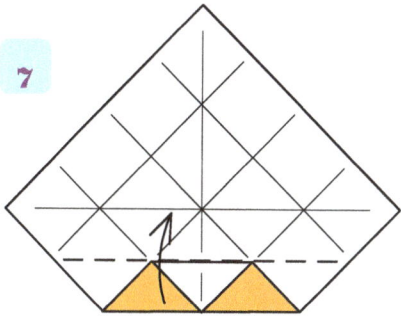

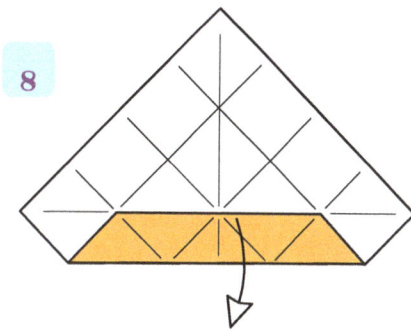

Unfold and rotate 90°.

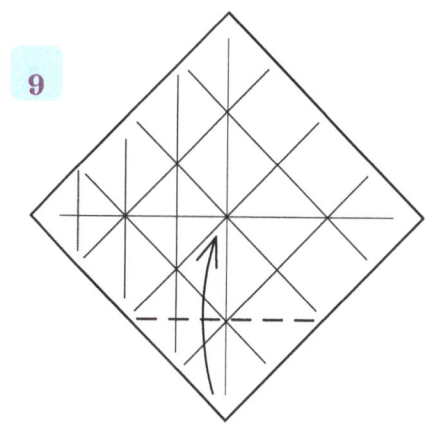

9

Repeat steps 5–8 three
times. Rotate 45°.

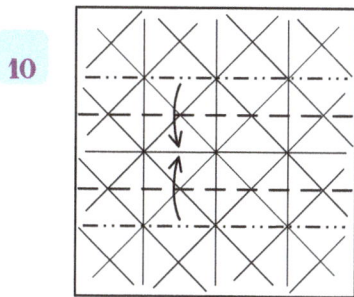

10

Pleat-fold to the center.
Mountain-fold along
the creases.

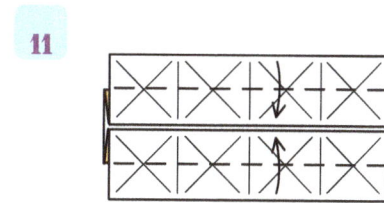

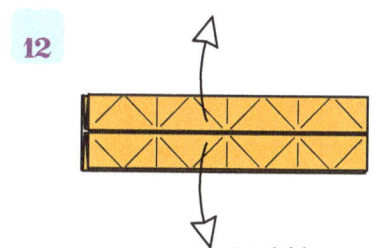

11

12

Unfold.

13

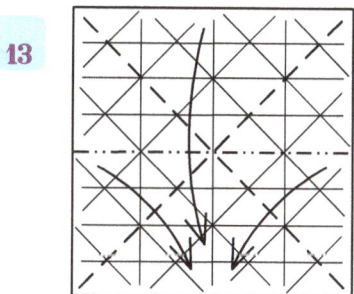

Make a waterbomb base.

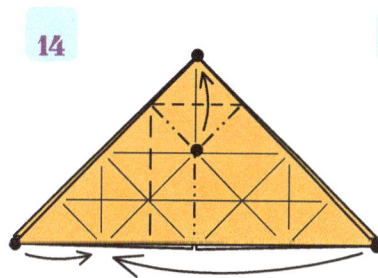

14

Lift up the top layer at
the center dot. The pairs
of dots will meet.

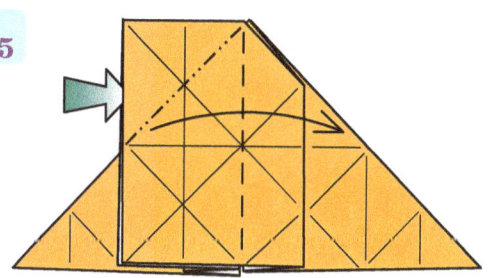

15

Squash-fold.

16

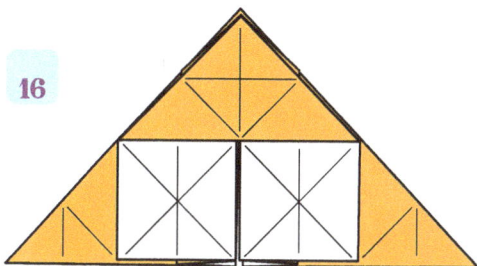

Repeat steps 14–15 behind.

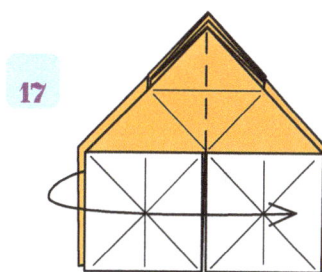

17

Fold the top layer.

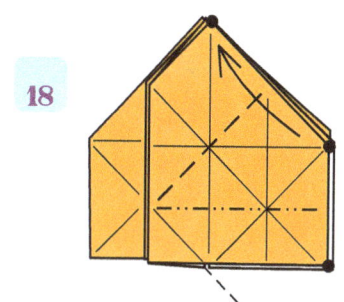

18

The three dots will meet at
the top for this combination
of squash folds.

19

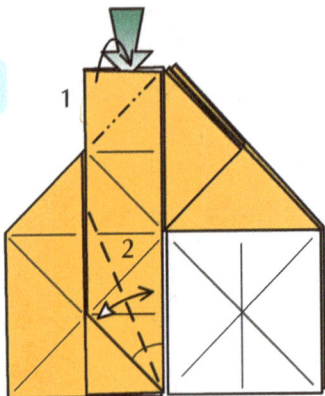

1. Reverse-fold.
2. Fold and unfold.

20

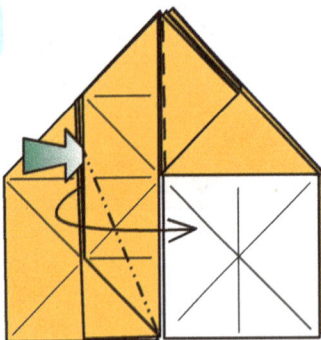

Spread-squash-fold.

21

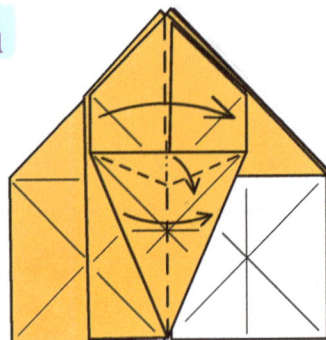

22

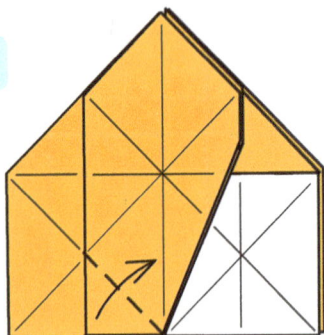

Fold along the crease.

23

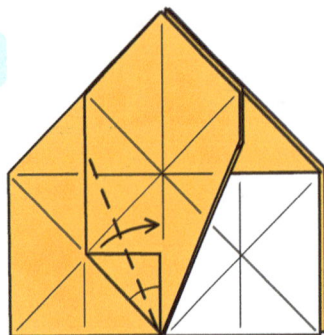

24

Unfold.

25

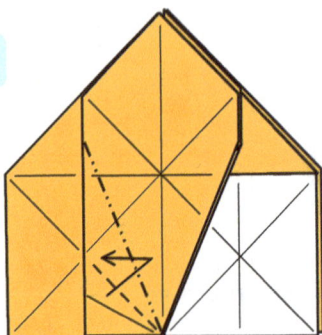

Crimp-fold along
the creases.

26

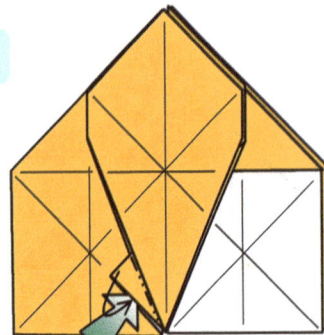

Reverse-fold.

27

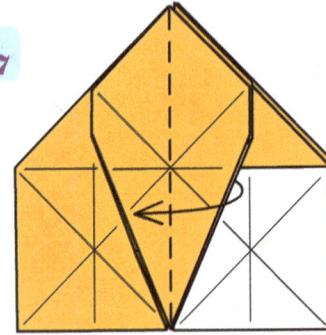

28

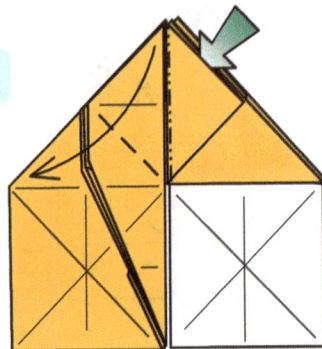

Squash-fold.

29

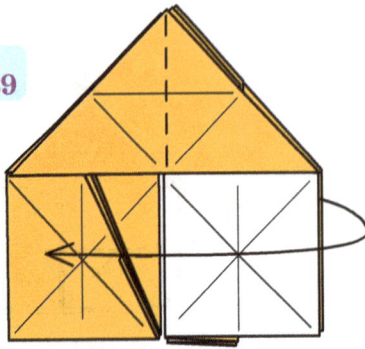

Repeat steps 17–28
on the right.

30

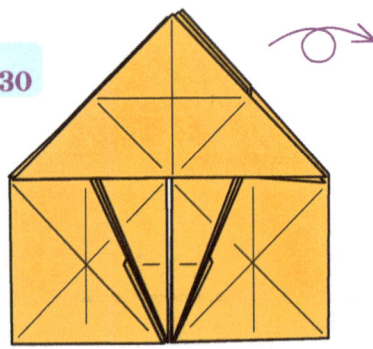

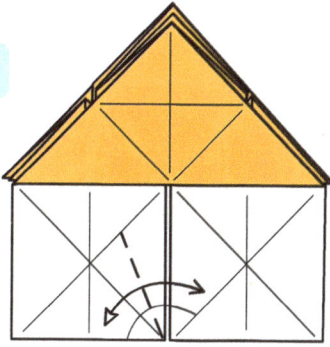

31

Fold and unfold.

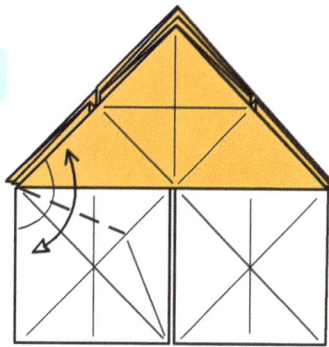

32

Fold and unfold.

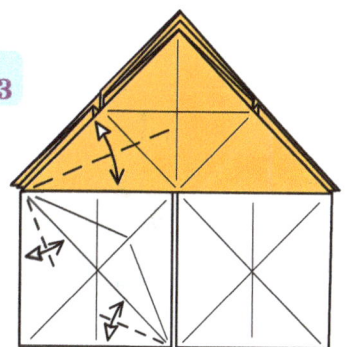

33

Fold and unfold.

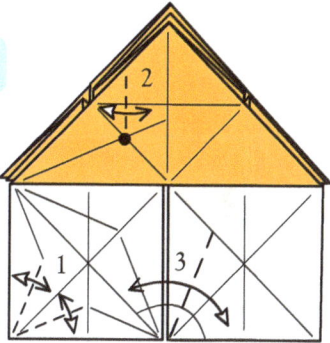

34

1. Fold and unfold.
2. Fold and unfold.
3. Repeat steps 31–34 on the right.

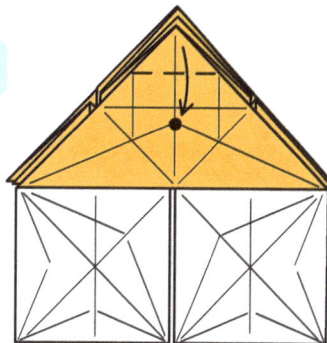

35

Fold the top flap down.

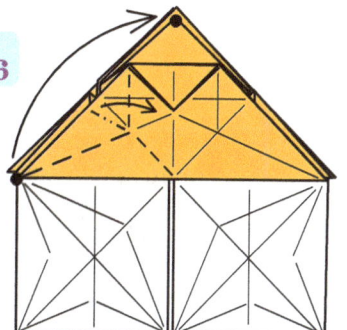

36

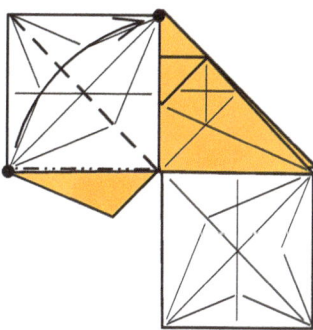

37

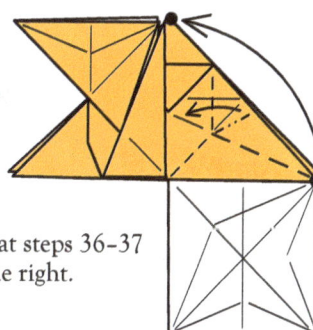

38

Repeat steps 36–37 on the right.

39

Make crimp folds.

40

Make reverse folds. Rotate 180°.

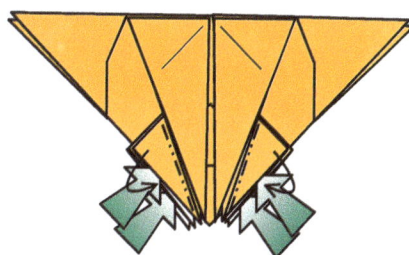

41

Make four reverse folds.

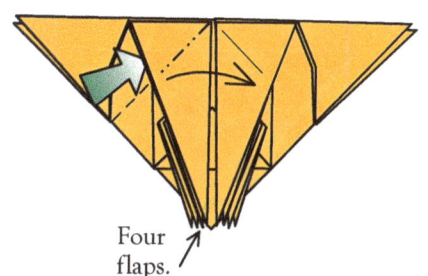

42

Four flaps.

There are four flaps by the arrow at the bottom. Squash-fold one and a half of the flaps.

43

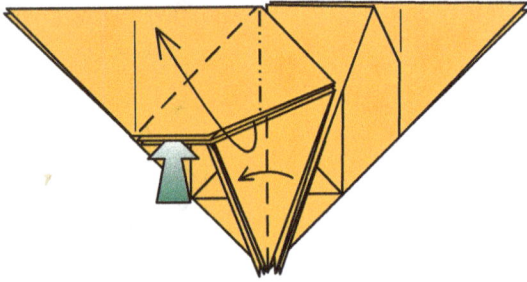

Place your finger into the second pocket for this squash fold.

44

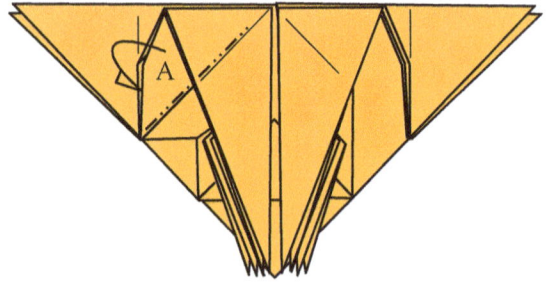

Tuck region A inside with a mountain fold.

45

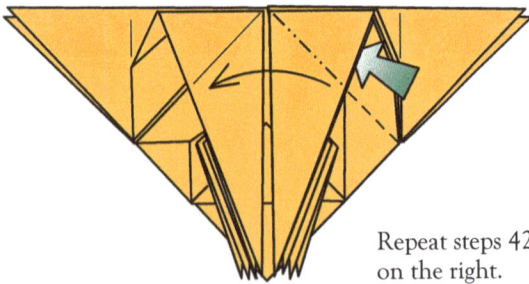

Repeat steps 42–44 on the right.

46

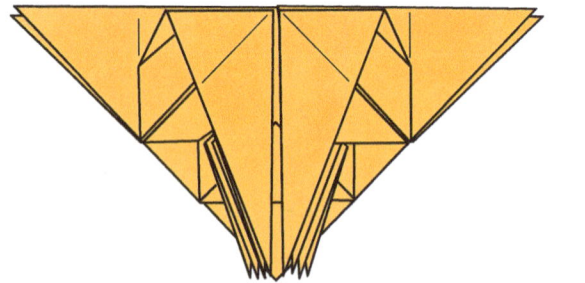

47

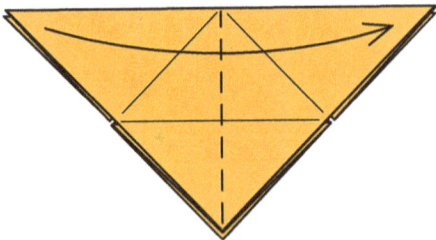

48

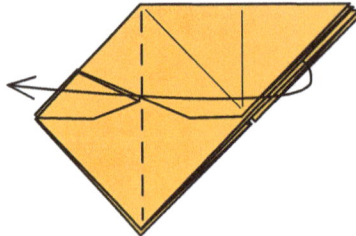

49

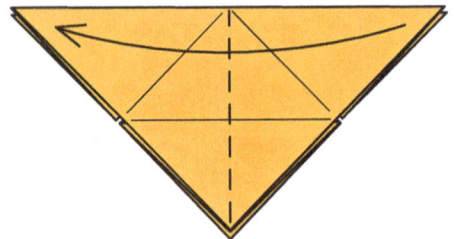

Repeat steps 47–48 in the opposite direction.

50

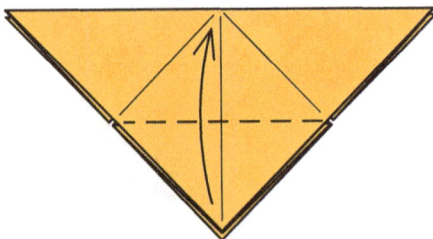

51

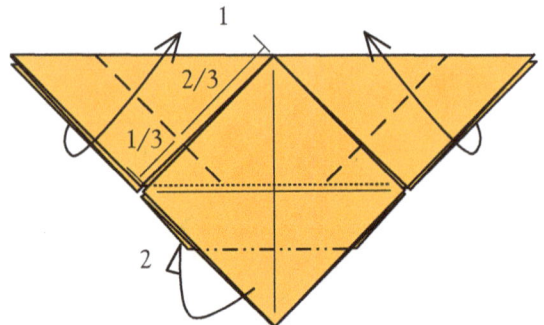

1. Fold the claws up at around one-third of the height on the left and right.
2. Wrap around the lower layers.

52

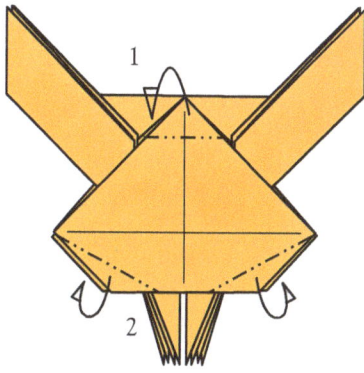

1. Tuck inside.
2. Fold all the layers together on the left and right.

53

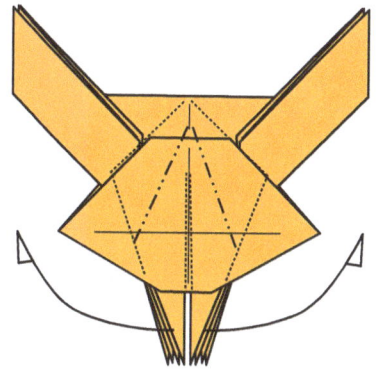

Fold all the layers together.

54

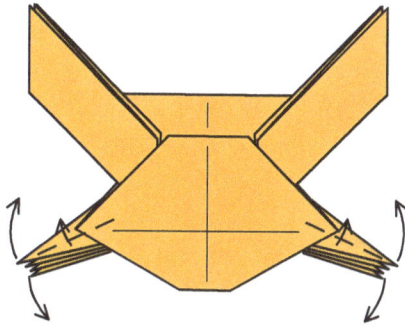

Thin each leg and spread them.

55

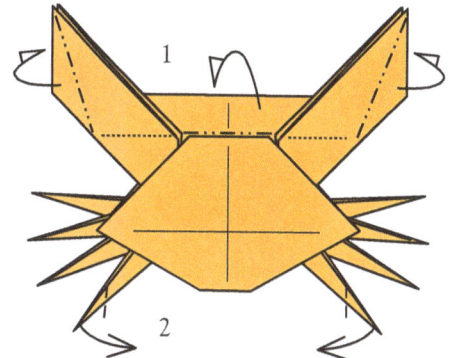

1. The layers are thick so fold carefully.
2. Make outside reverse-folds.

56

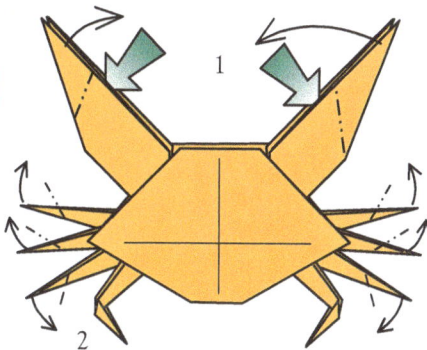

1. Make the claws different sizes with reverse folds.
2. Make reverse folds.

57

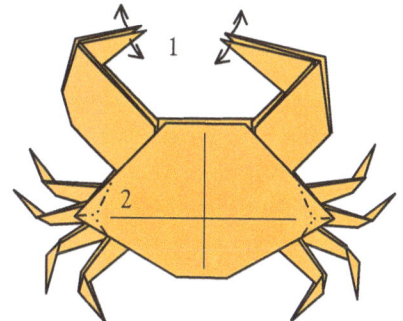

1. Spread and shape the claws.
2. Shape the shell on the left and right.

58

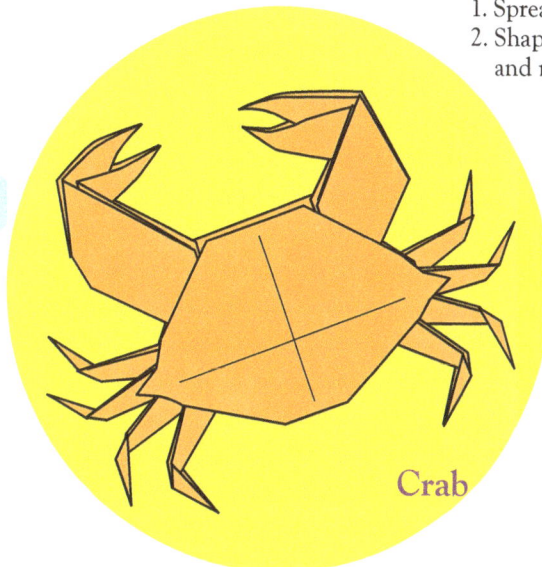

Crab

www.ingramcontent.com/pod-product-compliance
Lightning Source LLC
Chambersburg PA
CBHW080625030426
42336CB00018B/3083